27/11/

THE DISPOSSESSED

OTHER BOOKS BY AUSTIN STEVENS

Fiction

Time and Money
On the Market
The Moon turns Green
The Antagonists

Non-fiction

Making Money on the Stock Exchange

AUSTIN STEVENS

THE
DISPOSSESSED

BARRIE & JENKINS
COMMUNICA - EUROPA

FOR EILEEN, FIONA, AND PAUL

First published in Great Britain in 1975 by
Barrie & Jenkins Limited, 24 Highbury Crescent, London N5 1RX

Copyright © Austin Stevens 1975

ISBN 0 214 20052 3

All rights reserved
No part of this publication may be reproduced in any form or by any means without the prior permission of Barrie & Jenkins Limited

Printed in Great Britain by
Clarke, Doble & Brendon Ltd,
Plymouth

CONTENTS

Author's Note 7
1 The Jews of Germany 9
2 Britain as Host 42
3 Leaving the Reich 67
4 The New Arrivals 108
5 Enemy Aliens 151
6 War Effort 214
7 Entrenched Attitudes 235
8 Coming to Terms 256
9 Summation 303
Notes 307
Bibliography 310
Index 313

AUTHOR'S NOTE

This book is mainly derived from the personal testimony of many individual refugees. Sometimes they are quoted directly without being named; where necessary they have been given pseudonyms. Nothing has been invented, although I have on occasion used some of a novelist's freedom to dramatize and comment. I regret the necessity for pseudonyms but most of my informants wished to preserve their anonymity for obvious reasons. After nearly forty years this is still delicate ground.

I am most grateful to the many people who helped me and were kind enough to grant me personal interviews. Notable among them was Mr C. C. Aronsfeld, whose acute insight illuminated the whole subject for me, and Mrs Gerda Mosse, whose detachment and sense of history were of the greatest value. I must thank Lord and Lady Snow for entertaining me and answering my questions, and Dr Paul Tabori for showing me the typescript of his *Gift of the Exiles*. I am also grateful to Miss Joan Stiebel, Joint Secretary of the Central British Fund for Jewish Relief and Rehabilitation, for furnishing me with the Annual Reports of that organization. I am indebted to Mrs G. Auerbach; Mr Angus Calder; Mrs Doris Hamblen; Mr Michael Hamburger; Mr Fritz Hess and Mrs Ann Hess; Mr Wolf Mankowitz; Mr David Marcus; Mr Leonard Mosley; Mrs Mosley; Rev. Dr James Parkes; Mr Gerald Reitlinger; Karin, Countess von der Schulenburg; Professor Andrew Sharf; Mr Leopold Ullstein; Mr Phillip Whitehead. I received great help from Miss Janet Langmaid and Mrs Christine Wichman of the Wiener Library; from Miss Grogan of the Irish Central Library for Students; from Mr Sean Bohon and Miss Barrett of Cork City Library; from the staffs of the British Museum Library and the Library of Trinity College, Dublin.

I have been helped, as always, by the faithful support of Mr Richard Simon; by the sympathetic interest of Miss Vivien Green; and by the patient encouragement of Mr John Knowler.

Chapter One

THE JEWS OF GERMANY

The spring of 1933 was a memorable season in Germany. In March, Hitler gained control of the Reichstag and by April he and his party had achieved something neither Bismarck nor Kaiser Wilhelm had ever attempted: abolished the powers of the individual states and made them subject to the central authority of the Reich. This was something that went beyond politics and would soon affect every man, woman, and child in Germany. If they did not realize this immediately, they soon would.

Early in March Georg Joachim celebrated his ninth birthday. Soon afterwards he came home from school and asked his father an unusual question.

'Daddy,' he said, 'what am I?'

His father wondered what he meant. Georg explained. That morning the schoolmaster, Herr Grotwohl, had ordered 'all you Jews' to step forward and stand in front of the class. After some hesitation several boys had obeyed. They were told to fetch an extra bench from the lumber-room where spare furniture was stored. This was placed at a significant distance from the rest of the class. Herr Grotwohl said, 'This is the Jew Bench. You Jews will always sit on it.'

'Daddy, I didn't know what to do,' Georg said. 'Am I a Jew?'

'Yes, Georg,' his father said. 'You are a Jew. Tomorrow you will go and sit on that bench with the others.'

The next day Georg did. At first Herr Grotwohl appeared satisfied to have established the fact of segregation, contenting himself with remarks like 'No doubt our Jewish brethren can answer that' or 'May we have a non-Ayran approach to that question?' But the gentile boys were quick to implement the attitudes of their elders, ganging up on Jewish boys as they entered and left the school. Mostly they confined themselves to kicks and punches, but one group tore off a Jewish boy's shorts and exclaimed at the sight of his circumcised flesh. Soon Herr Grotwohl began to develop a policy. More and more of his time was devoted to the Jew Bench. From throwaway insults he progressed to an elaborate catechism. 'And your father, Karl—what did *he* do for Germany? We know what he did for himself, Karl – feathered his own nest while other men were dying for Germany! You know what *Schieber* means, Karl? – a moneybags, a profiteer, a Jewish leech sucking away the blood of the Fatherland . . .' Herr Grotwohl knew which of the Jewish boys' fathers had served in the war and he had another set of questions for these boys.

Georg's school was by no means the worst in Berlin. Herr Grotwohl was not an imaginative man. His colleagues at other schools showed far more skill in devising humiliations – especially his female colleagues. 'My wife and I tremble,' a father said, 'when our daughter sets out for school in the morning, and we tremble when she creeps home in the evening. We no longer ask questions – and she no longer tells us what happens.'

Sitting on the Jew Bench, seeing their race defined on the blackboard as *Untermenschen* – sub-men, 'akin to animals' – the Jewish children had to chant:

> The German land for the German man, the German man,
> The Jew may run to Canaan if he can, if he can.

There is little point in exploring the microcosm of hatred offered by the German schools. But Georg's question was of great significance. His family were Jewish and they had lived in Germany for hundreds of years. Unlike many German Jews they had never sought to dissolve their Jewishness in Christian baptism. And yet Georg could ask, 'Am I a Jew?'

The extraordinary degree of assimilation of Jew into German is a phenomenon of history. It was hardly equalled even in Spain, and the Jews left Spain many centuries ago. It is easy to think of German Jewry simply in terms of persecution – and certainly persecution of Jew by German has been inherent in their relationship for at least a thousand years. They have been described as playing the roles of executioner and victim alternatively, but that overlooks the one-sided nature of the conflict. The persecution of the Jews in Germany reached its climax under the Nazis: the horrors of that time have been described so often that they will be dealt with as briefly as possible here. This is the story of the German and Austrian Jews who survived that persecution and escaped to Britain where they made new lives for themselves. But to tell their story one must first consider their origins and characteristics; what they had in common and how they differed from each other; why some became refugees and others remained in Germany. The fact of German-Jewish assimilation underlies all these questions.

In the first place, it determined the way the German Jews thought of themselves. Throughout their history the Jews have been the victims of the stereotypes their enemies have projected. Such labels have a profound influence on those condemned to wear them. The classic, hostile image of the Jew is immediately familiar. The face is that of an old man. He has a beard and wears a skull-cap. He is at once oily and bullying, crafty and hysterical. It is the face of Shylock and, later, of Fagin. This Jew is trying to sell you something and if you do not buy he turns nasty and complains shrilly that you have wasted his time. Such images have been the stuff of anti-semitic fantasy all over the world: used as emotional fuel for pogroms and to justify keeping the Jews as a race apart, holed up in ghettos, pursuing minority trades and professions.

In no country were such fantasies unleashed with more effect than in Germany where there was an anti-semitic tradition going back a thousand years. All the more remarkable then, to find that by the 1920s, when Hitler had already begun to plot their destruction, a large number of German Jews had come to think of themselves as wholly German and only incidentally Jewish. They had not so much rejected their Jewishness as overlaid, forgotten it. It no longer seemed relevant. Hence the shock to Georg Joachim when Herr Grotwohl confronted him with the Jew Bench.

It may be asked why these Germans of Jewish origin should not have considered themselves wholly German. And what of the thousands of German Jews who had embraced Christianity and been baptized? What did it matter? They were all Germans.

They were indeed all Germans, and they represented an influential and varied group of great value to the community. At the beginning of the First World War their ambience went far beyond the traditional areas of banking, medicine, and the law. Jews tended to be excluded from big business and heavy industry so, apart from private banking, they often engaged in small manufacture and independent crafts – for instance the textile industry – and of course the professions and the arts. Medicine, pure science, economics, law, the novel, the theatre – the Jews were pre-eminent in them all. The only historical comparison is with Moslem Spain.

It is not enough to see the Jews only as a leaven, an enlivening and at the same time sobering influence, although no doubt they were that: German obsessions, German hysteria needed Jewish subtlety as a counterpart. But the degree of Jewish assimilation in German life went even farther. The extent to which Jews of the Diaspora (that is, any Jews but those of Palestine itself) have been absorbed by the people of their host countries has varied a great deal at different times and in different places. In the Scandinavian countries the rate of Jewish-gentile intermarriage was always the highest in Europe, and there the Jews hardly exist as a separate community. By contrast the Jews in America have survived as a distinct and powerful group because America, more than any other country, is a vast total of such groups, each of which has good reasons for maintaining its ethnic identity.

In Germany the unique degree of assimilation between Jew and gentile established a distinctive way of life. This 'gentilism' of German Jewish life had a beneficial effect on every aspect of German society. The German Jews had a life-style which might be somewhat bourgeois but which was eminently solid and civilized. ('Yaeche' was the nickname this evoked.) The German Jew differed in several respects from the East European or Russian Jew who, through emigration, became the English, French, or American Jew. Any study of the German Jewish refugees must take account of these differences and also recognize that other factor in the equation, the attitude of the 'real' German – whose tortured, ambivalent relationship with the Jew down the centuries was to culminate in Hitler's Final Solution.

In 1934 the famous Jewish scientist, Professor Richard Willstätter, returned to Germany from Palestine. 'I know that Germany has gone mad,' he said, 'but if a mother falls ill it is not a reason for her children to leave her. My home is Germany and I must return.' A year earlier the German Jewish leaders had reiterated their devotion to the Fatherland, protesting that they would cheerfully accept any form of government that would give them dignity, work, and freedom. Their attitude, even at that late hour, was almost Goethe's: 'If I love you, what's that to do with you?'

The first German Jews have been identified from terracotta bottle-stoppers from the later part of the third century: sculptured manikins with unmistakably Jewish noses. These manikins probably lampoon the Jewish traders who travelled with the Roman legions. They sold the soldiers what they needed and naturally they also came in contact with the barbarians – the Teutons, the Franks, and the Goths. The barbarians in their turn had much to offer the Jews: bracelets and rings of gold and silver, furs and hides. Soon the Jews were functioning in a role that has become familiar. A Jewish community existed in Cologne in the fourth century; by the fifth there were Jewish enclaves all over Europe. At that time the Jews were not yet segregated and forced to live in ghettos; they enjoyed equality under Roman law.

Later, under Charlemagne, they followed the conquering armies in his *Drang nach Osten* (thrust to the East): each of the pioneer towns had its Jews. The Jews lived their lives apart: dominated by the canons of the Torah and the Talmud. The medieval rabbi was a figure of omniscient importance, at once religious leader, scholar, schoolmaster, legislator, administrator, and judge. The rise of German cities brought competition from Christian merchants; more and more the Jews turned to money-lending and this increased the hostility towards them that was already stirring in the dark, squalid towns and cities of medieval Germany. Both noble and peasant began to hate the Jew. He walked apart and – it must have seemed – aloof, often clad in rich silken robes. The noble resented the Jews because they were often wealthier than he and yet lacked the prestige of blood. The peasant wondered at the comfort the Jews enjoyed; they were too remote for envy, perhaps, but not for hatred. The fate of Rabbi Gershom's academy in Mainz was an instance of what was soon to happen all over Germany.

The Rabbi Gershom ben Judah was born in 965. His academy in Mainz is described as having been a fine brick and stone building that even boasted a swimming-pool – a *mikvah*. The swimming-pool underlines the grotesque contrast between life inside the academy and the pullulating darkness outside it. To the Jewish scholars of the academy the native Germans must have appeared like savages; to the Germans of the town, grubbing out a day-by-day existence at a near-animal level, the Jews must have seemed infinitely privileged. Privileged but not invulnerable. The people of Mainz attacked the Rabbi Gershom's academy. It was burned and every Jew either killed or driven out of the town.

A greater tragedy impended. The Crusades have been explained by different historians in different terms. As a resolution of economic rivalries: as the implementation in action of the belief that the combined strength of France, England, Germany, and Italy could destroy the Moslem domination of the Levantine trade and also smash the Jewish monopoly of that trade in Europe. That is one explanation, simplified and thus falsified, as every such explanation must be when presented in modern terms. It overlooks the dark forces of medieval religious feeling, part-mystical, part wholly barbarous. The Crusades represented a tortured amalgam of motive and emotion: many of those who fought in them probably accepted the child's history book version of a God-inspired war to free the holy places. But as Marvin Lowenthal, the historian of German Jewry, says:

when the ruling classes go out to save something, whipping their underlings into an idealist frenzy, it is generally to save themselves.

With the Crusades emerges a strand that will become familiar, not only in the history of the German Jews but in every discussion of anti-semitism: the concept of the Jew as scapegoat. The holy places were a long way off, but there were Jews in every town. The Jews had crucified Christ: why not make a start with the ones to hand? Godfrey de Bouillon swore:

I will avenge the blood of my little Jesus on the blood of the Jews ... I will avenge the blood of God on the blood of Israel.

In Spires a mob that included the local burghers besieged the Jewish quarter. The bishop managed to save its inhabitants; the

THE JEWS OF GERMANY

riot was quelled and only eleven dead Jews 'sanctified the Holy Name'. In Worms all the Jews were slaughtered with the exception of those who had taken refuge in the Bishop's Palace. But Bishop Adalbert was either indifferent or powerless, for his palace was stormed and many Jews killed themselves rather than perish on Christian swords. The same thing happened at Mayen. Again and **again** Jews thwarted their would-be murderers by committing suicide. The resolve to spare a fellow human being the guilt of one's blood may have influenced them. Lowenthal speaks of the 'lure of a divine *liebestod* wherein death brings the lover to a perfect union with God'. Whatever the reason, this is another pattern of behaviour that emerges again and again right up to the coming of the Nazis nine hundred years later when many Jews killed themselves rather than face what they knew lay before them.

In Cologne the local inhabitants surprised the Crusaders by protecting the Jews. If they wanted to attack their Jews, the burghers said, they would have to take the city by storm. The crusading knights hesitated, uncertain. Unfortunately the burghers then decided that the Jews would be safer if they went into hiding in neighbouring villages. The knights discovered this and surrounded each village in turn, killing every Jew. At Mors hundreds of Jewish bodies were seen floating in the Rhine. In Mainz – again – the Jews took refuge in the Archbishop's Palace but, as at Worms, the Crusaders stormed the palace and massacred the inmates.

It was the same all over Germany and it set the pattern for the future: rich opportunities for plunder and a chance to translate into action the religious anti-semitism that had begun with the Emperor Constantine in the fourth century. In the Middle Ages Christian fanaticism excelled itself in providing charges against the Jews. Not only had they murdered Jesus but they undertook the ritual murder of children; they desecrated the Host; they intrigued with the enemy (whoever the 'enemy' might be at the time – and this has a familiar ring: Jewish traitors plotting the downfall of the state). It was from the Crusaders that the German Jews first heard the cry 'Hep! Hep!' – that snarling bark of hatred that has echoed down the centuries, always revived when anti-semitism was at its most intense. ('Hep' is said to be an abbreviation of the Latin *Hierossolyma est perdita* – 'Jerusalem is destroyed', although some think it comes from the old German *habe* – 'give'.)

Five centuries of horror and darkness were to follow the First Crusade with everything conspiring to separate the German Jew from his neighbours and to develop in him certain attitudes towards his persecutors: attitudes that were to persist in the persecution under Hitler. A passivity, an acceptance, a baring of the throat before the knife of his enemies that has evoked either impatience or admiration, according to whether it is seen as a ritual defeatism that verges on masochism or a triumph of the spirit of the Deutero-Isaiah (the Unknown Prophet) that enables the Jew to see himself as one chosen to expiate the suffering and pain of mankind. Indeed the medieval liturgy of the Jews abounded in *selihot* – penitential prayers which are full of agony and self-accusation.

In 1348 the Black Death struck Europe and the Jews were again the scapegoats. At first the rich blamed the poor; then they united in blaming the lepers; finally the Jews. The torturings and the burnings multiplied. But now the conditioned hatred of the Christian for the Jew gained a new dimension: the hatred of debtor for creditor. In other words, 'money was the poison that killed the Jews'. More and more of them had been forced to become money-lenders and by the fourteenth century the nobility owed them large sums. In Strasbourg two thousand prisoners were burned alive in the Jewish cemetery and the money of the victims was divided among the artisans of the city. The poor got their hands on some money; the rich disposed of a creditor. This went on all over Germany: in Worms, Mayen, Spires, Erfurt. Often the Jews set their own homes afire and died in an inferno of their own making. The only city of any size to protect its Jews was Regensburg. At that time few Jews elected to save themselves by baptism. Instead they fled to Bohemia and to Poland, where under Casimir the Great there was only the plague to fear.

There is no need to follow the German Jews in detail into the twentieth century. Certain patterns remain consistent. But this historical excursion is necessary if only because many books on the Nazi persecution of the Jews tend to imply that German anti-semitism was invented by Hitler – or at least by Luther. In fact

Luther was only exploiting a tradition that was already ancient in Germany. Curiously enough he had begun by speaking *for* the Jews:

If a man wanted to be a true Christian, he might better become a Jew.

Later he reverted to the anti-semitism of the Church he was rebelling against, contributing a boiling venom of his own:

They are thirsty bloodhounds and murderers of all Christendom ... for more than fourteen hundred years, and indeed they were often burned to death upon the accusation that they had poisoned water and wells, stolen children, and torn and hacked them apart, in order to cool their temper secretly with Christian blood.

It was all there then, by the sixteenth century: all that the Nazis attempted in the twentieth. *Plus ça change, plus c'est la même chose.* The Final Solution was not born in a vacuum. The history of German Jewry offers not only all the weapons with which the Nazis tried to exterminate the Jews, but all the responses of the Jews themselves.

Between the fourteenth and the seventeenth centuries the figure of the *Hof-Jude* or Court Jew emerged.

Germany after the Thirty Years' War was in ruins. It was not one state but three hundred: each a little kingdom in miniature. Each had its standing army and a circle of tiny dignitaries revolving around a toy monarch.

The *Hof-Jude* was a privileged figure who suffered none of the traditional disabilities of the Jew. He was free to trade, travel, and live how he liked, under the protection of the king. The *Hof-Jude*'s function was to lend money to the ruler, superintend his finances, and arrange supplies for his army. The Court Jews achieved their greatest privilege and influence in the late seventeenth century, although their position always tended to be a difficult one. They functioned against a background of jealousy and intrigue; they were exposed to the machinations of rival financiers; in times of defeat or of a bad harvest they often served – inevitably – as scapegoats. Let them slip from the monarch's favour and they could face disgrace, imprisonment, even death. But the *Hof-Jude* exemplifies the interdependence of Jew and gentile that was to grow stronger and stronger in Germany.

The *Hof-Jude* was relied on, even courted – and yet readily blamed. One cannot help suspecting that this, like so many Jewish-gentile relationships, was essentially one-sided; that the princeling used the Jew who, although he was aware of this and despite his own racial integrity, allowed himself to be used.

But the *Hof-Jude* enjoyed great advantages. The disabilities inflicted on the ordinary Jewish community were so heavy that it was worth anything to escape them. A Jew paid to be born, to marry, and to die. Restrictions were calculated to limit and check the extent of the Jewish trade, so as to lessen the competition to Christians. Spies were posted near synagogues to make sure that the prayers making references to idolators (Christians) were not said. Families were limited by statute. One son or daughter was free to marry and then paid certain annual marriage-dues. Other children could marry only if their possessions equalled a certain figure – greater for the third child than for the second – and if they paid higher annual dues.

Not until Napoleon crossed the Rhine did the German Jews taste any real freedom. By 1806 Austria and Prussia were crushed. West and South Germany were incorporated in a Confederation of the Rhine, which included Saxony and Westphalia, Württemberg, and Bavaria. Westphalia, Bavaria, Baden, Württemberg, and Mecklenburg liberated Jews completely. Saxony, 'the Protestant Spain', refused to do so. Frankfurt was reluctant, but finally agreed. Prussia granted Jews full citizenship, but did not allow them to hold positions in the state.

During this period of liberation and enfranchisement financial power tended to flow away from individuals – the *Hof-Jude* figures – towards banking dynasties like the Rothschilds, who first came into prominence at this time.

The Napoleonic respite was brief. The Jews were cheated at the Congress of Vienna in 1814. They were allowed to retain all the privileges already granted by the German states. The catch lay in the substitution of the word 'by' for the word 'in'. As in every state except Prussia and Mecklenburg reforms had been enacted by the French, not by the states themselves, this left the Jews as badly off as before. Worse off in fact, for the mood of the time, with its romantic cult of the medieval, bred anti-semitism. There were riots in Carlsruhe, Frankfurt, Würzburg, and Hamburg. Once again the hideous 'Hep! Hep!' sounded in German streets and with it *'Judah verrecke!'* (Perish Judaea). Only in a few states were the rights bestowed by the French preserved : in Hessia and to a lesser extent in Baden with Württemberg. In Prussia the Jews retained some rights; everywhere else the old conditions were revived in a modern atmosphere.

In the period that followed baptism was to offer itself as 'an admission ticket to modern civilization', as the poet Heine put it. He himself had been baptized in 1823 in order to overcome professional discrimination and become a Doctor of Laws, and he always remembered this with bitterness. It was during this era that conversions of German Jews became numerous : to Protestanism in the north of Germany, to Roman Catholicism in the south. By the beginning of the twentieth century there were more Christians of Jewish descent in Germany than anywhere else.

It is not a coincidence that this period also saw the beginning of the Reform movement in German Judaism. This started with the singing of hymns and the saying of prayers in German. Although this can be seen as a kind of 'Protestant' reaction to traditional rituals, such as the cantor intoning the prayers in Hebrew as he had done for centuries, it was also a move away from the ghetto, an instinctive attempt to identify with the outside world. The dropping from the liturgy of many prayers referring to the faith in a messianic return to Palestine was a gesture of loyalty towards the German state – and thus, perhaps, a tacit plea for emancipation. The synagogue was called a 'temple', a description hitherto reserved for the fallen temple in Jerusalem, for whose restoration the Jews had prayed for centuries. The 'temple' could now be in Berlin or Breslau just as well as in Jerusalem. The reformers felt they were moving towards unity with their fellow-countrymen. Some Jews, of course, reacted against Reform towards Orthodoxy; later a compromise group emerged : the Conservative. Among those Jews who still practised their religion at the beginning of the twentieth century the greatest number were Conservative. They kept to the dietary laws; observed the Sabbath; used the orthodox Hebrew prayers, but listened to sermons in German.

The Reform movement can be seen as another instance of the craving towards assimilation working in the German Jew, and this urge towards identification showed itself in various guises throughout the nineteenth century, against a widespread anti-semitic undertow. After the war with France in 1870 thousands were ruined in a wave of speculation followed by a disastrous collapse – *Der Grosse Krach* (the Great Panic) – and of course they reacted against the Jews, damning them as usual as alien spoilers in the German heartland.

The second half of the century also saw the outcrop of an intellectual anti-semitism that has been borrowed as a 'philosophic' basis for Nazism. Count Joseph Arthur de Gobineau was a French writer and diplomat. His *Essay on the Inequalities of the Human Race* (1853) advanced the theory that there were 'higher' and 'lower' races. Only the white races possessed true creative power and of these the so-called 'Aryan' group ranked highest. And, on Gobineau's ascending order of merit, of the Aryan group the Germanic or Nordic section are supreme. While exalting the Aryans, Gobineau degraded the Semites whom he said were totally uncreative. Gobineau's Aryan and Semite theories are important in the psychopathology of Nazism; and it is curious that this Frenchman should have been followed by an Engishman in creating a National Socialist rationale. This was Houston Chamberlain, who became a German and married Wagner's daughter. His *Foundations of the Nineteenth Century* (1899) influenced Kaiser Wilhelm II and later Hitler himself. For Chamberlain, as for Gobineau, the key to history was race. The Jews were a menace. While careful to maintain their own racial purity they were prepared to infect Indo-European stock. The Jews were a negative race, a 'bastardy'. The Germans on the other hand are the race most richly endowed. They have the right to be masters of the world.

Among the writers who swum in this trend Eugen Dühring, 'the philosopher of Jew hatred', is said to have sown the seed of Zionism in the mind of its founder, Theodor Herzl. Reading Dühring first aroused Herzl's sense of racial identity. This was sharpened by insult when, years later, entering a bar, he was greeted by a loud 'Hep! Hep!' In 1896 he published *Der Judenstaat*, which set out his dream of a Jewish state. When it was proposed to hold the first Zionist congress in Munich, several rabbis protested. According to them Judaism required its followers to 'give all their heart and strength' to the land to which they belonged. Herzl told the rabbis that they were not free citizens; that they 'belonged' – *angehören* – to Germany : a comment on those whose dominant passion it was to be first of all German and only afterwards Jews.

The majority of German Jews under Wilhelm II remained indifferent to Herzl and his dreams. It was during this era that they developed the kind of collective persona, hard to define but easy to recognize, summed up by the untranslatable 'yaeche'. Most German Jews were middle-class, contributing heavily to the professions – although the proportion of Jewish doctors and lawyers has been exaggerated. Certainly many of the problems of the Jewish refugees who were to leave Germany fifty years later derived from their being so overwhelmingly middle-class. The solid 'German' qualities developed by the German Jews were further evidence of their assimilation into the ambitious, expansionist Germany of Kaiser Wilhelm – the 'new' Germany that other nations had begun to dislike and even fear. Like other countries, it was being developed by a rising commercial bourgeoise that had replaced the old burgher-merchant class. But in Germany other factors were added: a fiercer chauvinism; a traditional respect for the military caste; and – anti-semitism. The paradox of the German Jewish position lay in their absorption into a society that carried within it an urge towards their destruction. An aspect of this Germany was personalized by Heinrich Mann in his trilogy *Das Kaiserreich* (The Empire) in the character of Dietrich Hessling: the 'new man', the ruthless bourgeois who rises to great heights in the Germany of Kaiser Wilhelm – on whom he models himself, even to imitating his aggressive moustache. Hessling claims that 'blood and iron' are still the most effective remedies. He is, of course, anti-semitic. Involved in a doubtful business deal with a member of the Junker class, he proclaims his satisfaction that two 'honourable' men should be doing business – so unlike the dirty dealings of the Jews. Naturally he is intensely patriotic. In the later part of the trilogy he becomes an arms' manufacturer – typical of the kind of German capitalist for whom the Jews served as scapegoats.

In the years before the First World War both anti-semitism and Jewish-German assimilation proceeded along strange, parallel lines. Most Jews tried to ignore expressions of anti-semitic feeling. They were helped in this by a belief in that fashionable nineteenth-century concept, the ideal of progress. The fashionable 'intellectual' anti-semitism was merely an aberration, something that must pass. Anyway, the violence – the riotings and burnings – these must belong to the past. This was how many Jews argued, and the farther they had moved from traditional Jewish attitudes the more necessary such arguments became. Germany needed the Jews, they told themselves. And, indeed, with a few exceptions the German Jews had never fled during a thousand years of persecution. They had stayed; they rode out the storm; and in part this was because they knew that while the pogrom might bring their enemies a certain amount of loot in the end one does not 'kill the cow that one wants to milk'. Despite popular anti-semitism, the development of a more complex system of capitalism made the Jews more and more necessary to the state. (Just as, centuries before, the *Hof-Jude* might be reviled or deposed but still remained indispensable.) After the First World War Hugo Bettauer wrote a novel, *Die Stadt ohne Juden* (The City without Jews), that postulated the expulsion of the Jews from Vienna. The city cannot get along without them and they are soon recalled. Bettauer's thesis crystallizes the myth of Jewish indispensability that many Jews clung to long after Hitler came to power.

It was not hard for the majority of German Jews to convince themselves that they were unassailable. After all, they did their part in the war. Although the army class had never welcomed the Jews – for many years only a doctor could be granted commissioned rank – 100,000 Jews served, 80,000 at the front. 12,000 were killed; 35,000 decorated for bravery. A Jew wrote the 'Hymn of Hate'. Jewish patriotic enthusiasm never waned at any time, even when a member of the High Command suggested that the impending defeat be blamed on the Jews. The fantasy that a 'Jewish international conspiracy' had sold out the country was seized on by millions of Germans and even given official endorsement by General Ludendorff. But the Jews ignored all the signs, no doubt helped by the fact that in its early years the Weimar Republic threw every door open to them: the government services, the universities, and the judiciary. The Weimar Republic, the first democratic constitution Germany had ever had, even had Jews among its ministers.

The Weimar honeymoon was brief enough. In June 1922 the dollar rose to two and a half trillion marks. A million German bank accounts were wiped out. American investors in German currency and securities lost a billion dollars. New foreign loans, including another two billion dollars from America, gave a momentary appearance of solvency. Walter Rathenau, the Minister of Foreign Affairs, was negotiating to save Germany from the worst consequences of inflation. A Berliner, son of a Jewish industrialist and a director of the great electrical trust A.E.G., he had organized the economy against the British blockade during the war. Now the indispensable financial expert of the Weimar Republic, he had secured monetary agreements with France and the U.S.A. earlier in the year. Undoubtedly his gifts transcended those of the usual financier-politician. On 22 June 1922 he was murdered.

The trial of his assassins momentarily illuminated the blank yet sinister world of post-war Germany. The men who shot Rathenau seem anonymous: conventional masks for the forces in whose pay they were. The Junkers? The 'capitalists'? 'International Jewry' itself? The Rathenau trial was no Dreyfus case. No one was there to rally the forces of liberalism and republicanism as had happened in France. There was only cynicism and evasion: symptoms of a mood that would soon overwhelm all Germany.

The Inflation hit everyone. Everyone suffered but especially the middle classes. The million bank accounts that had been wiped out stood for that fragile wall which the middle class in every country erects between itself and the fear of poverty. Now that wall was down. The German people did not know what had hit them.

Everything was calculated to produce a 'they' and 'us' mentality. 'They' are always omnipresent, powerful, and merciless. 'They', of course, may be anyone – anyone whom the underdogs visualize as being responsible for their suffering at the time: the government, the capitalists, or even, with middle-class groups who have sunk in the economic scale, 'those people who keep striking for more money'.

In the Germany of the twenties – the Germany of the *Schieber*, the war profiteer who has grown fat in the peace – it did not take long to convince a large section of the people that 'they' were the Jews. *Schiebers* undoubtedly existed and naturally there were Jews among them. But there were plenty of gentiles among them too – financiers, bankers, entrepreneurs – and it suited these to hide behind the traditional scapegoat. Hugo Sturmer, a gentile and a Christian, was perhaps the biggest *Schieber* of all, but he attracted little popular odium, any more than did the impersonal façade of the Reichsbank itself. The Jews were there to take the blame: a reflex conditioned through a thousand years. The Jews had murdered Christ. The Jews had taken Christian children for ritual sacrifice. When pestilence raged, the Jews had poisoned the wells. The Jews had organized the French Revolution. A Jewish 'stab in the back' had lost Germany the war. Three Jewish financiers – Strauss, Goldschmidt, and Gutman – had arranged the devaluation of the mark in order to gain control of German industry. 'International Jewry' had planned the Bolshevik revolution in Russia. (By now *The Protocols of the Elders of Zion*, that extraordinary and potent anti-semitic fantasy, was circulating throughout the world.) Finally, as the Nazis began to grow in power and influence, it began to be said that the Weimar Republic had itself been some kind of Jewish conspiracy.

Although they did not realize it, time was running out for the Jews. By 1932 there were six million unemployed in Germany. Hindenburg was elected president with nineteen and a half million votes; Hitler received thirteen million. In July 1932 the Nazis polled fourteen million votes in the elections for the Reichstag; the Social Democrats eight million; the Communists five million. But – deceptively enough – by November 1932 the Nazis had lost two million votes and the Communists had gained 101 seats in the Reichstag. It seems likely, however, that this success by the Communists was actually of benefit to the Nazis for it was to frighten many people into supporting them as a 'bastion against Bolshevism' (a phrase that will become familiar); and it enabled Hitler to take advantage of the stupidity of his political rivals and come to an arrangement by which Hindenburg made him chancellor: this set in motion the series of events which ended in the Reichstag fire and the final seizure of power by the Nazis.

And the Jews themselves? If in the years preceding Hitler's triumph the blaming and the hating had gone along traditional lines, so had the Jewish reaction to it. (With one hopeful exception perhaps. In the twenties Zionism first began to be taken seriously by the German Jews, particularly among the youth at the universities.) And there were other Jews who, ironically and pitiably, even managed to find a scapegoat for a scapegoat: the

Ostjuden. There were the East European Jews who had been deported from Lithuania and Poland by their thousands by the German Army during the war. In the twenties their numbers had been swollen by many more who had fled from Poland. They were 'different' from the German Jews; in fact nearer the bearded, gesticulating Shylocks of the stereotype. (Hitler offers the same stereotype when he mentions his encounter with some Galician Jews in Vienna, with their caftans and side-curls.) If the German Jews did not welcome these newcomers, they treated them fairly and generously; but they tended to deplore their noisy behaviour, their money-grubbing lack of taste. No wonder gentiles were anti-semitic if they saw Jews going on like that!

Of course only a minority found satisfaction in making the *Ostjuden* a surrogate for the feelings against themselves. The rest ignored and rationalized hostility as they had always done. Not long before Hitler came to power a number of prominent Jews placed a signed advertisement in the *Vössiche Zeitung* in which they deplored anti-Jewish riots – in Palestine.

We profess the Jewish religion but reject any kind of Jewish nationalism. We regard ourselves, along with the overwhelming majority of German Jews, as members of the German, not of the Jewish people.

As the Nazi party got more and more powerful, as academics and professional men and even the clergy began to see the advantages to themselves in supporting the Nazis, the Jews waited: ignoring, dreaming, or arguing, according to temperament. There was, in any case, little they could do. They might have certain attitudes in common; but they were too diverse a group to 'unite'. They were divided by all the usual social and economic factors and by their religion – or their lack of it. A tailor in Berlin; a banker in Hamburg; an Orthodox cattle dealer from southern Germany; a journalist of Zionist views; a Conservative manufacturer in Dresden; an agnostic physician – what did these have in common? Jewish representative bodies usually represented only minority elements. The Jews could only wait and hope, as they heard the words of the 'Horst Wessel' song,

Und wenn's Judenblut vom Messer spritzt, ja dann geht's nochmal so gut. (When Jewish blood flows from the knife things will go twice as well.)

that the Nazis were indulging in menacing gestures of a kind to which the Jews were accustomed. Or if deeds were to follow words, that the traditional pattern of what Raul Hilberg has called 'alleviation and compliance' would be fulfilled. He has identified certain Jewish reactions to force which have been repeated again and again over the last two thousands years. He instances the Jews in Alexandria in A.D. 38. They were driven into the Delta, their food supplies cut off; every escape route sealed. They then petitioned the Emperor Caligua for relief. This Hilberg calls 'alleviation'. He describes as 'anticipatory compliance' the Jewish readiness to do what is wanted before it is even asked for and cites the mobilization of forced labour in the Warsaw ghetto before the Gestapo ordered it. The Jews never run from a pogrom: they live through it. Thus the German Jews tried to live peaceably under Hitler. They were, after all, only following the pattern that had saved them in the past. Even the Nazis would realize how essential the German Jews were.

But many Jews simply clung to the fact that they were Germans. How could anyone take that away from them? 'If I love you what's that to do with you?'

The testimony of the Jewish refugees from Germany is necessarily fragmented. Refugees may remember certain key-incidents, but the sheer weight of years has usually flattened memory into a grey summary. The refugees were in any case a small minority who decided to leave Germany. The majority who made another decision or who decided to go too late are necessarily silent. One can only look for answers among the few survivors.

Georg Joachim feels that the safety of himself and his sister weighed largely with his parents. His father was a professor in the medical faculty in the University of Berlin who also had a large private practice. Although the Joachims felt pride in their Jewish ancestry they had no religious affiliations with Judaism and played no part in any Jewish activity. Their identification with the German professional classes was as complete as it could possibly be. Financially their position was very good; socially and in every other way the family led an attractive and agreeable life. And yet, early in 1933, within a few weeks of Hitler's coming to power, Professor Joachim and his wife decided they must leave Germany. This was an unusual decision for such a time. While emigration was obviously comparatively easy, most Jews failed to recognize the necessity for it. The air was already thick with anti-Jewish threats but Professor Joachim had as yet no reason to feel threatened personally, except indeed through his son and daughter's humiliations at school. As a temporary measure he put them at a school which catered for Jewish children only : the numbers attending such schools had, of course, increased enormously during the first weeks of the Hitler régime. But his mind had been made up from the first : he was going to take his wife and children to England and make a new life there.

This decision showed great determination and clarity of mind. Not only was Professor Joachim turning his back on an established social and financial position, a degree of acceptance in his own world which the Nazis could hardly threaten – or so the professor's colleagues were busily assuring themselves – but he was going to throw aside all the honour and prestige he had won in thirty years of medicine. At fifty-four he was relinquishing a university chair and a large practice to go to a strange country where he knew no one. Once there, he would have to go back to the beginning : study for years in a foreign language in order to qualify as a doctor all over again. German medical qualifications were not recognized in Britain and hardly anywhere else; in fact the only place where the professor could have taken up his career again without re-qualifying was Shanghai. And yet Georg does not remember his mother or father uttering a word of doubt or complaint. Georg and his sister Helga were bewildered. They could not make the imaginative leap their forthcoming emigration required. Their parents tried to make England real to them by showing them old bound copies of English periodicals like the *Strand* and the *Illustrated London News* and trying to conjure up places like the Zoo and the Tower of London, making the children see them as part of an attractive, colourful future.

After Professor Joachim had come to his decision but before he left for England (he was to go first, the family following), on 7 April 1933, the German Government enacted the Law for the Reconstruction of the Civil Service which represented a blanket proscription of all state employees of 'non-Ayran' descent. (Four days later a regulation defined a 'non-Aryan' as a person one of whose parents or grandparents was Jewish.) This law, proliferating through a number of ordinances and decrees, led to the dismissal of thousands of government and municipal employees, members of the judiciary, public health officials, school teachers, and university professors and lecturers. Professor Joachim's chair would not have been immediately threatened, since he had served as a medical officer at the front during the war and was thus exempted under the so-called Veteran's Clause, but he did not regret his decision, hard as it was.

At that time it was comparatively easy to enter the United Kingdom, and the National Socialist Government had not perfected their machinery for mulcting the prospective emigrant, so the Joachims were able to get a good part of their capital out and even tranship their furniture to England.

Professor Joachim left Berlin in April 1933. A week later Frau Joachim received a letter from him, giving the address of his lodgings in Edinburgh. He had enrolled as a first-year student of medicine at Edinburgh University. Soon afterwards Frau Joachim arranged for Georg and Helga to start learning English. They had lessons from a Fräulein Eckermann who lived in one of the western suburbs of Berlin. But they made little progress. England was still unreal to them, despite pictures of Tower Bridge and the Changing of the Guard; and Scotland still more so, although they knew now that they would be going to live in Edinburgh.

Meanwhile their mother waited, full of anxiety, longing to see her husband again. They had many friends and they were all full of rumours, good and bad. The Joachims were both musicians of great accomplishment and, unlike some of the professor's colleagues, their circle did not consist merely of other doctors and their wives: they also knew many people connected with the arts. Inevitably, some of these were Jewish and thus Frau Joachim found herself watching the barometer of Jewish hopes and fears. Few had yet suffered material harm from the new régime, although everyone knew someone who had lost their job through the Reconstruction of the Civil Service Law. None of their friends had been physically attacked by the Nazis, but every day brought a new story. (At this time the Jews were not the sole targets of the Nazis. The Communists, Socialists, and Trade Unionists still occupied some of their attention.) Seven Jews had been brought to an S.S. barracks where, at gun-point, they were ordered to flog each other. Early in March a Dr Wilhelm Spieger, a lawyer and a Socialist living in Kiel, was awakened at 2 a.m. by a loud pounding on his door. Two brownshirts stood outside. Frau Spieger tried to telephone the police, but one of the brownshirts shot Dr Spieger. Then they left. Dr Spieger died in his wife's arms a few minutes later. Elderly Jews had been beaten up in the streets. A contemporary of Frau Joachim was spat on and threatened by Nazi youths.

And yet Frau Joachim got the impression that some of these things were hardly real to the people who told her of them. Certainly most of their friends disapproved of her husband's decision. Anyone who approved was thinking of going himself. Some doctors and their wives could hardly contain themselves when they thought of what Karl was giving up professionally. To go back to the beginning! And in a foreign country! At his age! It was clear that they doubted his ability to re-qualify at all. And herself and the children? When were they going? In a week or two's time? Such an upheaval . . . They pitied her: she could see that. What could justify such a thing? The Nazis? Well, they were extremely unpleasant and it was obvious that nasty things were going to go on happening, for a time at least, but these were the fanatics, the kind of people who are always to the fore when a revolution begins. The moderates always stay in the background at first; soon they would take over and a saner state of things prevail. Anti-semitism wasn't new; the Jews had been through this before. There were sensible men in the government: Schacht for instance, that was a clever fellow. Men like Schacht knew that Germany needed the Jews: that the Jews were involved with too many things for the country to be able to do without them. The Civil Service law just wouldn't work. It was the work of the extremists, and it would soon be quietly shelved. Hitler? Well, it was known that Thyssen was *using* Hitler . . .

So they talked. And then someone else would be beaten up, or a swastika or a '*Judah Verreck*' daubed on a wall, and they would be all a-flutter again, talking of getting away while the going was good, asking Frau Joachim how Karl had got away so easily with all his responsibilities. But they were still talking, still swinging from panic to reassurance and back again, when she and Georg and Helga got on the train at the Zoo Station.

A few of the waverers eventually followed them, some soon

after and one or two much later, when it was almost impossible to get out of Germany and anyone who did manage it got to Britain penniless. But mostly they stayed and died in the concentration camps and killing-centres of the Reich.

Hugo Neher also left Germany in the early months of 1933. He was young; he had little interest in politics; he was in no immediate danger. And yet he was overpowered by a sense of disgust and outrage. He could not go on breathing the air of 'that polluted land' – as he was to call his native Germany.

He came of a family that had been in Germany since 1400. Although the Nehers had not shed their Jewishness to the extent the Joachims had, they too considered themselves Germans and only incidentally Jews. Hugo's father was a nineteenth-century liberal at heart, devoted to the ideal of progress. The anti-semitism of Gobineau, Wagner and the rest had been a temporary madness: everything was working towards future happiness and brotherhood. Herr Neher was opposed to Zionism, rejecting like so many Jews of his generation Herzl's dream of a National Home. 'Jerusalem' might figure in the Nehers' family prayers, but this was symbolism, nothing more. Every German Jew held Jerusalem in his heart.

Hitler's triumph shattered the young Neher's belief in progress and eventually converted him to Zionism. But in those early days of 1933 he was conscious mainly of feeling trapped. He was a young man with a passionate craving for freedom. He still quotes a line from the first English poem he ever learned, by John Barbour 'Fredome, all solace to man giffith'. He knew, instinctively, that the air of Germany lacked this essential oxygen. 'I was haunted by the *passion de malheur*. Everything seemed to be unclean and it made me positively choke.'

His, then, was a leap in the dark. He simply felt he could not stand Germany any longer. In the years to come he would often be congratulated for his foresight in leaving Germany so early. He denies any special prescience in doing so. His foresight was born of a passionate resentment – and he wonders that more did not follow their resentment to drive them to escape.

He remembers one incident: the catalytic episode that was needed to turn emotion into decision for him. He was walking down a quiet Berlin street one afternoon when he saw a platoon

of storm troopers marching towards him. He knew he would be
expected to give them the Nazi salute as they passed. If he
didn't . . . No one took that risk, let alone a Jew. But Hugo knew
he could not raise his arm in that salute.

He ran into the first house he saw. What would he have done
if he had found Nazi sympathizers inside? In fact it belonged
to an elderly couple who did not understand what he wanted.
When he emerged on to the empty street ten minutes later, he
promised himself that this should never happen again.

Lothar Kahlmann was an exception among German Jewish
refugees in that he did not belong recognizably to the middle class.
He was a tailor, who lived and worked in a room in an old working-class district of Berlin, high in an alley through an archway
where the walls were daubed with Nazi crosses and plastered
with tattered bills. His clients were all gentile and all poor. They
knew he was poor too and this coloured their dealings with him.
They all came from the mile or two of tenements and decaying
high houses divided down the centre by the overhead railway.
Lothar made clothes for these people, and sold them on the instalment plan. It was a rule of his never to press for payment.
He would make a suit and allow the customer up to a year to pay
for it. By then he might need a new overcoat; and, by the time
both debts were cleared, Lothar might have made him more clothing, perhaps to the extent of another hundred marks or so. The
whole district owed him money, with Lothar rolling before him
a kind of snowball of credit, sometimes swelling, sometimes
diminishing. He had been told that the Nazis would call this
usury. Lothar could not see how this could be. Was he not helping
his neighbours? If he did not give credit, he would have no customers and these poor people would have no clothes. He knew
that his customers, decent working-class people, had grumbled
about the Jews for years. But only the *rich* Jews. They didn't
think of him, Lothar Kahlmann, the way they thought of the
bankers and the big store owners. They liked him. They needed
him. They were good people. He could say of them, 'These are
the real people: they have the true heart of Germany beating
inside them.'

Lothar lived an isolated life and this perhaps made him less
conscious of the Nazis than he might have otherwise have been

– this and the fact that anti-semitism was more virulent in the country and small towns than in a poor quarter of Berlin.

He had been aware of Boycott Day, but it hadn't meant too much to him, in his quarter of Berlin. He had heard of the Civil Service laws but knew no one who was affected by them.

The Nuremberg Laws were a different matter. Lothar read all about them and, within a month or two of their being passed, they were to lead to the first of the two traumatic incidents that brought him to the decision to leave Germany.

The Nuremberg Laws were passed on 13 September 1935 after a propaganda campaign to prepare public opinion. They had been evolved in a few hours against a Wagnerian background of roistering and brawling at the Nazi party rally, the work of a group of legal experts who feverishly drafted them in the music-room of a villa belonging to Wilhelm Frick, the Minister of the Interior.

The Nuremberg Laws were actually two laws: the Reich Citizenship Act and the Blood Protection Act. The first of these introduced the concept of 'Reich Citizenship'. No Jew could be a citizen of the Reich ('a horse which is born in a stable is still no cow' as an anti-semite had once remarked in the Reichstag), and a Jew could not vote on political questions or be appointed to any office of state. The Blood Protection Act was concerned with 'racial purity'. Legal definition was given to what had been theory. Marriage and extra-marital relations between Jews and Germans were prohibited in the interest of 'the survival of the German race'. Nor might any Jew employ a German woman under forty-five in his household.

The Reich Citizenship Act spawned a number of regulations. The first of these was designed to sort out Aryans from non-Aryans and in doing so it created a new entity, a *Mischling*. Full Jews were people with three Jewish grandparents; people with two Jewish grandparents who belonged to the Jewish faith at the time of the passing of the Nuremberg Laws; anyone married to a Jew; the child of any marriage of which one partner was a Jew; the illegitimate child of a union between a Jew and another person. The new entity, the *Mischling*, was a half or quarter Jew. A *Mischling* of the first degree was someone who was descended from two Jewish grandparents, but who did not belong to the

THE JEWS OF GERMANY

Jewish faith on 15 September 1935 and was not married to a Jewish person at that time. A *Mischling* of the second degree was someone who was descended from one Jewish grandparent and who was not a member of the Jewish faith or married to a Jew.

This new category of *Mischlings* became important. Before November 1935 the people who were now defined as *Mischlings* would, by reason of their part-Jewish ancestry, have been treated simply as Jews; after that date they were not. In fact the *Mischlings* were to inhabit a no-man's-land in which they could encounter many possibilities, ranging from a grudging toleration that permitted a *Mischling* to serve in the ranks of the army (one reason for the creation of the *Mischling*: non-Aryan cannon-fodder) and only marry a German with official consent to *Befreiung* – liberation, which meant full citizenship of the Reich.

Many more regulations followed. Anti-Jewish measures were now given the force of law. Doctors, dentists, veterinary surgeons, pharmacists were either prohibited from practising or severely restricted. And the 'Aryan Clause' – as Lothar Kahlmann was to discover – was widely used as an excuse for breaking business contracts. In April 1938 an order was made for the 'Prevention of Camouflaged Assistance to Jewish Undertakings'. This was designed to prevent Jews from using gentiles as nominal owners of their businesses while retaining control themselves. And on 26 April came an order for the 'Disclosure of Jewish Assets'. This was really a levy: a proportion of the assets were to be retained as a kind of deposit. Not unexpectedly, this was the suggestion of Reichsmarshal Göring, who had always been interested in the financial aspects of anti-Jewish legislation.

Lothar Kahlmann realized how serious the Nuremberg Laws were for the Jews, but he didn't see how they could affect him. All along, these anti-Jewish laws were hitting at rich people – judges, high civil servants, and more recently, lawyers and doctors. But who would bother with him, a poor tailor living in a slum?

And then he thought he began to notice things. No one insulted him, but he thought he noticed a coldness. People were out more often when he called. When they were in, they didn't talk so long. Money got harder to collect. The snowball he trundled grew to alarming proportions. And then came the matter of young Norval's overcoat.

The Norvals had been his customers for years. On this occasion Lothar had called to collect an instalment that had fallen due. These people were customers but Lothar, a solitary man, would have called them friends. The horrible shock, then, of having young Hans Norval, who was barely sixteen, snarl and spit and shout *'Jude!'* Then of having the father, Otto, whom Lothar had always thought a very decent man, remain silent while Hans abused Lothar with Berlin gutter-words. And then the humiliation of having Hans throw the 'Aryan clause' of the Nuremberg Laws at him as an excuse for cancelling the debt.

This was the first of the two incidents. The second was less personal but more frightening.

It happened on a Tuesday night. Lothar had been to see one of his few relatives, a female cousin. The long street he was walking along was empty; then he saw groups of people coming towards him, all moving the same way. They were men and, as they came closer, he saw they were brownshirts. There must have been a Nazi meeting that evening.

Lothar tried to keep at the same pace as before. If he turned, it would look as if he was running away. He would soon come face to face with them, but if he kept walking they might ignore him. That was the best chance.

It worked, for they all passed him, most of them with scarcely a look. They were shouting obscenities and singing the 'Horst Wessel Song'. Lothar had tried to look relaxed as he passed them. The more at ease he seemed, the better his chance. These men could smell fear as an animal smells it. But he told himself that these were just young Germans dressed in a kind of Boy Scout uniform. Some would be bullies, but others would be decent lads, just going along with the crowd...

They had all passed him. Lothar had noticed how quiet many parts of Berlin were now except for the times when the Nazis were demonstrating. He began to walk faster. He daren't let them see he was hurrying: now it didn't matter.

Almost before he realized it, he came up to some stragglers from the main group: four young men who carried Nazi banners shouldered like rifles and walking in the same direction as Lothar himself.

He slowed down, to let them draw away from him; then he saw two men hurrying along on the other side of the street. The brownshirts saw them too; they crossed the street and confronted the two men. The men tried to run but the Nazis were too quick for them. They jumped on them, pairing off with military precision, two to each man, knocking them down and starting to kick them as they lay on the pavement. One of the men squirmed away, pressing his face to the ground; the other managed to get up, struggling on to his knees. As he did so, the Nazis drove at him with their banner-staves, which had sharp metal ends pointed like arrow-heads. Lothar saw the sharp points stabbing the man's face; saw the face tear across and then the gouts of blood bursting through it like blobs of jam bursting a paper bag. He heard the man screaming and the Nazis shouting, and then the man was lying on his back and all four brownshirts were kicking him. (Their other victim had managed to crawl away, somehow.) Lothar stood there, paralysed. Then he saw the four brownshirts moving away, shouldering their banner-staves in the most matter-of-fact manner possible. Lothar began to vomit. The vomit gushed out over his shirt and collar, soaking them with a hot, disgusting acid. Then he started to tremble so violently that he had to hold on to the iron railings beside him. All this time the man lay where the Nazis had left him. Lothar could hear him groaning but he did not go to him. He didn't even think of helping him; in fact, when the trembling grew less, he walked slowly away in the direction he had come, without even looking at the man, whose groaning had stopped by now.

Afterwards his own self-accusing guilt made him ask himself again and again: was there anything he could have done? In his own disgust and terror he hadn't even thought of the other man. He could have done nothing when the brownshirts were attacking the man: that was obvious. But later, when they'd gone? Lothar had been so sick with squeamish horror and fear for himself that he had simply run away. He kept thinking of this, but he knew that if he saw the same thing happen again he would always be too frightened to do anything.

He thought about young Norval's insults too: and that night, for the first time, he thought of leaving Germany. He had no idea how he could do this but he knew he had to go.

In the months that followed, in the time between his decision and his actual departure, Lothar scarcely left his room. Working away there, he still felt safe, anonymous, as if all this hatred were passing over his head. But he knew this was really a delusion. He was a Jew and he was not safe anywhere in Germany.

Today Ilsa Geiss can look back on the thirties in Germany and analyse the complacencies, the fears, and the courage of the group to which she belonged.

More clearly than most refugees she sees the paradox of the German Jews' relationship to the 'real' Germans, the passionate, bred-in-the-bone desire of some of them to be Germans and nothing else. All her judgements are illuminated by a sense of history. She sees in the French orientation of the early German Jewish refugees – some of the first to leave went to France rather than Britain and got trapped there when the Germans invaded – an atavistic reaching-back to Heine, that attractive and symbolical figure, and to the fact that Napoleon was the first to grant 'civil rights' to the German Jews.

Ilsa Geiss differs from most refugees in that she has always preferred the country to the town. Although she came from the professional class and lived in Berlin, she always had a country house near Potsdam and spent as much time as she could there. Her husband Kurt was a physician, a professor in the same faculty of Berlin University as Karl Joachim, and her father's family had connections in journalism and publishing. She came, then, from that section of German Jewry to which most of the refugees to Britain belonged: solid, metropolitan, financially secure, and intellectually distinguished.

She had been appalled and distressed by Hitler's rise to power, but neither she nor her husband had considered leaving Germany. Then, in April 1933, something happened to change their minds.

Kurt Geiss's brother Max was a German Jew who defied all the vulgar, slightly hostile views as to what a Jew should be like, and this was not any deliberate choice on his part but simply a matter of temperament. He was an outdoor man, a physical man; a farmer and a soldier. He had held a high rank in the war and had been accepted by members of the officer class as one of themselves. His personality seemed to fit his life-style: bluff, direct, rather irascible. Now he farmed several hundred acres and was a pioneer of agricultural mechanization in that part of Germany.

Max Geiss treated his employees well and, so far as he knew, none of them resented his being a Jew. (Until the Nazis came to power, he had almost forgotten that he was.) He didn't see why they should and anyway he did not differ in any particular from the other gentlemen farmers in the region, except possibly in his vigorous and progressive ideas. But he always spoke his mind and damned the consequences and he had been from the beginning a bitter opponent of the Nazis. He took his stand as an ex-soldier, an ex-officer, and was fond of directing his arguments at his old friends among the Junkers, the officer class: men with whom he had served. By 1933 he had a number of Nazi supporters among his own employees and he made a point of tearing down the stickers which they plastered over the farm buildings, advertising party rallies and meetings. But the Nazis went on fixing the posters and stickers – the anti-semitic slogans on them got uglier and more menacing as time went on – and even painted swastikas on the walls of Max's house.

Kurt Geiss, more sensitive and imaginative than his brother, had feared the Nazis from the beginning. He knew Max was pitting his courage against men who had no respect for courage or anything else. He knew too that Max, like all physically brave men, felt invulnerable in himself, whatever the dangers. But he couldn't make him see the risk he was running. Max would say, 'Once you let them see you're frightened, you're finished.'

1 April 1933 was Boycott Day. Hitler had decided to institute a nationwide boycott of Jewish businesses. No doubt this would also be a signal for a Nazi show of strength; for brownshirt demonstrations and probably for anti-Jewish violence. Characteristically, Max Geiss decided to bring his weekly trip to Berlin forward by twenty-four hours and go on Boycott Day.

In fact many people in Berlin were to ignore the boycott, although uniformed S.A. men were posted outside all the big stores to point out to shoppers when they were buying from a Jewish concern. But some Berliners still had enough of their traditional independence and toughness of mind to pay little attention. In some of the smaller towns, however, anyone who chose to ignore the boycott got a rubber-stamp mark on his forehead.

Nevertheless Boycott Day was an occasion of great symbolic importance for the Jews. Leo Baeck, that revered father-figure among refugees, after whom the Leo Baeck Institute, still a focal point for German Jewry in exile, is named, said:

The first of April 1933 should be named historically The Day of Great Cowardice ... Universities had remained silent, so had the churches, the chambers of commerce, the courts of justice – all remained silent.

Ilsa Geiss chose to drive out of Berlin with her children and spend Boycott Day in the country. It was warm and sunny and she stopped the car by a stream. A hundred yards away the stream was crossed by a small footbridge; a dazzling white rail circled a clump of trees through which a farmhouse could be seen, toy-like and perfect. The boycott seemed very unreal to her at that moment. Her main concern was to see that the children did not start paddling in the stream while she was setting up the picnic. But she made herself think about the boycott and tried to visualize what was happening. The screen of her mind remained blank, however; then she thought of Kurt, presumably safe enough at the university.

When she got home that evening she heard what had happened to Max.

He had driven to Berlin that morning and had left his car at the garage where he always left it. He told the garage-owner that he would collect the car around four in the afternoon. No one knew how Max had spent the next two or three hours. He had probably been shopping and no doubt at Jewish stores: he would have wanted to defy the boycott. Certainly he went to lunch at his favourite café in the Kurfürstendamm. After lunch he sat drinking coffee at one of the tables outside the café. He wore his overcoat for although the day was fine it was still cold. Two men approached him (his brother Kurt was told by a witness who refused to go to the police) and said something that the witness could not catch. Max Geiss half rose in his chair and the two men drew pistols. One of the men shot him twice; first in the stomach and then in the head. He fell forward over the table and the two men walked quietly away, mingling with the crowds in the Kurfürstendamm. Max lay slumped over the table, his blood dripping down into the shattered coffee-set. As the witness said, 'It was exactly like a shooting in an American movie. The killers – the way they looked, the way they came up to him – it was just like gangsters in a movie.'

No one was arrested for the murder. No one would tell the police anything. There must have been at least a dozen witnesses: only one of them ever came forward and that was to talk to Kurt Geiss under the promise of anonymity. Professor Geiss knew that any police investigation would be a farce. The killing had been done on orders from the party. Some of the dead man's employees were heard to say that Geiss had only got what was coming to him.

The murder had a profound effect on Kurt Geiss. Although he had always feared the results of Max's defiance of the Nazis, he had felt optimistic in a general way. He had argued that the Jews were indispensable to the modern German state, especially in the financial and scientific fields. The interests behind the government (those vague capitalist ogres whose creature Hitler was said to be) must see this and curb the excesses of the Nazi bullies. And more recently he had begun to echo the theory that the governments of the great powers would not stand by and see these things happen to the Jews – particularly Britain and France. He had got quite annoyed when the Professor of Pediatrics had said that the way Britain and France had acted over the reoccupation of the Rhineland didn't give him much confidence in their reactions now.

Now his views changed overnight. The Nazis would do anything and there was no one to stop them. He was going to leave Germany. Immediately. There was no time to lose. Not that he was going to imitate Joachim in his ridiculous course of action. Going to Britain and spending years studying in a foreign language! He had no intention of doing anything of that kind. There were two places in the world where he could begin to practise the day he got off the boat: Persia and Shanghai. He thought for a day and chose Shanghai.

The decision was so sudden and so drastic that Ilsa could not accept it immediately. And what about the children, just into their teens? Shanghai for them, now? Ilsa decided that the question must be postponed, at least for a month or two. She would never have believed that Kurt could even consider leaving without them; now, confronted by the sudden blankness in his face, she realized that he was so obsessed by the need to escape that he would leave her and the children without a second thought. He shrugged. 'Maybe that's a good idea. Think it over, then let me know when you decide to come out there.'

He had no visa or passport problems going to Shanghai. Soon he and Ilsa were travelling into the country together for the last time. It was early summer and, sad as she was, Ilsa sought the strength and renewal the country always brought her. But the last few days they passed together were tense with sadness; only one incident brought her a little comfort. The burgomaster of the village called the day before they went back to Berlin. He was a genial, rosy-cheeked man with a Kaiser Wilhelm moustache; solid in every way – in the depth of his responsibilties, the width of his shoulders, and the breadth of the acres he farmed. He knew that the professor was going away and he brought with him an unusual air of formality. 'Herr Doktor,' he said. 'I'm going to make you a promise. Nothing – nothing – shall ever worry your wife while I'm burgomaster here.'

After her husband left Ilsa spent more and more time in the country. Gradually she accepted the idea that she too must leave Germany, if only for the sake of the children. This was a conclusion she dreaded; and only by degrees, over months and even years, could she come to terms with it. But for the moment it seemed logical to send her eldest child, her daughter Maria, then thirteen, to school in Britain to learn the language which she herself hardly knew.

The memories of the surviving refugees offer certain patterns of thinking and feeling that constantly recur. Almost without exception they can recall some catalytic, last-straw incident that made up their minds for them; ended all argument and agonizing and decided their going. For Professor Joachim this loaded moment was his son being called to the Jew Bench. For Richard Freud the public burning of his father's books. For Hugo Neher the emotional certainty that he would never accept the Nazi régime. For Lothar Kahlmann the revelation of his own cowardice when confronted by a man savaged by the Nazis in the street. For Professor Geiss the horror of his brother's murder.

But what about the others? The German Jews who did not leave, or left when it was almost too late? During the period we have considered, and indeed for much longer, they stayed locked, impacted in doubt: victims of the contradictory impulses – some deep and basic, some almost trivial – that sway all human beings when danger threatens.

And so, in those still early days, the German Jews tossed the familiar arguments to and fro.

The most familiar of all – the 'practical' argument:

Hitler is no fool. Jew-stuff is good propaganda. He'll denounce the Jews to the masses – of course, but he knows he can't go on without the Jews . . . The Jewish bankers can break him. Jewish finance is international. Even if he's curbed them in Germany, what about Paris, Zurich, New York? He's in pawn to them – like every other government.

Nearly as common:

They dare not offend international opinion beyond a certain point. They're not strong enough – either militarily or economically. You're making a bogyman of them: they're more vulnerable than you think. Britain – they daren't offend Britain. And what about Jews in the United States? They'll have something to say.

Perhaps the most popular was the argument from history:

This is nothing new. We have suffered all this before. Whatever they do to us, they know we are German and that German we shall remain. It's happened before – and we're still here.

Unfortunately, history itself set a trap for the Jews. It offered them nothing to compare with what they were soon to suffer in Germany. Not even the Crusaders had shown the consistency of the Nazis. The Jews had always trodden out their classic pattern of alleviation and compliance – and always survived. Arguing, as he did, by analogy, the German Jew was making a deadly mistake. 'It's all happened before.' Nothing like this had happened before. Indeed, the long persecution suffered by the Jews of Germany, the anti-semitic tradition with which they had come to terms over the centuries, far from warning them of their danger only made their destruction more certain. History held no parallel for the Final Solution which Hitler offered the Jews.

Chapter Two

BRITAIN AS HOST

A quotation from Erskine May, the historian and jurist:

It has been a proud tradition for England to afford an inviolable asylum to men of every rank and condition seeking refuge on her shores from persecution and danger in their own lands. Through civil wars and revolutions, a disputed succession and treasonable plots against the State, no foreigner has been disturbed. If guilty of crimes they were punished, but otherwise enjoyed the full protection of the law.

These words were true when they were written. Britain had a high tradition of hospitality to the foreigner: one that was maintained for many centuries. Some will argue that this tradition has not ceased to be maintained, but it would be hard to deny that the ideal set out by Erskine May had decayed between 1830 and the 1930s when the first German Jewish refugees came to Britain. This decline must be considered in relation to various important questions. Did Britain behave fairly to the German refugees? Was her immigration policy as humane and flexible as the circumstances permitted? Did not the exacting procedures, the rigid policy of demanding financial sponsorship for the refugees, result in thousands dying who might otherwise have escaped to survive in Britain? And what of Palestine? How many Jews might have been saved if only Britain had facilitated, instead of prevented, Jewish immigration to that country?

These are difficult questions and they have elicited some very different answers. Many Zionists find it hard to disentangle Britain's role in Palestine from her general approach to the refugee problem, so they see in her government's attitude a heartless legalism which refused to open the doors until the eleventh hour and then only to hopelessly inadequate numbers. The British Government was aware of what was happening in Germany, so their insistence that the refugee organizations financially guarantee all refugees is seen as bureaucratic callousness. In British dealing with Palestine her critics see only a perfidious cynicism which led the British Government to go back on the Balfour Declaration simply to gain political favour from the Arabs.

The opposed, British Establishment view sees things very differently. It stresses how well Britain treated the refugees in comparison with other countries (the United States in particular is implied). Statistics are quoted. Britain, it is argued, simply had to operate the restrictions she did – and after September 1939 there was, after all, a war on. The refugee lobby in the House of Commons, it is said, always ignored this; they talked as if the refugee problem were isolated from the general war situation; as if Britain had not been fighting for her life.

If one accepts the terms of reference that the British Government set itself, then its policies were as fair and honourable as was possible in the circumstances. In a recent book Mr A. J. Sherman has used hitherto unpublished Foreign and Home Office papers in an examination of British official policy towards the refugees, and he concludes:

The standard charges, based on a narrow view of the Palestine problem, of British Government lack of generosity or indeed of indifference to the fate of refugees from the Nazi régime must receive the verdict 'not proven'.

It would be hard to dispute this conclusion, reached at the end of a long and exhaustive survey. But Mr Sherman had to accept the same terms of reference as the British Government set itself. Obviously British policies – and British public opinion – no longer reflected the ideals proclaimed by Erskine May. How far was this change a matter of necessary expediency; how much a change of heart, a surrender to the winds of prejudice that were blowing all over the world?

It is necessary to examine the history of the British tradition towards foreigners seeking refuge, just as it was necessary to examine the origins and attitudes of the German Jews who were to seek refuge in Britain from 1933 onwards. The two contrasting views on British policy both have some validity, but one must try to bite deeper, to assess the climate that bred the attitudes behind the policy. The 'realistic' Establishment arguments invite the reply that if this was the best Britain could do then it was hardly good enough – and if other countries, including America, did no better, so much the worse for them. The Establishment argument has a certain smugness in the light of the millions of Jewish dead: it can be seen ballooning from the mouth of the British Government spokesman stereotype – as persistent a character as the Jewish stereotype – a morning-coated, striped-trousered figure who starts every sentence with the words 'Her Majesty's Government' and who still arouses the frenzied hatred of Nationalists, be they Irish, African, Arab, or Welsh, all around the world. In the period we are concerned with this gentleman usually spoke for the appeasers, the Englishmen who were hysterically eager to come to terms with the Germans. The Nazis' treatment of the Jews was an intolerable embarrassment to men who wanted to believe that Germany was a 'glorified public school'.

On the other hand the hostile Zionist argument ignores several important factors, the most important being the war itself. What if Britain had not fought Germany? All the refugees say they heard the declaration of war with relief. 'Now at last,' Ilsa Geiss says, 'we could permit ourselves to hope.' If Britain had not defeated Germany, how many Jews would have survived anywhere in the world?

So in such matters as the internment of refugees, there was some justification for the official attitude that a nation fighting for its life could take no chances. It must be remembered that at different times the Foreign Office, the Colonial Office, and the Home Office all had conflicting attitudes. And the question of Palestine was always there, relevant to the refugee problem and yet in many ways apart from it.

Many different strands of thought and emotion unite together in British attitudes towards refugees.

It is often said that Britain is not a country of immigration, but in fact successive waves of foreigners – Danes, Angles, Saxons, Normans, Belgians, Dutchmen – have kept arriving over the last two thousand years. In 1540, thanks to immigration from the Low Countries, one third of those who paid subsidy in London to the king were aliens. London was so crowded with Protestant refugees that they were dispersed by an order in Council to neighbouring towns. Canterbury, Yarmouth, and Colchester were full of immigrants. In 1569 there were nearly 4,000 Walloons in Norwich. When, in 1685, the Edict of Nantes was revoked, 80,000 Huguenots fled to Britain. In the reign of Queen Anne 10,000 Palatinates were admitted.

In the nineteenth century the Irish began to arrive; but this was a different kind of immigration: these were economic rather than political refugees, fleeing from destitution not persecution. They came in their hundreds of thousands to work in the factories of the Industrial Revolution. Many went to the north of England; still more to Scotland.

All these immigrants encountered great hostility. This has never been emphasized in the case of the Huguenots, perhaps because their Protestantism was approved by English historians. The Irish aroused the greatest antagonism, particularly in Scotland, and this went deeper than the traditional hatred of 'Papists'. There were anti-Irish riots in Glasgow and the Clyde valley; it was alleged that the Irish were diseased and that many of them were criminals – stock charges that one sees levelled again and again at every kind of immigrant. But no *political* interest was aroused. No one suggested controlling the entry of the Irish (who were technically not immigrants at all as Ireland was part of Britain). Immigration legislation was non-existent at that time. A Royal Prerogative to expel any alien who did not please the monarch was never invoked. The French Revolution and the Napoleonic Wars had produced several Aliens Acts, but when the wars ended these were repealed. The Aliens Act of 1826 and the Aliens Registration Act dealt simply with registration. The situation of freedom, of tolerance, described by Erskine May prevailed through the greater part of the nineteenth century. The concept of freedom was of course essential to the thrusting, expansionist British society of that time. It was an era of Free Trade; goods moved freely over national boundaries, so why not people? The later argument for immigration control – that the foreigners would take jobs away from native Englishmen – would have seemed absurd then, when there was not enough labour to satisfy the demands of the dark Satanic mills of industrial England.

The tradition of Britain as a host to the persecuted foreigners reached its apogee then, in the middle of the nineteenth century. There were intellectuals exiled from Tsarist Russia like Herzen, Ogarev, and Bakunin; there were Garibaldi and Mazzini; and there was Karl Marx. These distinguished subversives posed so small a threat to British values that Victorian politicians actually welcomed their presence and made speeches extolling the Elysium they themselves had created. Only when men with more violent theories began to arrive did this attitude change. 'Anarchist' and 'nihilist' were bogy-words in late nineteenth-century England. The government did not sign any agreement to refuse entry to foreigners wanted for political offences, but the police kept a close watch on ports of entry and exercised surveillance on political activists after they arrived.

Then the Extradition Act of 1870 gave the government power to deport criminals wanted by other countries. It was hedged around with exceptions which were supposed to keep the right of political asylum alive; in fact it marks the beginning of the end of free immigration into Britain. The given target of this legislation was the anarchist, but the net was really set to catch someone much more vulnerable: the Jewish immigrant from Russia and Eastern Europe.

These people had been arriving in small numbers for many years; but by the 1880s the endemic anti-semitism of Tsarist Russia had become organized persecution. The lot of a majority of the Russian people at that time was misery and starvation; the misery of the Russian Jews was sharpened still further by the laws against them. In the reign of Alexander III Jews had been generally banned from the villages and towns of interior provinces. The rich among them, who could pay a special tax, and artisans were allowed to remain. The others were forced to live in the ghettos of the southern provinces, which meant that a majority of the Jews of Russia were concentrated in certain areas. There were towns where over half the inhabitants were Jewish and these were inevitably the seat of the worst anti-semitism.

The situation of the Russian Jews grew steadily worse throughout the eighties and nineties and this resulted in a flow of immigrants to Britain and America. During this time the transatlantic fare required by some German shipping lines was only £2. This meant that a Russian Jew could set out, ostensibly bound for

America or Canada, but intending in fact to land at the first British port.

Most of these Russian and Polish immigrants settled in the East End of London and it was there, in the 1890s, that the first rumblings of anti-refugee feeling made themselves heard. What was to become a familiar complaint was made: that foreign Jewish workers were putting Englishmen out of jobs. The phrase 'cheap foreign labour' was used: these immigrants had touched the xenophobic nerve in the British working-class that is always exacerbated by economic uncertainty and unemployment.

Although no one realized it, these were classic reactions to the first example of what was to become the most tragic phenomenon of the twentieth century: the enforced migration of thousands, even millions of people. These Russian and Polish Jews were the forerunners of millions of refugees of many nationalities – White Russians, Armenians, German Jews – driven from the country of their birth and finding no welcome in any other.

Anti-semitism in Russia continued to increase up to the end of the century. Defeat in the Russo-Japanese war threw the whole country into a state of hysterical chauvinism that discharged itself in sadistic massacres of the Jews. The more Jewish the area, the worse the pogrom. In Byalistock, in Russian Poland, Jews were crucified and burned alive. Children were thrown to animals in a menagerie. Several elderly Jews were put into a vat in a distillery and boiled alive.

Such excesses caused a frenzied rush to emigrate. The steady stream of Russo-Jewish immigrants became a great torrent (between 1899 and 1902 figures for immigration into the United Kingdom trebled). The reaction of the British Parliament was slow at first but gradually gathered momentum. A Select Committee had investigated immigration as early as 1889. At that time it was concluded that the number of aliens was not 'large enough to cause alarm'. Control was not suggested, but the Marquis of Salisbury introduced a bill for that purpose in 1894. He did not succeed, but a few years later, when Salisbury himself was prime minister, the bill went through the Lords but never reached the Commons. Paul Foot in his *Immigration and Race in British Politics* sees this unsuccessful attempt to introduce control as the signal for the formation of a 'powerful and dedicated anti-alien lobby in the House of Commons'. This lobby sought to push control legislation through the Commons as quickly as possible. Several Conservative Members were particularly active in this, notably Sir Howard Vincent, an ex-A.D.C. to the king and a vice-chairman of the Primrose League. Allied with him was Major William Evans Gordon. He was Member for Stepney, which could be described as a reception-area for Russian-Jewish refugees. As immigration continued to grow, these two men pressed relentlessly for controls. Speaking in 1902 Evans Gordon paraded all the stock racist accusations:

English families are ruthlessly turned out to make way for foreign invaders. Out they go to make way for Rumanians, Russians, and Poles ... It is only a matter of time before the population becomes entirely foreign ... Among the thousands who came here is a considerable proportion of bad characters ... I should have thought we had enough criminals of our own ... These [the quarters inhabited by the refugees] are the haunts of foreign prostitutes and souteneurs, of gambling dens and disorderly houses ... Our working classes know that new buildings are erected not for them but for strangers; they see notices that no English need apply placarded on vacant rooms ... A storm is brewing which, if it is allowed to burst, will have deplorable results.

Evans Gordon did all he could to precipitate that storm. He was an example of the English Tory anti-semite whose latent xenophobia (in his case perhaps aroused by the influx of refugees into his constituency) becomes obsessional, pursued far beyond the limits of political interest.

The government promised they would appoint a Royal Commission and let him sit on it. This did not satisfy him. He kept up the pressure: in 1904 his friend Vincent moved an amendment in which he compared Jewish immigration to the entry of diseased store cattle from Canada. When the Royal Commission finally made their report in 1903 many of the charges against the refugees were dismissed as 'wild and inaccurate'. There was no job-snatching from the gentile; no crime; little disease. There was terrible overcrowding among the immigrant population, but no more than among the native residents. Even so – although the findings of the commission had actually refuted the Evans Gordon–Vincent lobby – stringent control of immigration was recommended. The commission also coined that familiar and emotive phrase 'the undesirable alien'.

After this Vincent and Evans Gordon intensified their campaign. Beset by problems, Balfour's Government realized that the alien could offer a useful diversion. The King's Speech for 1904 mentioned a bill to deal 'with the evils consequent on the entry of destitute aliens'. Although the Liberals were at first uncertain whether or not to support this bill (the Liberal Member for Poplar said if he didn't support it he would lose his seat), they eventually opposed it and it was defeated. In the course of the debate the Liberals suggested that the evils of 'low paid alien labour' would best be met by legislation; they wanted to retain the traditional right of asylum.

The controversy about the bill exposed the anti-alien stance of what was then called the Yellow Press: the papers founded by Lord Northcliffe to cater for the vast new readership created by primary education. Articles appeared with titles like 'Foreign Undesirables' and 'Invasion of Destitute Aliens'. A strong anti-semitic note began to be apparent in reference to the immigrants. At a by-election a speaker referred to 'foreigners who are criminals, who suffer from loathsome diseases, who fill the streets with profligacy and disorder'.

A modified version of the bill was brought forward in 1905 and, thanks to the atmosphere of suspicion and hostility that had been created, it was passed. It was, however, fairly moderate in its provisions. Aliens were required to land at certain 'immigration ports': Cardiff, Dover, Folkestone, Grangemouth, Grimsby, Harwich, Hull, Leith, London, Newhaven, Southampton, and the Tyne.

Then in 1914 all liberal ideas were abandoned before the threat of war. The Aliens Restriction Act passed in that year met with no opposition, and the Commons were assured that, as soon as the emergency passed, the act would be repealed. Immigrants were prohibited from landing in the country and all aliens had to register. Distrust and hatred of foreigners steadily increased. Spy fever raged. The German wives of English husbands were refused food in shops. D. H. Lawrence's Cornish neighbours denounced him and his German wife as spies. Dachshunds were disembowelled in the streets. The internment of all enemy aliens was demanded – although it must not be forgotten that in the First World War most aliens of German nationality were not persecuted Jewish refugees but native Germans with every reason to be loyal to their Fatherland.

The end of the war brought no change of mood. In the debate on the Aliens Restriction Act (which was to replace the act of the same name of 1914) some speakers opposed the entry of any aliens at all. Mr Noel Billing asked:

Why not have badges? Why not badge these aliens? So that at least people might say, 'This fellow is a German. I will have nothing to do with him.'

This debate was notable, not only for the naked racism of some of the speeches, but for the speech of a man who twenty-five years later was to emerge as the greatest champion the refugees coming to Britain ever had. Josiah Wedgwood, of the famous Staffordshire pottery family, was a radical in the old tradition. (His niece C. V. Wedgwood called her biography of him *The Last of the Radicals*.) He was a sympathizer with Zionism and a pioneer member of the Labour Party. He said bluntly that the English had always hated aliens. The mob has always been opposed to them but

that mob has always had leaders in high places ... a mob of entirely uneducated people who will hunt down foreigners and you always have people who will make use of the passions of the mob in order to gain their ends politically ... [there is] a desire to show on the hustings and platform what has been done. Members will come forward: 'I voted against these foreigners and I voted to keep them out of it.' This bill is devised to satisfy the meanest political spirit of the age.

The act had few other opponents. It was remarkable for the power it gave a single official, the immigration officer. He had complete control over the immigrant's destiny. He decided whether the alien could enter the country or not – and he was bound to refuse him admission if the alien could not support himself financially, was seeking 'unauthorized employment', or was medically unfit. Normally the alien's stay would be limited to three months unless he held a Ministry of Labour permit or could prove that he had visible means of financial support. The alien could at any time be deported by order of the courts or by the Home Secretary. There was no right of appeal. (Since 1956 such a right has existed. The alien can appeal in a magistrate's court, but he could not do so during the period covered by this book.)

With the passing of the second Aliens Restriction Act the ideal set out by Erskine May had been degraded and diminished to vanishing point.

Immigration was sluggish throughout the next decade and no significant legislation was enacted before the first German Jewish refugees began to arrive in the early thirties. But the anti-alien lobby went on working, playing on the xenophobic nerve that throbs near the surface in every society. There were too many foreign jockeys. French onion-sellers were threatening the livelihood of Britishers. Nothing, it seemed, was too bizarre or trivial to attract their attention.

During this period several future enemies of the German Jewish refugees were heard from for the first time. Among them was Edward Doran, Member for Tottenham, and Captain Ramsay, Member for Peebles. 'Josh' Wedgwood persisted in his lonely championship of humane values. In a debate in 1923 he was supported by a future prime minister, Clement Attlee, who said that the Aliens Restriction Acts were 'thoroughly bad'.

Neither Wedgwood nor Attlee, unfortunately, was typical of the Labour Party. Paul Foot has pointed out that Ramsay Macdonald, Clynes, Thomas, and their colleagues had by this time rejected internationalism in their struggle for parliamentary power. When he was Home Secretary Clynes actually boasted that he had naturalized fewer aliens than his Tory predecessor. It was the old question of foreign labour flooding into Britain, the old fear that 'foreign Jews' would put true-born Englishmen out of their jobs that forced these Socialists into attitudes that denied their principles. In fact these fears concerning the German Jewish refugees were not so much to influence Labour Members in the Commons as to exercise a less public but still important influence through the trade unions.

Most of the Russian Jewish immigrants came either through the port of London and settled in the East End or through Grimsby and Hull to settle in Leeds or Manchester. They practised the usual occupations of the poor Eastern European Jews – tailoring, cabinet-making, cobbling and boot-making, saddling and leather-making – and as far as possible they tried to follow these trades in Britain. They had come in ever-increasing numbers from 1880 onwards and the Jews of this first considerable Jewish immigration into Britain differed in many respects from the German Jews who were to follow them some forty years later.

Like the German Jews, these Russian refugees were Ashkenazi Jews, but this was almost the only aspect they had in common. While the German Jew often thought of himself as German first, many of these Russian Jews were almost theatrically Jewish. To the often illiterate, sometimes hostile inhabitants of the slums of London or Manchester they must have represented the familiar, hated stereotype come alive: exotic, bearded, gabbling in a strange tongue. Many of them knew no English; they were nearly all literate, but their language was Yiddish and at first they could not read the names on street-corners or shop-fronts. They were helped by the Jewish Board of Guardians in the big cities, and could be seen queueing for aid at the offices of the Board. It was the habit of poverty – not so much their poverty on landing, for many of the German Jews fleeing from Hitler arrived penniless – that marked them off from the middle-class German Jews. The majority of these had led comfortable, financially and socially secure lives. The Russian Jewish refugees came from a background of suffering and hardship. This gave them an important advantage over the German Jews, for it is easier to rise from an accustomed poverty than to fall from an assured status and then fight one's way back. The Russian Jews were also a more homogeneous group than the German Jewish refugees. With a few exceptions they were devoutly Orthodox. They lived by the Torah and the Talmud; they lit the Sabbath candles and drew support from the sense of their identity as Jews. A number of the later German Jews were of course equally devout; but some were not, especially those who were the most German, who had identified most with the mainstream of German life and culture. When the Nazi persecution began, these were the most vulnerable: they had surrendered their sense of racial identity to a Germany that had used and then rejected it.

The last and perhaps greatest advantage the Russian immigrants had over their German successors lay in the fact that many of them were, in an important sense, possessed by a dream.

This was a dream of opportunity. While for historical reasons the German Jew tended to look towards France, England remained the land of welcome and potential for thousands of Eastern and Central European Jews. How far these dreams coalesced around the figure of Disraeli it is not easy to say. But certainly Disraeli, the archetype Jew, with his big nose and black oiled locks – 'Sheik Ben Dizzy' as *Punch* once called him – became a figure of legend to many of these deprived and downtrodden people. England must be very different from Russia if a Jew could achieve what Disraeli achieved. Why should not a bright young Jew from Byalistock or Grodno win greatness in the England of Disraeli? So, despite the hostility they often encountered, England remained to many of these Russian Jewish immigrants a land of hope. Anything was possible when you landed in London or Grimsby. This attitude, of course, was not shared by members of the anti-alien lobby like Evans Gordon, whipping up prejudice with talk of criminality and disease, or even by Socialists like Ben Tillett who told a group of newly-arrived immigrants: 'Yes, you are our brothers and we will do our duty by you. But we wish you had not come.'

But the dream persisted. For some it materialized. Some famous names emerged from the new ghettos of London and Manchester, among them Chaim Weizmann, first President of Israel.

The German Jews, most of them middle-class, many of them middle-aged, would have found it hard to capture a comparable vision. Unlike the Eastern immigrants, most of them had already known comfort and success in the land they had left. Despite the undertow of anti-semitism, they felt that Germany had accepted them, given them the sort of life they wanted to live. England offered survival; but for some of the older German Jews it must have seemed little more than that.

Very different from the Jews of the Russian diaspora was the small enclave of German and Austrian Jews who settled in Britain during the nineteenth century. Although these never exceeded a few thousand in number, they represented a distinguished leaven in the solid mass of English Victorian life. These prosperous immigrants came mostly from northern Germany: from such cities as Hamburg and Cologne, from Berlin itself, and from Austria. Compared with the poor peddlers and shoemakers from Eastern Europe, most of them were already rich when they arrived in Britain. They had come as young men, not in the grip of any romantic dream, but in search of solid business opportunities that were lacking in Germany and available in Britain. They were, moreover, clear-eyed about the anti-semitic possibilities in their native land. Sir Felix Semon, who was to become Edward VII's physician, left Germany in 1875 because of 'religious intolerance'. Ludwig Mond, the great chemist, left because his mother 'had always suffered from the persecution put upon her race by the German people'. And the exile of the most distinguished of all Hitler's refugees was foreshadowed when Sigmund Freud visited his half-brother Emanuel in Manchester in 1875. Freud envied Emanuel the right to bring up his children in a society 'far from the daily persecution Jews were subjected to in Austria'.

In the main, however, the incentive was a financial one. Germany in the middle of the nineteenth century was a poor prospect compared with burgeoning Britain; and these German Jews saw horizons before them in London and Manchester that did not exist in Germany.

This was a period when Germany and England felt closer to each other than ever before. The English and the Germans were almost cousins. How right and appropriate the marriage of Victoria and Albert seemed. The English at that time appear to have had a genial, idealized picture of the German (perhaps dating from the time of Metternich, when the thirty-eight states that made up Germany were a threat to no one). That had been the era of *Gemütlichkeit*, when the German was a gentle, jovial creature who drank beer out of tall steins, smoked a long pipe, and wept for the sorrows of young Werther. Lovable if rather slow-witted Germans crop up in fiction right through the century. (Towards the end of it, after Kaiser Wilhelm's jealous disposition had become apparent and the naval arms race had begun, the 'Hun', the sinister spy and trouble-maker, took over.)

But in mid-century the rapprochement was complete, and these prosperous merchants benefited from it. Whatever they thought about them, the anti-alien lobby ignored their existence: one has only to compare the success and esteem these Germans enjoyed with the attitude towards the Russian immigrants to realize that this was the classic *Ostjuden* situation.

Indeed, by a curious paradox, at the very time Vincent and Evans Gordon were busy stirring up hatred against 'foreign Jews', Edward VII was surrounding himself with a number of German Jews. The most famous of these was Sir Ernest Cassel. Without his aid, it was said, the king could not have gone on sustaining his very high level of expenditure. The extent to which Edward depended on Cassel is not fully known, but the relationship gave rise to a number of stories. One of the aristocracy remarked that Edward VII had a strong German accent. 'What is odder, he had a German-Jewish accent. I wonder' – the aristocrat paused – 'where he got it? Perhaps from his creditors.'

But Sir Ernest Cassel was not merely the Edwardian equivalent of the *Hof-Jude*. He gave Sidney Webb, the Fabian, £250,000 for the building of the London School of Economics and played Maecenas to a number of artistic and cultural causes, but his relationship with the king aroused jealousy and he never achieved the acceptance won by Ludwig Mond, later Lord Melchett, the founder of Imperial Chemical Industries, or by Jules de Reuter, who created the news-agency named after him. Reuter arrived in England in 1851 and, in the words of *The Times*, working against every obstacle he made himself a world power through his character and integrity.

A number of the German Jews settled in the north of England. Some German Jewish manufacturers in Lancashire and Yorkshire concerned themselves with the social and educational welfare of their employees to an unusual extent. German Jews were responsible for creating and supporting the famous Hallé Orchestra. J. B. Priestley has written of the enlivening influence of the German woollen merchants in the Bradford of his youth. These men, he said, brought more to the city than bank drafts and lists of customers.

But the death of Edward VII brought a reaction against all his circle and the German Jews felt the backwash. Wilfred Blunt wrote of the clean sweep that had been made of 'the Jews and the second-rate women that the king preferred to his aristocracy'. A general anti-German feeling became apparent, deriving from Germany's growing threat to Britain as an imperial power. Some of the prejudice that had been concentrated on the penniless Russian Jews was now directed at the rich German Jews who had become part of the Establishment. There is a tragicomic story from this period. Two German Jews living in England are commiserating with each other. 'What's going to happen to us,' one asks, 'if we English go to war with us Germans?'

When war actually began, the virulence that had marked the alien debates in Parliament was unleashed against men like Sir Ernest Cassel and Sir Felix Semon. People who had enjoyed Cassel's hospitality turned on him as a 'Hun', while Semon wrote:

Because I have the courage of my opinions I have been ostracized by my native country; because I was born a German, I am boycotted by my adopted country.

These German Jews represented a pocket of talent and energy, distinctively German in all they did. They were soon absorbed into the dominent class of their new country – as opposed to the Eastern Ashkenazi, most of whom remained isolated in their Stepney ghettos, only a few miles distant from the Cassels and the Semons, but socially and financially a world away. It was not the fault of the latter that the war set racial prejudice festering against them, of the kind that their less fortunate Eastern brethren had long learned to endure.

Between 1900 and 1920 then, the attitude towards the foreigner seeking asylum in Britain underwent a radical change. A longstanding tradition of hospitality was destroyed: that destruction had begun with an attack by a small but determined group and had then been sealed by the war. Up to 1914, subject to some rather half-hearted regulations any refugee could come to Britain and stay there – unless the authorities could prove his presence was a danger to the state. The immigrant was presumed innocent until he was shown to be guilty. After 1920 he lost this moral right. It was up to him to prove his case; persuade an immigration officer that he was a suitable person to enter Britain; and, even when he had done so, he only stayed on sufferance.

Since American policies towards the German Jewish refugees closely followed British ones, it is interesting to compare the development of alien-control legislation in America with that in Britain over the same period. Some close parallels are apparent.

The great Jefferson had said:

Shall we refuse the unhappy fugitives from distress that hospitality which the savages of the wilderness extended to our forefathers arriving in this land? Shall oppressed humanity find no asylum on this globe?

and these ideals had certainly been adhered to throughout the greater part of the nineteenth century. The United States had been proclaimed throughout the world as the haven of those fleeing from poverty and persecution. The New World welcomed those abused and rejected by the Old. Up to the 1880s most of the immigrants came from northern European countries: Germany, Norway, Sweden, Denmark, Britain, and of course Ireland. (The Irish immigrants tended to congregate on the eastern seaboard; the German and Scandinavian to move farther west.) Then from the 1880s onwards the victims of the great Russian pogroms began to reach America: brothers of the same *Ostjuden* who were flooding into Britain. The influx into America was proportionately greater and it met with reactions predictably similar to those aroused in Britain. Restrictions against 'aliens becoming a public charge' were brought in as early as 1882; and the Alien Contract Labor Law in 1885 (against 'cheap foreign labor'). Anti-semitic and anti-alien prejudice was worked up in much the same way as it was in Britain. Madison Grant castigated the new arrivals in familiar terms:

Jails, asylums, and almshouses filled with human flotsam, and the whole tone of United States life, social, moral, and political has been lowered and vulgarized by them.

In 1920 the House of Representatives tried to stop immigration altogether, but the Senate would not agree. In 1921 the quota system was introduced. This geared immigration from any European country to 3 per cent of that country's population according to the census of 1910. The maximum quota was 355,000 in any one year. The phrases used in House of Representatives and Senate debates bear a wearisome resemblance to those heard in the House of Commons when the alien legislation was discussed. 'Barbarian hordes . . . a threat to our religious and cultural heritage . . . Crime . . . Disease . . .' The pivot of the alien-control machinery was the provision excluding any immigrant 'likely to become a public charge', and this was implemented more vigorously after 1929. The mass unemployment of the Depression naturally made the American labour market sensitive to the threat of foreign workers and on President Hoover's instructions the State Department refused visas on these grounds. It is hard to assess how far popular isolationist thinking (to say nothing of anti-semitism) influenced this attitude to immigrants, but in the years of German-Jewish emigration, from 1933 onwards, the State Department officials appeared to be at least as sensitive to the 'threat of mass-immigration' as were their British equivalents. It almost appears, indeed, that both British and American authorities disliked immigration on principle and felt an irrational but scarcely suppressed irritation that the Jews should pose a problem of such magnitude. The head of the State Department's Visa Department claimed that the Nazi persecution of the Jews was exaggerated.

All through the vital years after 1933 the Department waved the ignoble red herring of communists infiltrating America in the guise of refugees. Section 7 of the Immigration Act was also invoked. This required a certificate of good character for the past five years from the police of the country in which the intending immigrant had been living. This request seems almost cynical when one imagines the German Police giving a Jew a certificate of good character in 1937 or 1938! (But no doubt some such certificates were forthcoming – at a price.)

In essentials, the attitude of the American and British governments was very similar. Both resented the moral challenge represented by the Jewish refugees; both stood on the letter of their immigration laws; both did too little, too late. The State Department's attitude was just as harshly legalistic as that of the Foreign Office or the Home Office; only President Roosevelt's genius for public relations obscured the fact more successfully.

The machine, then existed in both Britain and America to control immigration: to prevent or allow it as the authorities determined. What was the attitude of the men in England who controlled that machine, the members of the government whose policies the civil servants administering the immigration laws had to follow?

These were the men who wanted above all to please the Germans: the Appeasers, the Men of Munich, the Guilty Men, the Hollow Men – they have been called many names. The thirties in Britain evoked a multitude of symbols, and these names are among them, along with Chamberlain's umbrella, the Oxford Union resolution that this House will not fight for King or Country, and 'Peace in our time'. But despite the clever hindsight, the wealth of phrase-making, it is hard to penetrate the heart of the thirties. The Britain of Chamberlain seems to us now irritable and self-obsessed, soon to purge its self-hatred by turning against the drab men who were its scapegoats: Baldwin, Halifax, Hoare, Chamberlain himself.

No doubt Britain's share of the world depression and the huge number of unemployed that followed had its effect on everyone, resulting in a dangerous loss of nerve. But the Tory Government's anxious, propitiatory attitude to Germany went back for several years. It was rooted in social and economic factors; and there can be no doubt that this bias, this anxious lust to propitiate, had its influence on the way immigration control was exercised on Germany's helpless victims – the Jews.

The romanticized version of the 'good' German had long been dead and during the First World War anti-German feeling had run riot. But the Treaty of Versailles had aroused some compensatory reactions. Many considered that the Germans had been harshly treated and endorsed the Germans' own resentment of the War Guilt clause. J. M. Keynes's *Economic Consequences of the Peace*, which attacked the policy of seeking reparations from the defeated countries, had contributed to this attitude. And the question of reparations leads to an important aspect of the ambivalent British attitude towards Germany. The City of London – pro-German and anti-French – had, with Wall Street, lent many millions of pounds to Germany. The City naturally hoped to get some of this back with a profit. Peace and stability on the Continent would benefit everyone. A revived and prosperous Germany would mean a European market for British goods and would end the threat of 'Communism on the Rhine'. A prosperous Germany meant an expanding market for Britain and badly needed opportunities for British capital. The City was therefore pro-German and anti-French because it saw in French intransigence and uppishness a threat to the desired status quo.

This state of mind was cleverly expoited by the Germans, particularly by their supreme manipulator, Dr Hjalmar Schacht. Germany had got millions from the City to pay her reparation debts; once she had got the money, however, the Germans asked to be absolved of these 'political' debts on the grounds of poverty. (The German national income in 1929 was 77 per cent higher than it had been in 1913.) They were so persuasive that the whole reparations scheme was eventually cancelled. (Lord Vansittart called the transaction 'a genuine but shady miracle'.) Moreover the great banking houses of Wall Street and London, attracted both by high interest rates and the legendary efficiency of the Germans, poured money into the German economy, underwriting the recovery of armament firms like Krupps and Thyssen. The Germans had no warmer friend in the City than Montagu Norman, the enigmatic governor of the Bank of England – 'the banker's bank', which had special power to pass on all foreign loans from the City market: standing, as Montagu Norman himself said, in its relation to the British Treasury as Tweedledum to Tweedledee. Norman had close links with Germany and particularly with Dr Schacht (he was godfather to one of Schacht's children). Norman's reaction to the Nazis' rise to power was to bring together a group of international bankers and to call their attention to the great stabilizing influence that had arisen in the shape of Nazi Germany. He described Hitler as 'the only bulwark against Russia'. National Socialism was in essence a planned economy with a great future before it. He invited those present to help to finance Hitler and his regime.

In 1934 the Third Reich needed a huge loan and Norman met Schacht to arrange this. The Bank of England bailed out the Reichsbank; in fact, as Professor Margaret George has said, England saved Nazi Germany from her creditors.

It cannot be said for Montagu Norman that, like thousands of others, he was fooled by the Nazis at the beginning and later saw through them. As late as 1939, after the German invasion of Czechoslovakia, he made the Bank of International Settlements (a kind of clearing house for international and reparation payments) order the Bank of England to transfer some six millions in Czech gold to Germany: a totally gratuitous and partisan act.

Montagu Norman's description of Hitler as the only bulwark against Russia uncovers another, equally important strand in the British attitude: the Communist obsession of the British right wing. (And of course the City was largely made up of right-wing Tories: Evans Gordon of the anti-alien lobby had given his name to a well-known stockbroking firm.) Like Norman they saw Germany as 'a bulwark against Bolshevism' – that phrase recurs again and again in the writings and speeches of the period. Journalists and politicians throughout the preceding decade had spoken constantly of 'the menace of Bolshevism', feeding a middle-class obsession that was partly a genuine dread of something alien and barbarous, partly a paper tiger manipulated by politicians to make moneyed flesh creep. Again and again the Tories played the Bolshevik card – in the strike of 1919, the Zinoviev Letter, the General Strike of 1926 (which Stanley Baldwin called 'a challenge to Parliament and the road to anarchy and ruin').

The bulwark against Bolshevism theory bred a number of lesser superstitions and rationalizations. Germany had been treated shabbily at Versailles. The Germans were people just like ourselves: a civilized, cultured people. ('Hitler was given credit for Goethe' as C. C. Aronsfeld has said.) The English, after all, had more in common with the Germans than with the French. Ask anyone who'd been at the Front in 1914–18. They all preferred the Jerries. Hitler's complaints that Germany had had a raw deal at Versailles had a good deal of basis; and as for his attacks on the Jews – everyone knew what the Jews were like! If it were necessary to make certain gestures to satisfy Herr Hitler, well then, let them be made. No one wanted another war. Peace with honour. In fact, war was unthinkable.

In this last opinion, at least, the politicians were supported by a huge mass of English people who shrank from the very mention of war. They had signed the Peace Ballot; their sons had voted not to fight at the celebrated Oxford debate. Indeed the Tories might have argued that their attitude reflected the feelings of a majority of the English people; and certainly their policies mirrored a widespread element of pure fear: not so much a reasoned fear of the new German power, the German aggression, but a pervasive, generalized fear of the whole situation. Fear of the war just around the corner. Fear of the Russians. Fear of the poison-gas and disease-germs the Germans were going to use. Fear of a Nazi-style takeover in Britain itself. A dark, Horla-like fear lurking behind the cricket pavilion on the sunniest afternoon. There is a feeling of it in the apocalyptic ending of Orwell's *Coming Up for Air* when the bombs begin to fall.

It must not be forgotten that these men of the thirties were of mediocre calibre: compromise, conciliation came easily to them. This was the party that had preferred Stanley Baldwin to Winston Churchill, that had opted for 'the dim leadership' of Bonar Law. They disliked the ethos of 'the great man' (although they dallied with the Fascist grandees on the Continent) and had settled for a reliable image like Baldwin's. Baldwin was an artist in the obvious: the dullest voter would find nothing to baffle him in anything that was said or done.

These men told themselves that Germany was a bulwark against Bolshevism and yet at the same time they shared the general fear of Germany. Again and again in official utterances there occur plaintive expressions of the hope that German friendship, German cooperation are just around the corner – and this long after most informed people had decided that war between Britain and Germany was inevitable.

The fact that the British Government clung to these illusions must have had an influence on its policy towards the refugees, causing the cumbersome machinery of the immigration laws to be used in the unimaginative and often unfeeling way it was. But it must be stressed that these inimical forces worked largely in an indirect way. With the exception of a small group of Fascist extremists, no one among the right-wing propitiators and appeasers actually approved of the Nazis' treatment of the Jews. Instead they evaded the truth for as long as they could; they pleaded political expediency to justify their friendly attitude towards Germany; and later economic expediency, the threat to employment, as an excuse for not letting in more refugees. And naturally these appeasing Englishmen did not go quite unaffected by the various strands of anti-semitic feeling in English life. The Bolshevist obsession had always had an anti-semitic flavour. From the early twenties propagandists in both Europe and America had been saying that Bolshevism was part of a Jewish plot to destroy the world (the Jews having already been blamed for the French Revolution). The correspondent of *The Times* in Russia wrote that a statue of Judas Iscariot, the great Jewish hero, had been erected in Moscow. Right-wing sympathizers with Germany might not go that far, but they were certainly not reluctant to see a connection between Godless Russia and International Jewry.

The British Government's evasive and quasi-judicial attitude to the Nazi persecution of the Jews is best illustrated by comparing the official silence on the subject with what the British press had been saying for several years. The government maintained silence until after the war began. The White Paper issued on 31 October 1939 was in fact the first utterance the British Government had made on the Nazis' treatment of the Jews – and even then it was brought out not in defence of the Jews but as a retaliation for German propaganda on British concentration camps in the Boer war.

In contrast the press had treated the subject fully from the beginning. Naturally there were many differences in approach and emphasis, but it cannot be said that there was any deliberate suppression by any major newspaper. At the beginning there was perhaps incredulity. This sort of racial persecution surely didn't occur in Europe? In Tsarist Russia, yes; or in Bolshevik Russia. In the Balkans before the war. But in Germany, now? This sense of disbelief lingered on, even after a year or more of the regime.

Anti-semitism has been developed into the most essential symbol of this great attempt to unite a scattered people on a racial basis; to give seventy million-odd dispirited people a new superiority complex at the expense of those who cannot prove their Aryan blood and thus to make workers and peasants gentlemen ... The whole Third Reich should really be regarded as a glorified public school system aimed at doing for a whole people what Dr Arnold did for the upper middle classes.

Thus the *Spectator* in a series of articles on the New Germany. Such a bizarre pandering to what was no doubt mainly an upper-middle-class readership was the more remarkable in that Nazi Germany had never imposed any censorship on foreign correspondents. It was easy to find out what was going on. Newsmen were not confronted with any of the difficulties they encountered in Russia. And yet oddities of reporting persisted.

The quality and emphasis varied from one paper to another. There were then three dailies which could be described as catering to educated British opinion: *The Times*, the *Manchester*

Guardian, and the *Daily Telegraph*. (The old High Tory *Morning Post* was already dying.) Of these three the *Manchester Guardian* gave the most space to the Nazi persecution of the Jews; no doubt because the *Guardian* was traditionally radical and anti-authoritarian. While its coverage of these events was fuller than that of any other paper, it had a tendency to lump all the victims of Nazi persecution together: both Jews and Socialists were described as 'liberals'. *The Times* was equally objective and certainly did not minimize the dangerous situation of the Jews. Both *The Times* and the *Daily Telegraph* may not have been eager at first to print too much material damaging to a German Government that was of the right and thus a defence against Communism in that country. Certainly *The Times* and *Daily Telegraph* were more reticent than the *Manchester Guardian* in appearing to criticize the affairs of a friendly nation.

The more 'popular' papers had a different approach. They were naturally more concerned with whether or not the German Jews were news. Some time before Hitler had come to power the *Daily Express* had decided that Jewish affairs in general had news-value, and thus chose to print more items about Jewish life than its competitors. When the Nazi persecution began their reports had that liveliness that has always characterized the *Express* group; but a suggestion tended to emerge that the Nazi-Jewish confrontation represented two opposed points of view, that there were 'two sides' to report. Apart from this, the picture given was clear enough, although Boycott Day was treated less adequately than it was in the heavies, and there were oddities like

Jews could stroll along the Kurfürstendamm, gay and unmolested, in a country which is at least 60 per cent anti-semitic.

The report added that a fat stormtrooper in brass and braid seemed to be on the best of terms with one of the Jews . . . Then, in 1934, it was decided in an article 'Hitler's First Birthday' that National Socialism on its first anniversary 'lacks charm': there was nothing in it to indicate that the Nazi proscription of the Jews might go farther than merely barring them from certain jobs.

The other dailies and the evening papers hardly appeared to have any clearly defined policy at this stage. The *Daily Worker* and the *Catholic Herald* each had an orientation of their own.

The *Daily Worker* spoke of the occasion of the issue of the new Prussian state bonds.

Jews and guaranteed Aryans stand side by side. No fewer than twenty Jewish bankers appear . . . Not merely tolerated but endorsed as pillars of the Fascist State, decorated with the glory of the eagle and the swastika – bankers are bankers and business is business.

The *Worker* also implied that the Nazis were only driving out the poorer Jews; that the rich Jews would remain in Germany, secured in favour by their possessions. In fact, paupers and millionaires were to die together in the killing-centres of the Reich.

The *Catholic Herald* always stressed that, however badly the Jews were being treated in Germany, Catholics were receiving even worse treatment in other parts of the world.

[Other newspapers] to whom wholesale murder and incendiarism in Spain are of no consequence – as they are anti-Catholic – while far lesser wrongs done in Germany are most infamous because done against Jews.

These distinctive attitudes are significant because they foreshadow reactions when the sufferings of the German Jews had ceased to be items of foreign news and become matters of domestic concern. When the Nazis first achieved power comparatively few refugees came to Britain; as war approached and their numbers increased, they became people instead of statistics; no longer remote atrocity stories but mouths to feed, a possible threat to British jobs. As Arthur Koestler said, a dog run over by a car is more distressing than three million Jews killed in Poland; and as the refugee problem sharpened, different editorial policies appeared. In the main, the 'serious' papers remained sober and objective; the more 'popular' – the successors of the Yellow Press that had been active against the 'undesirable aliens' at the turn of the century – were inclined to see themselves as watchdogs guarding British rights against an invasion of predatory foreigners.

No single attitude, no single group of friends or enemies awaited the German Jews who were to come to Britain after 1933. There were, of course, the Jewish organizations that devoted themselves to the care of the refugees; but these were more than friends: they were family in the true sense of the word and although their relationship with the refugees may have developed some of the tensions a family may display under unusual strain, these organizations undertook the enormous responsibility of sponsoring every Jewish refugee who landed on British shores. But, apart from the support of these fellow Jews, the refugees faced a government that, almost up to the outbreak of war, had stood in a conciliatory stance to the very country that threatened their lives. They faced, too, rigid immigration laws that had not been intended to embrace any situation resembling theirs; a press that would in part yield to the bogy of the refugee threat to employment; and a mass opinion vaguely good-natured, certainly less anti-semitic than that of most European countries, but largely ill-informed, both about Germany and the German Jews.

In their turn, the ideas of the refugees were often as vague and ill-informed as those of their hosts. The most confident among them were those who spoke English and had, perhaps, visited England on holiday. Others had inaccurate or old-fashioned ideas of English life derived from books. A great number, of course, regarded Britain as merely a stepping-off place on the way to America. By a peculiar irony some of these, overtaken by the war, stayed in England; others, who had wanted to remain in England, drowned on the *Arandora Star* on their way to internment in Canada.

Chapter Three

LEAVING THE REICH

A number of German Jews are said to have welcomed the Nuremberg Laws. 'At least we know where we stand,' they consoled themselves. 'Now we have our laws and we know our position.' None of the refugees echoed this attitude, which is almost a parody of 'anticipatory compliance' and seems to represent a certain kind of Jewish temperament. It was, of course, a last-ditch attempt to rationalize a desperate situation. 'We have our laws' could only mean that the position of the German Jews, despicable and inferior though it had been declared to be, was now regularized; that the Nazis having taken from the Jews their very existence as citizens – they were now only *Staatsbürger*, not of German or related blood, and therefore only guests on sufferance in the country of their birth – would now be satisfied and take away no more. And indeed the number of anti-Jewish demonstrations and acts did seem to decline. The Jews reminded themselves that the Nuremberg Laws contained no reference to Jews actually having to leave the Reich.

The apparent slackening of anti-Jewish activity which followed the passing of the Nuremberg Laws was only momentary – in fact an illusion. The German Jews swung between fear and hope. A fear that grew every day, as murders and assaults multiplied; a hope that the Nazis would, after all, need international opinion. And if they, the Jews, showed that they bore no ill-will, that they were anxious to cooperate? Then surely a limit would soon be reached. This was nearly the state of mind that would welcome the Nuremberg Laws as 'regularizing' the situation. Thus far and no farther. 'Now we have our laws.'

Similar attitudes were reflected in the reactions to the later injunction to 'wear the Yellow Badge with pride'. (The Yellow

Badge that marked the Jews apart was not the invention of the Nazis but of the Fourth Lateran Council in 1215 which stigmatized the Jews as 'moral lepers suffering from noxious and contagious beliefs'. The Nazis revived a medieval ordinance and enforced it with unique cruelty and venom.) The slogan 'wear the Yellow Badge with pride' was coined by that remarkable leader and father-figure of the German Jews, the Czech-born Dr Robert Weltsch. Some chose to endorse his words, feeling that if the badge distinguished victim from persecutor, it was indeed a privilege to wear it. Others saw in the phrase the traditional compliance and rejected its use – although they understood the attitude of the courageous man who first uttered it. Ilsa Geiss felt that one could indeed wear the Yellow Badge with pride – if it meant proclaiming one's difference from the Nazis and their ways. Hugo Neher disliked the phrase and saw in it only subservience to the hated enemy.

Ilsa Geiss remembers the general confusion of mind. The pervasive apathy: how people argued, 'How can we go? Where shall we go?' And so they stayed, looking for and finding excuses to remain. Often they were the victims not of fear, but of imaginations atrophied through years of middle-class living. They knew what the Nazis had done already; they could not visualize what they would do in the future. And so they stayed; usually till they were taken away to a concentration camp. As Ilsa Geiss put it, 'They died for their sideboards', and indeed these sideboards, 'little houses', massive creations of oak or mahogany, could stand as symbols of the age that produced them: the post-Bismarck era when money was easily made, the apotheosis of the materialism that had triumphed at the end of the nineteenth century. How could any good German be expected to pull up such roots? To carry this solid German past that cradled them here in Frankfurt or Breslau to another country across the sea?

Of course not all the German Jews were confused, dazed and irresolute before the threat that confronted them. Some saw exactly what lay before them. Almost immediately after Hitler's coming to power, German Jewry had sought to organize itself with the help of the Jewish communities in other countries. The Jewish Agency for Palestine opened a Central Bureau for the settlement of German Jews. The Jewish Colonization Association (concerned with the settlement of Jews in agriculture, particularly in South America) joined with the Hebrew Immigrants Aid Society of America in organizing a department for the movement of German refugees from Europe to host countries elsewhere. In England the Central British Fund for German Jewry was established (later it was known as the Council for German Jewry). This fund reflected the concern of all sections of the Jewish community in Britain and was in close touch with the Reichsvertretung der Juden in Deutschland, the Jewish representative body that functioned throughout Germany.

There is no doubt that the policy of this organization was realistic enough with regard to the implications of Nazi policies towards the German Jews. Whatever the heart-searchings and vacillations of individuals, the long-term plans of the Reichsvertretung recognized that the Jews of Germany had no future there. The Reichsvertretung acknowledged that, whether individuals admitted it or not, German Jewry had to adapt itself to a new kind of ghetto – a ghetto not limited by physical boundaries but by ever increasing pressures and ever diminishing opportunities. With great courage and vision the Reichsvertretung organized a Committee for Relief and Reconstruction which dealt with education, vocational training, and retraining for emigration. Recognizing the great disadvantage of the overwhelmingly middle-class orientation of most German Jews, this committee announced that the young must be trained for 'productive manual occupations' which would be readily acceptable in the lands to which they would emigrate. So while Nazi hostility and persecution grew steadily more vicious and oppressive, the Reichsvertretung established training-centres all over Germany where both young Jews between seventeen and thirty and school-leavers between fourteen and seventeen could be taught more marketable if not necessarily simpler skills than their parents, most of whom were business or professional people. The main subject of training was of course agriculture, not only because it was hoped that a majority of those trained would go to Palestine and contribute to its development by cultivating its land, but because farming also offered opportunities in South America, Australia, and many other countries. Young men were also given training as mechanics and in the building industry.

Even to plan along these lines required considerable courage and vision in the circumstances. Unfortunately, all these training schemes hinged on emigration and the factors controlling this were not in the hands of the Jews. And from 1935 onwards the situation began to deteriorate much faster than the Jews could train or organize against it.

The attitude of the British and American governments towards the refugees were, as has been seen, very similar at the outset. Out of a number of considerations that determined the entry or exclusion of a refugee one was paramount: the question of money. Did the refugee have enough of it? Could he or she support themselves financially?

In both countries this principle was already enshrined in legislation, but the British authorities' reliance on it was strengthened by a historic guarantee made by the Jewish community that was to have in some respects unfortunate consequences.

As early as April 1933 the Home Secretary had conferred with the Cabinet, informing them that there had recently been an influx of German Jews. These were mainly professional people and although they had managed to satisfy the immigration officers as to their financial status they were certainly refugees. The Home Secretary went on to describe a visit by the representatives of Jewish organizations to the Home Office. They had requested that:

1. All Jewish refugees from Germany should be admitted without distinction.
2. Jewish refugees already admitted as visitors or those who may be admitted as visitors in the future should be allowed to stay indefinitely.

For their part the Jewish representatives had guaranteed that all the expenses of maintaining the Jewish refugees, either on a temporary or permanent basis, would be met by the Jewish community 'without ultimate charge to the State'.

This was an offer of immense importance – of much greater importance than was realized by either party at the time. Once accepted, this guarantee was rigidly invoked on every possible occasion through the crucial years frrom 1933 to 1939. (When they gave the guarantee the Jewish organizations estimated that there would be some 3,000 to 4,000 refugees coming to Britain.) One could indeed argue that a generous and humane gesture was seized on, as a matter of bureaucratic tactics, and then used as an excuse for evading a gigantic dilemma. But none of this can have been fully apparent in April 1933.

The British Government considered the Jewish proposals and rejected the possibility of relaxing the regulations so as to allow entry to German Jews lacking financial means or in search of employment. It was considered necessary to keep the present regulations unaltered, except that the refugee should register with the police on entering the United Kingdom. Where refugees wished to extend their temporary stays they could do so – provided that the Jewish community would guarantee maintenance. Thus the principle of 'no admission without financial guarantee' was confirmed.

At a later Cabinet meeting the question of distinguished refugees was discussed. While it regarded the prospect of any large-scale Jewish immigration with fear and distaste, the British Cabinet wondered whether it would not be possible to give sanctuary to refugees eminent in science and the arts. This, it was said, would 'create a very favourable impression in the world'. Thus the principle of quality before quantity was translated into human terms.

Shortly afterwards the Cabinet faced a parliamentary question as to whether the government would consider the granting of asylum to refugees from Germany on a self-supporting financial basis. The official reply approved by the Cabinet was as evasive as might have been expected. Having said that the interests of Britain itself must come first and that the case of every refugee must be considered on its merits, it was pronounced that in accordance with time-honoured tradition no obstacle would be put in the way of foreigners seeking admission. These were admirable sentiments but rang hollow before the actual facts of the situation.

(And this indeed typified the British official attitude – and still more the American – when words were preferred to deeds again and again at a time when deeds were still possible.) The hope was expressed that the Germans would take note of the British attitude to the German treatment of the Jews, but the only reaction to this was a predictable protest from the German Ambassador in London.

As the refugees continued to arrive, the Foreign Office began to wonder if the problem could not be turned over to the League of Nations. Pressure to this end was being applied by the Labour Party. The Foreign Office pointed out that since the German Jews were not 'stateless persons' (it must be remembered that this was before the passing of the Nuremberg Laws) they still had passports and they did not come within the scope of the Nansen Office (which had given stateless persons a passport between the wars which the League of Nations had persuaded most countries to recognize). The Foreign Office also pointed out that any approach to the League by Britain might be considered 'interference' by Germany. Later that year, however, the International Labour Organisation Conference at Geneva requested the International Labour Office to study the matter and advise what might be done for the German refugees. The Home Office had doubts about even this mild initiative as it might 'encourage' more refugees from Germany. The Colonial Office was worried lest German Jewish emigration to Palestine be increased. But eventually the Foreign Office put forward the view that it might look bad if Britain opposed the inquiry as it might then appear that the British Government lacked sympathy with the refugees.

Representatives of the Jewish community in Britain thought that the refugee problem was a matter for the League of Nations Assembly itself. But the Foreign Office was reluctant to raise it before the Assembly; as must never be forgotten a paramount consideration in British policy was the ever hoped for détente with the Germans. Naturally this was not the reason given by the Foreign Office for opposing an approach to the League of Nations. The comparatively small number of refugees then in Britain was mentioned (about 1,000) and it was admitted that it would be very awkward if, Britain having brought the matter up, the League then asked Britain to take more refugees.

But the Jewish organizations persisted, refusing to drop the question of League intervention. For months they argued with the Foreign Office; eventually the Netherlands Government sponsored a resolution inviting the Council of the League of Nations to evolve a plan to solve the refugee problem. With some reluctance the British Government conceded that Britain could hardly oppose the League Council's considering the matter. The British delegate was, however, instructed to say nothing that could offend the Germans.

The meeting of the League Council revealed that the British were not the only nation anxious to respect German susceptibilities. Discussion was strictly limited to technical and financial aspects of the problem. In October 1933 a High Commissioner for Refugees coming from Germany was appointed. An American was chosen : James G. MacDonald. There was some criticism on the ground that MacDonald lacked experience, but his being American was important for it was hoped to get funds from the American Jewish community. The High Commissioner was responsible not to the League of Nations itself but to a governing body consisting of representatives from twelve countries who were concerned with the German refugee problem.

The British Government attitude to the High Commissioner and his task was lukewarm if not actually hostile. When in September 1934 the High Commissioner requested the British representative at the League of Nations, Anthony Eden, to ask his government if Britain could make at least a token contribution to the cost of his work (£2,000 was the figure mentioned), he was rebuffed. The refugees, he was informed, must remain an occasion of private charity. Later, when it was suggested that the High Commissioner and the governing body be made an integral part of the League of Nations, the British Government opposed this out of their familiar tenderness towards Germany. Nothing must be done to offend Herr Hitler and his government.

In September 1935 the Nuremberg Laws were passed. The situation of the refugees continued to deteriorate. Although the problem they posed and the question of international assistance to them had been discussed at the League of Nations – an acknowledgement that for the first time the League regarded the refugees as its proper concern – James MacDonald had been growing more and more despairing in the face of the ineffectual lip-service the great nations paid the matter. In December 1935 he resigned and in a letter which received wide publicity he said :

an even more terrible human calamity within the German frontiers [is] inevitable unless present tendencies in the Reich are checked or reversed . . . I cannot remain silent . . . When domestic policies threaten the demoralization and exile of hundreds of thousands of human beings, considerations of diplomatic correctness must yield to those of common humanity. I should be recreant if I did not call attention to the actual situation and plead that world opinion, acting through the League and its member-states and other countries, move to avert the existing and impending tragedies.

The letter attracted considerable attention in Britain and America. The British Foreign Office, however, thought it somewhat exaggerated in tone and suspected MacDonald of Zionist tendencies.

By a freak of timing, MacDonald's resignation coincided with a scheme devised by several leading British Jews, the most prominent among them being Sir Herbert Samuel, Lord Bearsted, and Mr Simon Marks. This envisaged the assisted emigration each year of 16,000 young men and women and 7,000 children; at least half of these, it was hoped, would settle in Palestine. And almost as many older people were to emigrate annually, paying their own way. The three instigators of the scheme went to America in January 1936 as a first step towards organizing a fund of £3 million to carry out the scheme. The weakness of the plan was that it presumed the German Government would allow German Jews to take some quantity of money out of the Reich. In fact the scheme foundered on the German Government's refusal to do anything of the kind.

The Foreign Office welcomed the Bearsted proposals as a reasonable solution to the problem, but the obdurate attitude of the Germans made any progress towards it impossible.

In the summer of 1935 the refugee organizations approached the Foreign Office and argued that Britain should take action at the League of Nations Assembly. In addition the representative body of the Jewish community requested the British Government to make representations to the German Government urging a cessation of persecution and to allow the new High Commissioner to negotiate directly with the German Government.

The British Embassy in Berlin deplored the effect of anti-Nazi speeches at the League of Nations – not only on the situation of the German Jews themselves, but on the delicate equipoise of Anglo-German relations.

In September 1937 the new High Commissioner, Sir Neill Malcolm, reported that the settlement of refugees was not being achieved to any significant extent. In the League Assembly Lord

Cranborne reiterated the British Government's view that the League should give political and legal protection to refugees while at the same time the costs be met out of private resources. It was decided that the League Council should formulate a comprehensive plan to assist the refugees before the 1938 meeting of the Assembly.

The Home Office was concerned that the formation of a new organization to help the refugees might create problems for itself. The Home Office favoured mass emigration of the Jews to a 'suitable' country overseas – and this is why the Home Office was often at odds with the Colonial Office. The Home Office found itself the target on the one hand for the jabbing of the anti-alien lobby about the 'influx of foreigners'; on the other, the Jewish organizations and champions of the refugees like Josiah Wedgwood were not slow to point out that fine sentiments at Geneva were not matched by any great readiness to admit refugees to the United Kingdom itself.

The general position of the refugees continued to deteriorate. By the beginning of 1938 the most optimistic were beginning to despair – and then came the Anschluss.

The savagery of the Anschluss, the annexation of Austria by Germany in March 1938, was an augury of accelerated and intensified anti-Jewish action within Germany itself. What took months and even years to do to the German Jews was done in Austria in days and weeks. Moreover the Anschluss, by greatly enlarging the number of Jews in flight from the Nazis, not only exacerbated the plight of the refugees themselves but also created new problems for the host nations.

The old Austro-Hungarian empire had been multi-racial, the Germans only being one among eleven nationalities. When the empire disintegrated and a new Austrian republic was created on the Swiss model, there was a lack of any cohesive national feeling. Whatever pride in being Austrian there was existed mainly in Vienna. Most of the new republic was divided between a narrow regional patriotism, some nostalgic yearning for the Habsburgs – and a fierce German nationalism. The young Adolf Hitler, growing up in the provincial town of Linz thirty years earlier, had been imbued with this, identifying himself with everything German, hating all the other, to him inferior, races in the empire. In the years between 1920, when the Austrian republic was created, and 1938 when the Anschluss was forced upon it, nothing happened to bring any distinctively 'Austrian' feeling into being.

At the time of the Anschluss there were nearly 200,000 Jews in Austria, many of them living in Vienna. While there were wealthy Jews in Austria – Jews almost monopolized banking and were pre-eminent in the arts – there was a greater proportion of poor Jews than in Germany. The Austrian Jew was more likely to be a shopkeeper or small trader. Many of these Austrian Jews or their parents had already been refugees once before. These were Galician Jews who had fled during the war. When Austria recaptured Galicia many had returned, but some 60,000 had settled in the so-called Jewish quarter of Vienna, in the second and twentieth wards of the city. To some extent they were subject to traditional prejudice against the *Ostjuden*. When the Nazis launched their attack on the Austrian Jews their greater poverty and insecurity made them more vulnerable than the German Jews.

Anti-Jewish action in Austria after the German takeover had a greater impact on the sluggish imagination of other countries than the slower process the Germans had set in motion against the Jews. Indeed up to that time the German Jews had not suffered anything, collectively, as savage as the attack the Nazis now launched against the Austrian Jews. Some who had known Austria and particularly Vienna found this savagery incredible. William Shirer described the Viennese as more attractive, more gifted at enjoying life than any people he had ever known.

And yet it was not only the German invaders who participated in what Shirer has called 'an orgy of sadism'. It was hard to accept the conventional legend of the carefree, music-loving Viennese in the weeks following the Anschluss. It was as if all the coagulated hatred that lies under the surface of any society had been suddenly released in a boiling tide of violence against the Jews. Newspaper reports describe how the mob forced Jews out of their homes and made them kneel on the payments to scrub off such slogans as 'Hail, Schuschnigg' (Schuschnigg was the former chancellor, who had tried to resist the Anschluss). Jewish women were made to clean public toilets and even the latrines of the S.A. barracks. Some elderly Jews were rounded up in the

Prater, made to strip, and then forced to run around like dogs on all fours. Fleeing from his persecutors, a Jew climbed a tree in a public park and stayed up there while stormtroopers pelted him with mud and stones and promised to cut off his testicles when he came down. Suicides were common, paralleling those of the medieval Jews who had thrown themselves on their own swords rather than wait for the Crusaders. A young doctor gave his mother poison and then took it himself. Many Jews jumped from balconies and upstairs windows, not always dying but sometimes only crippling themselves. This did not save them from the concentration camps. Jews were taken by the truck-load to the central prison, the first step on the way to the camps.

The Austrian Nazis were aided by the fact that this was a smaller country than Germany and it was therefore easier to bring all the Jews into the net. To a great extent they were concentrated in Vienna and in the case of the poorer Jews in one or two districts of the city. But the Nazis were no respecters of persons. Sigmund Freud, who more than half a century earlier had thought longingly of living in England, was brought by the Nazis to the decision actually to go there. He had, of course, been aware of their hostility; his books had been burned, along with those of every other writer of European significance, in May 1933. But he had been living in Austria and Austria was not Germany. Although his son had urged him to leave, Freud was reluctant. His pupils were in Vienna and so was the specialist who treated the cancer of the tongue from which Freud suffered. Freud was reluctant to leave him and put himself in another's hands.

For a time he was left alone. In April his biographer and disciple, Ernest Jones, came to Vienna to try to persuade him to leave. Later, his pupil, Princess Maria Bonaparte, came from Paris with the same intention but Freud would still make no move. A relative of his believes that President Roosevelt let the Nazis understand that any interference with a man of Freud's eminence would have a disastrous effect on public opinion in America.

Then the Gestapo called on the Freuds. They were not particularly menacing or insulting, although they were clearly interested in the contents of the Freuds' home. Frau Freud treated them throughout with a courtesy that masked an implacable irony, addressing them as 'Gentlemen', deferring to them as one might to especially honoured guests. Eventually they left and in Freud's case too this visit appears to have aroused his sense of irony rather than his indignation. But he was both angry and alarmed when his daughter Anna was taken to the police station and interrogated. She was released, but her detention was for Freud the catalytic, last-straw incident, although it was June before he left for England.

Leah Sachs was the daughter of a middle-class family in Vienna. Her father was chief accountant in a large manufacturing firm; he lived with his wife and his son and daughter in the southern suburbs of the city. Leah remembers him as an essentially pessimistic man, although this did not mean he was always gloomy or never played or laughed with Leah and her brother Paul. But her father never said, as did so many Viennese Jews, 'They [the Nazis] will never come here. It can't happen here.' Marcus Sachs always believed that it would happen, that the Nazis would come. His daughter thinks there was an element of fatalism in his attitude, especially when he prophesied what would happen with such clarity: 'It's like standing on a hill and watching a tide engulf your neighbours,' he would say. 'First the streets and then right up over the houses, over the roofs – and then it's all gone. It's happened.'

Leah was eleven at the time of the Anschluss. She remembers the hysterical demonstrations by the crowds – her mother kept her and Paul at home – but they heard later of the mob that surged towards the inner city shouting 'Sieg Heil!' and 'Heil Hitler!' The police merely watched, making no attempt to control the crowds.

That was the Friday of the Anschluss. Frau Sachs kept the children at home on the Saturday too. German tanks and guns were grinding through the streets; all day they could hear the roar and drone of aircraft overhead. The noise went on and on till it seemed to fill the flat and echo back from the walls and ceilings. 'It is a form of torture,' Herr Sachs said. 'A demonstration of power, designed to have its effect on the impressionable Viennese.' He then made another prophecy. 'Part of the charm of the Viennese is that they are so imitative – just like monkeys.' He paused. 'That is why they will outdo the Germans in their treatment of the Jews.'

For a long time – until they left Austria in fact – the Sachs family lived in what seemed like a state of siege. Frau Sachs insisted that the children stay at home, only going out for an essential hour of exercise each day. And this was taken in the early morning, in accordance with their father's careful logic. So each morning Paul, who was eight, and Leah set out off on their walk, which never took them beyond the Belvedere Palace.

Most mornings their mother went with them, but one day she stayed at home with a headache and of course that day they walked farther than usual. Coming towards the Sudbahnhof, they saw a group of S.S. men lounging at the curb. Before them, down on their knees, were three Jews. Two of them were old: Leah saw the early sun glinting through the thin grey hair on to the shiny bald head of one of them; but one was not much more than a boy. The Jews were engaged in scrubbing something off the pavement; they kept their heads down while their arms moved in unison.

Then one of the S.S. men shouted something at one of the old Jews. The old man stopped scrubbing and slowly rose to his feet, turning to face the man who had called him. Another S.S. man pushed him back with the flat of his hand; a roar of laughter went up and then Leah saw one of the stormtroopers fumbling with the front of his breeches. A second later he had exposed himself brutally and was directing a stream of urine into the face of the prostrate Jew. As he tried to turn away, another of the S.S. men kicked him. He fell forward and now the other Nazis fell on the other two Jews, kicking and beating them.

A few weeks later the Sachs family were having breakfast when they heard a loud knocking on the door.

It was about half past seven [Leah Sachs said]. I don't think my father was up and I know my mother wouldn't have gone to answer the door. I was afraid to. Anyway, I don't think it mattered because they had kicked the door in before we knew what was happening. You saw the panels and then the toes of their boots coming through them. Then they came in, the brownshirts. They didn't say much; they were quite calm and well-disciplined. They didn't say much at all, really. They simply started to strip the flat of all our belongings, calmly and systematically like professional moving-men. I don't know how they knew we had anything worth taking: they must have gone around assessing or who told them? They took the best things first – like the silver that belonged to my father's family who had in fact been silversmiths themselves at one time; an old clock that looked unusual – I've never seen another like it since; some ivory figurines. And then they started taking the furniture itself. My father was up by this time and of course he came out and started protesting. They didn't take any notice of him; then – suddenly – they either decided they'd got as much of the furniture as they wanted or else they didn't want what remained, for they started smashing things up. That was very frightening – because they were just as systematic with the smashing as the taking . . . I'll never forget that.

A strong predatory element existed in the Vienna pogroms. The unrestrained brutality of many of the attacks on Jews contrasted with the organized way in which Jewish homes were wrecked and despoiled. The manner in which Jewish property in Austria was looted was crude and arbitrary compared even to the equivalent process that was taking place in Germany. Indeed, the whole Austrian Jewish tragedy took in every feature of the German Jewish tragedy as it stood at that time, but parodied it in exaggerated and brutal terms.

The months and years had gone by in futile discussion; in suggestion and counter-suggestion; in wrangling between different departments of state – but all this had led nowhere and now the Anschluss had greatly enlarged the refugee problem by increasing the number of refugees to be dealt with. In July 1938 the concern of the refugee organizations and the reluctant interests of various governments were to be voiced at an international conference. This had been proposed by President Roosevelt who, with his usual sensitivity to public opinion, realized that the refugees posed a problem of obsessive international proportions.

In March the United States had sent a note to ask whether Britain would cooperate in setting up a special committee composed of representatives of a number of governments to facilitate the emigration of refugees from Germany and Austria. This was to be financed entirely by private organizations and no country was to be asked to receive a greater number of emigrants than was permitted by its existing legislation. (This invitation was sent to thirty-two countries in all.)

The proviso about 'existing legislation' focused doubts that existed even before the conference took place. The proposals seemed vague and – it was noted – Roosevelt had no intention of changing America's rigid quota system which bore so heavily on the immigrant. There was doubt even of the sincerity of Roosevelt's motives in suggesting the conference. Was he calling it as a diversion to forestall pressure from American Jewish groups to relax his own immigration laws?

The conference was to be held at Evian-les-Bains on the French shore of Lake Geneva. The American delegate was Myron C. Taylor, a former president of United States Steel; his deputy was to be the man the Foreign Office had already labelled a troublesome idealist, James G. MacDonald, the High Commissioner who had created such embarrassing publicity by resigning.

Each of the British Dominions, with the exception of South Africa, proposed to be represented at the conference. The head of the British delegation was Earl Winterton, an unfortunate choice. He has been described as 'no friend of the Jews' and his speeches in the House of Commons had shown some anti-semitic bias; he was well-known as a supporter of the Arab cause. (In the event, however, it is doubtful if he did any better or worse than any Tory politician of the day would have done, granted the general context of futility at Evian.)

The conference opened in the Hotel Royal at Evian. Myron C. Taylor spoke first. He announced the fact that his government had decided to unite the German and Austrian immigration quotas, which would enable some 28,000 immigrants to enter the United States in a year. He also suggested the formation of a permanent committee to carry on the work of the conference.

Earl Winterton spoke in general terms. He warned against any attempt to include Jewish refugees from any country beside Germany and Austria. (He was probably thinking of Poland and Rumania, both of whom had sent an observer to the conference.) He deliberately excluded Palestine from the ambit of the conference: this was a separate problem and (he implied) one only concerning Great Britain.

The French delegate was concerned to emphasize the large number of refugees France had already welcomed. Other countries like Switzerland and Belgium took the same line. To a detached observer the whole council was an elaborate set-piece designed to impress the onlooker with the conferring governments' concern for refugees, but in fact empty and futile.

Two sub-committees were created. The British hinted at the possibility of a limited settlement in East Africa (nothing was to come of this). All that actually came out of the Evian conference was an Intergovernmental Committee under the directorship of George S. Rublee, an elderly international lawyer. In theory the director would act as a broker on the refugees' behalf, negotiating with the German Government on the one hand and with the host countries on the other. This was admirable – in theory – but no one really believed that Rublee could influence the Nazis.

Such a meagre outcome made nonsense of the pretensions of Evian. Words once again had been preferred to deeds.

In the autumn of 1938, after the Anschluss and the Evian conference but before the Munich agreement, Fritz Stuckart, one of the architects of the Nuremberg Laws, made a significant remark. Many of the decisions reached in the Laws, he said, 'would lose their importance as the Final Solution of the Jewish problem is approached'.

At that time the words 'Final Solution' had not acquired their later hideous significance: they were not taken to mean then what they later came to mean. But it was clear that the phrase meant that the Jews must be got rid of; that they must leave the Reich.

And by now a new factor had entered the situation. The war that for years had been a symbolic obsession with the Nazis acquired a new reality. Despite the appeasers of Britain and France, war seemed not only probable but inevitable. It might break out while some Jews still remained in the Reich. What would happen to the Jews in a Germany committed to total war? The S.S. newspaper *Das Schwarze Korps* (The Black Corps) answered the question: annihilation (*Vernichtung*).

But a twist was given to this answer when Hitler triumphed over Chamberlain and Daladier at Munich. Hitler had always been obsessed with 'International Jewry', blaming it for a familiar catalogue of wrongs: it had influenced other nations to gang up against the Kaiser; it was responsible for the injustices of Versailles; it had excluded post-war Germany from world markets. Now Munich brought to his thinking a concept already exploited by Göring and the Gestapo: the Jew as hostage. 'International Jewry' might be less inclined to pursue an interventionist war against him if he had some hundreds of thousands of German Jews at his mercy.

Only a week after the Munich agreement, on 5 October 1938, a decree had been issued: the passport of all Jews had to be stamped with the letter 'J'. Holders of such passports would require a special permit before they could leave Germany. This was a Gestapo decree but in fact the inspiration for it came from outside: from Dr Rothmund, the Swiss Chief of Police. His aim was to distinguish Jews from tourists and thus keep refugees out of Switzerland while continuing to enjoy the German tourist trade. (The 'J stamp' agreement was later to cause the deaths of many thousands of Jews in occupied Europe because it enabled the Gestapo to identify them.)

The next development had been foreseen by the Polish Government, who realized that there were some 60,000 Jews of Polish nationality living in the Reich. The Poles therefore passed a decree making invalid the passports of Jews living outside Poland unless they were endorsed with a special stamp only obtainable within Poland itself. Those Polish Jews who did not get this by 29 October 1938 lost their nationality, becoming stateless persons.

The Germans acted fast. On 28 October 15,000 Jews with Polish passports were taken by train to the border, with the intention of deporting them *en masse*. But the border was closed and the trains had to turn back.

A few days later the Germans tried again. This time the Jews were herded into goods trucks and brought to the frontier town of Zbaszyn. There they were thrust out into the fields. Many of the older Jews died of cold and exposure during the next few days; thanks to American efforts most of the remainder were accommodated in Polish towns or they too would have died. The Polish Government naturally protested but further deportations across the border followed. It was admitted by the German Foreign Office that Poland had been selected as a dumping-ground because there were so many Jews there and because of the Polish tradition of anti-semitism.

The deportations to Zbaszyn have a double significance: as a new manifestation of anti-Jewish policy and because, through one of those apparently remote casual links that abound in history, they led to the events of *Reichskristallnacht* – 'Crystal

Night' or 'Night of Broken Glass' – and to a new phase in the persecution of the Jews.

On 7 November 1938 Herschel Grynszpan, son of one of the Jews deported to Zbaszyn, killed Ernst vom Rath, a German Embassy official in Berlin. The murder itself seemed meaningless – the unfortunate vom Rath was not even a member of the Nazi party – except as a most uncharacteristic symptom of Jewish affront, a generalized act of revenge by the son for what the father had suffered. Whatever Herschel Grynzpan's motives for his action, he could not have foreseen its effects.

There can be little doubt that the widespread and violent reaction to vom Rath's death was not as spontaneous as it was alleged to be. On the evening of 7 November, Goebbels told a group of party leaders in Munich that retaliatory riots had started in the districts of Kurhessen and Madeburg-Anhalt. Goebbels said that the Führer had decided that if similar rioting spread throughout the country, 'it was not to be officially discouraged'. This was taken as the green light: that rioting and looting be systematically organized throughout the Reich. The S.A. went to work at once to burn down every synagogue in Germany. In fact 191 synagogues and 171 apartment houses were set on fire and 815 shops looted. Only 117 rioters were arrested, but 20,000 Jews were taken into 'protective custody', at least half of them being sent to the concentration camp at Buchenwald. (The next day it was admitted that 7,500, not 815 shops had really been looted.)

The Nazi leaders reacted in various ways. Himmler spoke of Goebbels's 'craving for power'. Göring complained to Hitler that Goebbels was very irresponsible. While they were all willing to blame Goebbels for the pogrom, they were none of them averse to benefiting from its results.

A conference followed on 12 November to decide on official reprisal for the murder. This was held at the Air Ministry building. Apart from the Reichsmarshal Göring, Heydrich, Funk, Stuckart, and various lesser bureaucrats were present. Genial, esurient, looking like a wicked Father Christmas, the Reichsmarshal was in a jocular mood. His main concern was the responsibility of the German insurance companies: 'It is insane to clear and burn out a Jewish warehouse, then have a German insurance company make good the loss . . .' This practical approach was typical of Göring's attitude towards the Jews. Financial considerations were never far away. Whenever Göring appears to have acted with less anti-semitic bias than his colleagues, money was usually involved. In the autumn of 1941 he got a respite for the families of Jewish armament workers in the Reich, but this was simply because he wanted to maintain the arms production programme. His true feelings were reflected in his answer to Goebbels's suggestion that special railway coaches be provided for Jews: 'A good German should need no law to enable him to kick a Jew out of his seat and make him stand in the corridor for the whole journey.'

Heydrich, the willowly and hardly Nordic-looking head of the secret police, was no less realistic but had a different approach. He suggested that the insurance companies the Reichsmarshal was so concerned about should indeed pay up but that the money should go to the Reich Finance Minister and the real victims – the Jewish shopkeepers and householders – be compensated by their own Jewish tenants. A Herr Hilgard, representing the insurance companies, pointed out that the claims were likely to double that year's revenue. That was too much for Göring: 'I wish you had killed two hundred Jews and not destroyed so many valuables.' Wörmann of the Foreign Office warned against interfering with the property of foreign Jews. America could seize German assets in reprisal.

Herr Hilgard was told to make sure that fewer windows were smashed next time. He then withdrew from the meeting.

This conference was important not only because it spawned a number of measures which went still farther towards crushing and isolating the German Jews, but because it emphasized the strong element of financial greed that ran through the Nazi attitude to the Jews: the ransom principle that reappeared again and again.

The measures taken after the conference were the most sweeping yet enacted. A collective fine was levied on the Jewish community of one billion reichsmark (£84 million): the *Sühnesteur* or 'atonement tax'. Jewish owners or occupiers had to repair at their own expense damage done during Crystal Night. Jews could not visit theatres or any place of entertainment; own or drive cars; they were denied the right to public assistance. And the 'Aryanization' of Jewish property was made compulsory.

The German Jewish diaspora was a complex tragedy. Considering the existence of individual refugees, one must travel to and fro in time, taking some liberties with chronology.

Ilsa Geiss decided to leave Germany in 1935. Her husband had died two months after he arrived in Shanghai and, apart from the numbing grief she felt for him, his death had in some curious way made a decision seem less urgent.

Their house in Berlin had been sold. Ilsa led a quiet life in the country. Her life had always been quiet; now, since both her son and her daughter were away at school, it was almost that of a recluse. She was consoled by her love of country things. She read the newspapers, she knew what was happening, but the nature of her life insulated her from horror or insult. Then one afternoon, while she was on one of her rare visits to Berlin, the police called.

In the old days, before the Nazis came to power, Ilsa and her husband had been local gentry, deferred to by the police. In the intervening years their attitude had subtly changed. In some way the murder of Max, her brother-in-law, had something to do with it. The police were still perfectly polite; they didn't treat Ilsa or the children as the police in some places treated Jews. But there was a change.

When Ilsa heard the police had called in her absence she was terrified. She immediately thought of Maria, at Dartington Hall. There had been several cases of children at school abroad being arrested on returning to Germany for their holidays. Maria wasn't due to come yet, but suppose she had come earlier for some reason?

Ilsa felt very alone. Any contacts she or her husband had with the pre-Nazi Establishment had long since decayed; and, assuming that the people they had known still had any power, an approach from a Jew or Jewess was a two-edged thing: possibly dangerous to the person approached who might then vent his anger on the Jewish person for having involved him. Who then? She thought of the burgomaster and his promise to her husband.

He, at least, did not appear to have changed. He was still the same smiling man with moustaches so luxuriant that they almost looked false. And yet, as he invited her in, she realized that he had changed. His smile faded instantly; he was frowning as he led her to a room on the ground floor. As she was about to follow him in, he told her to wait. He went to the windows and closed the shutters. She realized for the first time what the isolated nature of her life had prevented her from realizing: that she was no longer Frau Geiss, the professor's lady from Berlin, but now simply the only Jewess in the village. Even the burgomaster was putting himself into jeopardy by talking to her.

He was as pleasant as ever but, as he asked her questions about Maria and young Kurt, she had the feeling that he wanted to put off hearing whatever she had to say. She told him the police had called. Would he have any idea what they could have wanted?

'No, Frau Geiss, I have not.'

He looked so grave that she was afraid he must know but was afraid to tell her.

'I thought from your experience as burgomaster . . .'

She let the words trial away.

'Ah, my dear Frau Geiss, I have to say that my position isn't what it was. Burgomaster?' he demanded. 'The Nazis have taken everything away. They leave the burgomaster his coat, hanging on me like a scarecrow's; they take away the heart . . .' he placed his hand on his chest in an expressive gesture. 'The power. Everything that makes the office of burgomaster.'

'You can't advise me then?'

'Only to stay at home. Be in the next time they call. One thing' – and he seemed to seize on this: he was almost smiling. 'It is the police. Not the Gestapo. That's something.'

'I suppose so?'

'Frau Geiss, of course it is! The police?' he shrugged. 'It is with them as with me. The Nazis have taken their power. So if they come looking for you it can't be so bad.'

'Don't the Gestapo sometimes make the police do their dirty work?'

'Let's pray it's not that way this time.'

'Thank you, Herr Burgomaster.' Ilsa stood up.

'Frau Geiss – I will find out what I can. I will let you know.'

'Shall I come to see you again?'

He was frowning. 'Maybe better if you don't come here to my house. I will send a messenger.'

She left then, after he had assured her again that he had not forgotten his promise to the Herr Doktor. But Ilsa did not feel reassured. The burgomaster wanted to help her. But did he have power any more?

For the next fortnight she stayed at home, scarcely stirring from the house. The days were hot and brilliant; the heat solid as it quivered over the fields. Normally Ilsa would have revelled in this, not spending a moment in the house except to sleep. Now, waiting at home behind closed shutters, she hated it. It was cool in the house; she felt the sunshine as something inimical, keeping her a prisoner. She kept wondering about the police. When would they call again? She dreaded their coming – and yet at the same time she wanted it. She told herself: Get it over. Let them come.

They were quite polite when they did. Ilsa tried to console herself with what the burgomaster had said about the Gestapo having the real power now. But the interview did nothing to lift her sense of dread, her tickling-thumbs sensation of something impending. The police asked a number of questions about Maria. Where was Dartington Hall? Why had she sent her daughter to be educated outside the Reich? And the Herr Professor, he had died, had he not? He was in practice in Shanghai, was that right? And then they had questioned her about her son, Kurt, at school in Germany. And Maria? Did she come home on holiday often? She would be coming again soon?

After they had gone, Ilsa simply wanted to go to bed and sleep, endlessly, on and on. But she made herself write a letter to a friend in Essex telling her that Maria was on no account to come home to Germany when the school broke up. She wrote a similar letter to the principal of Dartington Hall. She dispatched both letters express the following morning; and then set about fulfilling her intention of leaving Germany. There had been, for her, no conscious moment of decision: the decision had been made for her.

She had never taken any interest in financial matters and neither had her husband. Both had been content to leave everything to what Professor Geiss rather grandly called his 'man of affairs', Ludwig Mendl, a partner in a small private banking house.

Mendl was a spare, leathery little man, with a clean-cut, boyish face; this, and his total baldness, made him seem curiously ageless. He had looked exactly the same for as long as Ilsa could remember. He had a reputation for shrewdness as an investment counsellor and now he made no comment on her decision. She was a little chilled by this. Did he think she was doing the right thing? All he said was, 'You want to go, Ilsa? This is really what you wish to do?' When she told him her mind was made up, he simply nodded. She couldn't help wondering if he had ever thought of leaving Germany himself. He was careful to explain the financial aspects of her departure to her, emphasizing the unfavourable exchange rate which made it certain that she would lose most of her capital. But he never revealed what he thought of her going.

Then, a week before she left, she invited some relatives and family friends to a small gathering at a hotel in Berlin. It was not officially a farewell party, although an air of finality hung over it. Ilsa felt less depressed than she had expected. Her imagination wouldn't supply any picture of what England would be like. She didn't know what she was going to. It would be difficult – she knew hardly any English and neither did Kurt. If she possibly could, she would live in the country. She was determined on that.

Then she heard Ludwig Mendl talking to her cousin Walter, who was an actuary in Berlin.

'Me?' Mendl demanded. 'You must be joking. With the exchange rate as it is.' She couldn't catch Walter's reply, but Mendl went on, 'I can't afford to give my money to speculators.'

Ilsa showed no sign of having heard, but she wanted to ask Mendl if it was too late to change her mind. He obviously thought she was crazy to forfeit most of her capital. She saw that Walter was smiling; then, catching her eye, he looked away.

She did nothing to alter her arrangements and she never saw Mendl again, although she corresponded with him after she reached England. He dealt with her affairs as efficiently as possible: she never doubted that. Many months later she received a letter – an incoherent, almost hysterical letter – from his wife. Ludwig had been taken away to a concentration camp, she didn't know where. She had received no news of him and she expected to be taken herself, any day. She was appealing to Ilsa on behalf of her children, her two daughters. (A few children were still getting out at this time if they could find sponsors in Britain.)

Ilsa wrote back at once but got no reply. Later, after the war, she heard that the Mendl family, father and mother and two girls, had all died in the gas vans of the killing centre at Kulmhof.

By the middle of 1935, when Ilsa Geiss decided to leave, the situation had deteriorated. It was harder to get your money out, although not yet impossible. The *Reichsfluchtssteuer* or 'flight tax' had in fact been devised before the Nazis came to power, in January 1931. The government had intended to discourage the emigration of wealthy citizens from the Reich. The law applied to anyone who had property worth more than 200,000 Riechsmark or whose income for 1931 exceeded that amount. In May 1934 the National Socialist Government extended this decree, making it apply to anyone who had a capital of 50,000 Reichsmark or who had enjoyed an income of at least 20,000 Reichsmark in any year since 1931. The tax represented a levy of 25 per cent on the whole property of the emigrant: no exceptions were made. Thus, as Mendl told her, Ilsa had to give a fourth of all she possessed to the German state before she would be allowed to leave.

The 'flight tax' was only the beginning. The remaining three-quarters of her assets would have to be kept in Germany and paid into a *Sperrmark* – blocked marks – account. In order that the German Treasury might acquire badly needed foreign currency – dollars, pounds, francs – she would only be able to realize the money in this blocked account abroad at a loss, owing to the very unfavourable exchange rates obtaining (this was what Mendl had meant about giving his money to speculators). In the event Ilsa lost three-quarters of the assets that remained to her after the exaction of 'flight tax', finally retaining less than 20 per cent or one-fifth of her total capital.

The German Government had an equivocal attitude to Jewish emigration. They wanted to get rid of the Jews, they wanted them to leave – and yet they made leaving as difficult as possible. One of the biggest obstacles to Jewish emigration was the question of the money the Jew was allowed to take with him. Obviously, poor Jews would find it harder to gain admission to other countries than rich ones. But the Nazis wanted it both ways: they wanted to be rid of the Jews and at the same time they created a machine designed to wring the last pfennig from the prospective emigrant.

The desire to plunder the Jews, in the very process of destroying them, was nothing new. But it was some time before the Nazis were able to put it on a systematic basis. The people they had attacked first – Jewish civil servants, lawyers, judges, doctors – were the least interesting from this point of view. Visualizing the Jewish community as a pyramid, at the apex of which stood the judiciary and the professions, it will be seen that the Nazis had begun at the top of the pyramid and were working their way down to the broad base of shopkeepers, small manufacturers, and business people in general. These Jews, not yet directly attacked and fighting a rear-guard action to maintain their morale, told themselves that the business sector would be relatively free from interference. They were wrong, for this was the most attractive area of all and the Nazi dynamic now began to function through the despolation and expropriation of Jewish property. After all, the extent of Jewish private enterprise was one of the Nazi grudges against the Jews. Jewish business was the heart of Jewish 'exploitation'; the local agency, as it were, for the 'world Jewish conspiracy'.

The process known as *Arisierung* – 'Aryanization' – was evolved. At the beginning Aryanization was voluntary. Later – after Crystal Night in November 1938 – it became compulsory.

The 'voluntary' element was something of a mockery from the start. Every possible pressure was brought to bear on the Jew in an endeavour to force him to sell. There was coercion in the very air he breathed. And time was never on the Jew's side. The longer he waited, the worse he fared. It might be thought that the larger Jewish firms would have a better chance of avoiding takeover, but these represented a bigger prize for the Nazis and were therefore worth more effort in the grabbing. There were a variety of techniques available to the government. Wholesale firms could be induced to withhold supplies from the business under attack; cartels with control of raw materials could freeze out Jewish members; the government itself could refuse export or import licences and block and frustrate the target firm in a variety of other ways. Obviously, the larger and more complex the organization aimed at, the more diverse the methods required. A simple unit like a village store could be dealt with by a customers' boycott, smashing a few windows, or perhaps beating up the owner. But a large industrial firm might have to suffer organized strikes and sabotage by workers who were Nazi sympathizers.

The systematic nature of the German Government's plan to despoil the Jews is illustrated by the fact that a Boycott Committee, under the chairmanship of Julius Streicher, was established to mobilize pressure on Jewish businesses. The committee called mass meetings, which were addressed by Streicher and Goebbels, and arranged for the picketing of Jewish shops by the brownshirted S.A. or the black-uniformed S.S. Sometimes the word '*Jude*' was smeared on shop-windows.

In 1935 the government decided to withhold all public contracts from Jewish firms; and the usual subsidies were withdrawn from all civil servants for services obtained from Jewish lawyers, dentists, chemists, and doctors.

The banks were in a particularly favourable position to apply pressure on Jewish businesses by restricting credit, calling in loans, and through a variety of other tactics. They went a good deal farther than this, however, becoming virtual agents or brokers in the sale of Jewish firms. Not only did the bank get a commission for bringing buyer and seller together; they would lend a purchaser the money he needed to acquire the Jewish firm, and of course the new owner would remain a customer of the bank.

But despite these pressures some Jewish firms held out. As late as 1938 the Dresdner Bank complained that there were more Jewish firms than German buyers. The reason was obvious: there was a free market and competition for the more successful Jewish firms had forced up the price. To end this situation, various kinds of buyers' agreement were evolved. One allowed several buyers to join together in acquiring a Jewish concern; another allocated Jewish firms to specific buyers. Thus three German banks acquired three Jewish-controlled banks: the Dresdner Bank took the Böhmische Escompte Bank; the Deutsche Bank the Böhmische Union Bank; the Kreditanstalt der Deutschen the Länderbank. Such a directed sale deprived the Jewish owner of his bargaining power; he could sell at the designated buyer's price or not at all.

All the Nazi leaders were interested in translating anti-semitic measures into economic advantage but, as we have seen, none more than Reichsmarshal Göring. Göring was concerned from the first in dislodging the Jews from their foothold in German industry. Characteristically, he intended to increase his own fortune at the same time. To this end he created that unique institution, the Hermann Göring Works.

Despite its name, this was ostensibly a non-profit-making institution designed to benefit only the state. Göring's own position of power made the Works an almost irresistible instrument in the acquisition of large Jewish concerns. His method was simple. He sent what amounted to an ultimatum to all the major German steel producers (not necessarily Jewish) 'suggesting' that they transfer some of their property to the Hermann Göring Works. Most of those approached were wise enough to do as he asked; but the Jewish families who owned several of the largest firms in the central German coal belt came into conflict with the Reichsmarshal. The reaction of one of these families, the Weinmanns, was a classic example of anticipatory compliance.

The Weinmanns operated coal mines in the Sudeten area of Czechoslovakia, recently absorbed by the Reich. Göring was interested in acquiring these mines because the German steel industry always needed coal and the Weinmann enterprise would be a valuable asset to the Hermann Göring Works. At first he offered about half what the family asked. This was not acceptable to the Weinmanns. And the Germans were offering to pay, not in dollars or pounds, but in Czech crowns, a useless currency. Moreover, no doubt to soften up the Weinmanns, the Germans were refusing to issue a passport to one of the family, Hans Weinmann, trapped in Prague when the Germans invaded.

Before the negotiations with the Germans opened in Paris, Fritz Weinmann paid 20,000 Swiss francs for a genuine passport for Hans Weinmann (who actually escaped from Prague, mysteriously, without any passport at all). Meeting the Germans in Paris, Fritz Weinmann first demanded that they refund him the 20,000 Swiss francs. Still in this confident vein, he went on to require payment for the Weinmann coal mines in foreign currency – sterling or dollars.

The German negotiators, two experts in Aryanization from the Dresdner Bank, were taken aback. Their surprise deepened when Fritz Weinmann went on to argue that he was entitled to what he asked because he had himself 'done the State some service' and deserved well of the German people. Then he calmly claimed to have been a National Socialist before Hitler himself! While the two Nazis were still dazed with anger and surprise, Weinmann switched to more familiar ground. The family firm simply could not function without him. He was indispensable. Finally, he put forward yet another reason for deserving well of the Germans: he had not sold the mines to the Czechs in 1938 because it would not have been in the interest of the local Sudetenland Germans.

The German negotiators were baffled and angry. They could not accept Weinmann's claim to have served Germany or his pretended conversion to Nazi ideals. Far from seeing in his attitude the compliance that was intended, they thought he was mocking them. How could a Jew be a National Socialist? They brusquely rejected his arguments and negotiations broke down. In September 1939 the Economy Ministry ordered the Weinmann mines to be sold for the benefit of the Reich. The Hermann Göring Works were the new owners; to the annoyance of the German Finance Ministry the Works only paid some 60 per cent of the value of the mines – but who dared criticize the actions of the Reichsmarshal, the second man in Germany?

If the Germans had made rather a half-hearted attempt to use Hans Weinmann as a hostage, they showed much more determination in holding Baron Louis Rothschild to ransom.

This time Göring had his eye on a large steel complex owned by the Rothschilds, the Witkowitz Bergbau und Eisenhutten Gewerkschaft, again in Czechoslovakia. It was soon evident that the Rothschilds had taken more care than the Weinmanns to assure their position. More than two years before Czechoslovakia fell, they had transferred their Witkowitz holdings to the Alliance Assurance Company of London. This was important because, in the Rothschilds' eyes at least, it made Witkowitz a British company.

But if the first point had gone to the Rothschilds, the Germans soon struck back. When they invaded Austria in March 1938, they arrested Baron Louis Rothschild. It was clear that they intended to use him as a hostage in the negotiations.

These were only the first exchanges in what was to prove a long-drawn-out imbroglio. The scene changed from Paris to Berlin and back again. Millions of pounds were involved. The international character of the Rothschild family was to prove a great advantage to them. Apart from the Vienna Rothschild,

LEAVING THE REICH

who was being held by the Nazis, there was Eugene Rothschild in Prague, and Alphons Rothschild in Paris. This reflected the wide dispersal of the Rothschild interests which were spread over a number of countries, linked by a complex series of mutual shareholdings. Thus the French Rothschilds had holdings in Germany; the Vienna Rothschilds holdings in France. These interlocking interests gave the Rothschilds an advantage the Weinmanns had not possessed. On the other hand, the Nazis held the person of Baron Louis and this must have appeared to them to even the scales.

As early as 1935 the Hermann Göring Works had made overtures to the Rothschild complex at Witkowitz and the Länderbank had sent them a valuation report. Shortly before the invasion of Czechoslovakia in 1939, Baron Eugene Rothschild had gone to London to discuss the sale of Witkowitz to the Czech Government. The sum of £10 million in British currency was mentioned, but the meeting led to nothing. Then, in March 1939, soon after the invasion of Czechoslovakia, the Germans began negotiations with the Rothschilds. As usual, these negotiations took place in Paris. Baron Eugene Rothschild and Baron Alphons Rothschild confronted Göring's financial shock troops led by Dr Rasche of the Dresdner Bank.

The Germans started by offering approximately £10 million – the Rothschilds' price – but in Czech crowns. If the price was right, the proposed currency was useless. The Rothschilds demanded payment in sterling, pointing out that the sellers were in fact a British corporation: the Alliance Assurance Company of London.

The next day the Germans learned that all the Wikowitz assets, in every country, had been frozen. Court orders had been obtained to prevent payment from any Witkowitz account. The angry Germans pointed out that this was depriving the Reich of badly needed currency and was thus a violation of the law. They then offered the Rothschilds about a third of the price asked, but this time in sterling. For this the Germans were to get Witkowitz and a Swedish subsidiary, Freja.

The pivot of the deal, of course, was the captured Baron Louis in Vienna. The machinery of the sale had to be set in motion before the Germans would release him. The Rothschilds therefore instructed banks and finance houses all over the world to release the blocked Witkowitz accounts – on condition that Baron Louis Rothschild should have passed over the Swiss or French borders on or before 4 May. For their part the Germans arranged for one of their negotiators to meet Baron Louis in Vienna.

After his release everything seemed to be moving smoothly towards the completion of the deal. Aryanization of Witkowitz would mean many changes and the Germans were somewhat disconcerted to learn that the Witkowitz order-book included contracts for the British Navy still to be fulfilled.

The final agreement was drawn up in July 1939. The Germans planned to pay the purchase price, over £3 million sterling, with foreign currency belonging to the Czechs. The Nazis were pleased with their bargain. They complimented the S.S. for their shrewdness in arresting Baron Louis and thus smoothing the path of negotiation. Then, at the beginning of September, war broke out.

The transfer of Witkowitz never took place. The Germans accused the Rothschilds of having practised delaying tactics from the beginning. The contracts had been so drafted, the Germans said, that an impossible number of conditions had to be satisfied before the title was legally transferred. The Rothschilds had known the war was coming.

The Germans, of course, had physical possession of the Witkowitz works, although a lawsuit in the Swedish courts failed to get them the Freja subsidiary. But the Germans did not forget that the Witkowitz complex was still legally British and at that time Hitler still hoped to come to terms with Britain. So Witkowitz was leased to the Hermann Göring Works 'for the duration', and the Works took the profits made during the war.

The Aryanization of Witkowitz was not the complete triumph for the Germans that the Weinmann takeover had been. The Witkowitz Works were of great value to the German war effort but legal ownership eluded them. On the other side, had war not broken out the Rothschilds would have been forced to give up a valuable asset for about a third of its real value – to save the life of Louis Rothschild.

Göring's greed was on a scale befitting his eminence in the Reich, but in a cruder way and on a smaller scale the Gestapo was also holding thousands of Jews to ransom.

Their pursuit of the profit motive first became apparent in

1938 when effective control of Jewish emigration passed from two government departments, the Reich Ministry of the Interior and the Reich Office of Migration, to the Gestapo. All the refugees confirm that the two government agencies, particularly the Reich Office of Migration, had behaved efficiently and with as much humanity as was possible in the circumstances. They cooperated with the Jewish representative body, the Reichsvertretung der Juden in Deutschland, which in turn took in three emigration agencies, the Hilfsverein der Juden in Deutschland, dealing with emigration to all countries except Palestine; the Palestine-Amt, which was associated with the Jewish Agency and, as its name indicates, dealt with emigration to Palestine; and the Emigration Officer of the Jewish Community, which was concerned with the repatriation to other countries of Jews in Germany who were nationals of those countries.

For several years the Hilfsverein functioned on amicable terms with the Reich Office of Migration. The Migration Office showed themselves aware of the difficulties faced by prospective emigrants and no doubt many refugees owed their lives to the successful collaboration between the Jewish and the government agencies. But a shift in control was impending, although as late as 1937 the officials of the Migration Office still regarded themselves as masters in their own house.

In 1938 everything changed. In December representatives of the Hilfsverein called at the Office of Migration to inquire about the possibility of release for the 30,000 Jews who had been taken to concentration camps. The Reich Office of Migration informed the Hilfsverein that they had not been told of the arrests. The Gestapo had laid down a condition for the release of these Jews: immediate emigration. This was clearly a condition that it was impossible to fulfil at once. The Jewish representatives begged that the deadline might be extended. Mass emigration of this kind would involve the preparation of many documents; there would be many administrative problems to surmount. The new impotence of the Migration Office was illustrated by the fact that they were unable to tell the Jews if a memorandum they had submitted had even been read.

From now on all executive power over emigration lay with the Gestapo. They continually harassed the Jewish agencies with inquiries as to how many Jews had now left the Reich; and at the same time they proposed various schemes for emigration. The nature of these schemes, however, made the Jews wonder if they were put forward in cynical mockery or as deliberate provocation. A favourite with the Gestapo was mass emigration to Ecuador. Promises were said to have been obtained from the Ecuadorian Government. The Hilfsverein could only argue that such a scheme would represent a death-sentence for thousands of middle-aged Jews who would be exposed to hunger and fever and probably massacred by hostile natives in the South American jungles. But the Gestapo persisted. Eichmann, in charge of emigration, was angry that the Hilfsverein and the Reichsvertretung did not support the project. Another of its advocates was a shrewd businessman called Schlie who had already successfully charted the *Stuttgart* to take Jewish refugees to South Africa shortly before the South African Government halted immigration. Now Schlie's Hanseatic Travel Agency in Berlin hoped to do equally well out of the Jews for Ecuador.

Mass emigration was the catch-word with the Gestapo at this time. As might be expected, their cynicism was absolute. Once they asked the Hilfsverein in Frankfurt-on-Main why they weren't helping a certain Jew to emigrate. The man was an habitual criminal with a long record of convictions. The Hilfsverein said the emigration of such a man could only be engineered by using forged documents and, if this were ever discovered, it must prejudice the chances of later emigrants. The Gestapo official commented: 'So you keep the anti-social Jews in Germany while you get the decent ones out! That's your kind of patriotism.'

The Gestapo policy of forcing emigration came to a head with the so-called 'June Operation' of 1938. One thousand five hundred Jews with police records were arrested. The Gestapo described them all as 'anti-social' but in fact some were only technical offenders. A few were actual criminals. Those arrested in the June Operation were released from the concentration camps only if and when arrangements had been made for their immediate emigration. This in fact represented direct pressure on the Jewish agencies. From now on they had no choice but to get such hostages out by any means in their power – legal or illegal.

From the time of the June Operation in 1938 to Crystal Night in November of the same year, Gestapo pressure grew stronger and stronger. Associated with the Gestapo now was Goebbels's

Ministry of Propaganda. The government newspaper *Das Schwarze Korps* (The Black Corps) kept demanding that Germany must be made *'Judenrein'* – free of Jews. Harassment of the Reichsvertretung and the Hilfsverein was stepped up. Why were they not getting more Jews out of the country? At the same time the Nazis were quite indifferent to the ever increasing difficulties of emigration from the Reich. The regulations of most of the host countries were growing more stringent; they were more and more concerned to avoid an invasion of penniless refugees. Not only had the exchange rate for blocked marks grown even more unfavourable, but new taxes were imposed on Jews leaving the Reich. When Ilsa Geiss had left in 1935 she had been only relatively unfortunate in losing four-fifths of her capital. Refugees who left later fared worse. After Herschel Grynszpan murdered Ernst vom Rath in Paris in 1938 an extra tax was imposed, the so-called 'atonement tax'. This was on 20 per cent of the Jew's total assets – his assets *before* 'flight tax' and other exactions.

The attitude of the Gestapo grew steadily more brutal. In November 1938 a large number of officials of the Reichsvertretung and Hilfsverein were arrested. The situation was chaotic by now: a desperate catch-as-catch-can to get out of Germany. No one bothered about legality any more. Emigration – for those who had the money and the contacts – became a commercial racket for the civil servants, the Gestapo men, and (in some cases) the consular officials of foreign countries. If enough money passed, it was possible to emigrate with a tourist visa to South America – usually to Uruguay, the Argentine, or Brazil. Some got immigration visas for Paraguay and then went to the Argentine as tourists and remained there illegally. Other Jews obtained papers giving false details of their age and occupations. Many South American states offered easier immigration to farmers, so thousands of city Jews who had never even dug a garden presented themselves as experienced farmers. Brazil had special terms for anyone who owned land there, so a brisk trade sprang up in *'Llamados'* – the title deeds to land in unexplored territory, the Matto Grosso being particularly popular. The point was that the 'landowner' got a visa. Some states like Ecuador and Brazil favoured Catholic immigrants and this naturally led to a number of conversions. Some travel agencies like Schlie's Hanseatic

Travel or the French Travel Agency in the Unter den Linden made enormous profits by facilitating these devices.

It was even possible to buy passports direct from enterprising foreign officials. A Cuban diplomat called on the Hilfsverein and suggested selling any number of Cuban passports which would enable their holders to go anywhere in South America – but not of course to Cuba itself. It would even be possible to buy a passport that would enable its holder to live in Cuba but that would be more expensive. The diplomat warned the Hilfsverein that he only dealt in bulk – say 1,000 passports at 1,000 dollars apiece. The Jewish agency could not raise that kind of money; besides, even if they bought the passports, there were so many other people who would need to be bribed: Gestapo men and functionaries of the Interior Ministry and the Foreign Office.

Many German officials cooperated with these South American diplomats, taking a cut on the enormous profits that were being made. (There were exceptions among the diplomats, like the Brazilian consul in Berlin. He took no part in this passport-jobbing and granted hundreds of visas to refugees out of humane motives.)

Against this background of frantic corruption the Gestapo pressure went on. Throughout 1937 and 1938 the avenues of escape grew narrower. As we have seen, both Britain and the United States administered their immigration laws in a rigid and self-righteous manner, reiterating that 'no refugee must under any circumstance become a public charge'. Up to the war France had a more liberal policy (in 1933–4 the United States took 6,500 German Jewish immigrants; France took 30,000) but the general increase in the difficulties of 'legitimate' emigration only strengthened the black market in visas and passports. The travel agencies and shipping companies became expert at locating the consuls who were willing to do business. The French Travel Agency would find an Argentinian consul in France who would sell any number of visas – for cash. In this case the emigrants would leave through French ports. The Uruguayan consul in Berlin helped thousands of German Jews to leave Germany – at a price. He went all over Germany to get certificates for emigrants. One day he received a cable from his government. It said simply: 'Stop.' When it arrived there were Jews sitting on suitcases in his office awaiting the visas they had already paid for, but as the consul himself said: 'What can I do if they tell me in Uruguay: You have already made enough money. Stop.'

One by one the compliant South American countries began to tighten up their immigration procedures. The Brazilian Government chose to inspect the hands of some of the 'farmers' who were entering the country, and found most of them to be soft and unsullied by manual work.

It got harder and harder to escape from the Reich. For many, now, the decision to leave Germany had been made too late. Few Jews now told themselves that things would soon be 'stabilized'. All the rationalizations had been abandoned. The Nazis kept insisting that Jewish emigration must be stepped up. *Judenrein!* That was the ideal. Unlike the Reich Office of Migration, who had always tried to present emigrants in a favourable light to prospective host countries, the Nazis actually went out of their way to blacken them, claiming that Jewish refugees were physically and morally diseased. 'No one wants to have them,' they announced. 'People seek protection against Jewish immigrants.' The Propaganda Ministry and the Gestapo wished at this time to drive all Jewish emigration underground and into illegal channels.

Harassed by Nazi violence and abuse, the Jews tended to lose their nerve, to grasp feverishly at any thread of hope. As the chances of getting to South America declined, as European nations like Britain refused to ease their immigration laws, many Jews began to think of Palestine as a last hope.

Many German Jews had already gone there. After August 1933 they had taken advantage of the so-called Haavara ('transfer' in Hebrew) agreement between the German Government and the Jewish Agency for Palestine. It allowed a Jew with some capital to contract with a German exporter for the sale of German goods to Palestine. The German exporter would be paid from the blocked account of the intending emigrant who would then receive his Palestine currency from the Jewish Agency as soon as he got to Palestine. This was an arrangement that pleased both parties to the transaction; in fact, German goods were exported in great quantities into Palestine as a result of the agreement. A barter arrangement was later made that exchanged Palestine oranges for German timber, motor cars, and agricultural machinery.

The Haavara agreement had worked relatively well, but by now the situation had changed. The British Government had reversed its declared policy on Palestine in its White Paper of 1939. To propitiate the Arabs it had banned all but a trickle of Jewish immigrants into their long-promised homeland.

The most desperate period of Jewish emigration now began. With every escape route cut off, the Jews who attempted illegal entry into Palestine had nothing to lose – except their lives. Many of them gave all they possessed to anyone who promised to get them to Palestine. The consulates of Liberia and the Dominican Republic would issue transit visas and passports at a suitably high price. Even countries like France and Switzerland would issue safe-conduct documents to refugees who claimed to be going to obviously bogus destinations such as Cuba or China. Switzerland allowed groups of refugees to muster under the guise of 'tourists'. The Polish Government allowed large numbers of Jews to travel to Palestine for 'holidays'.

With the connivance of various governments, the refugees were organized in groups numbering up to 700. They then travelled by train or Danube steamer to the ports of embarkation. If they went by train, they usually travelled to Athens, there to go aboard the ship that would take them to Palestine. But mostly they travelled down the Danube to embark from Black Sea ports like Constanta and Sulina in Rumania or Varna (now Stalin) in Bulgaria. Local Jews organized welfare centres along the routes to give the emigrants food and such comforts as they could.

The Hamburg Amerika Line actually advertised illegal emigration to Palestine. With the alternative the concentration camp, few Jews hesitated. The Gestapo cooperated in the matter of documents, to the great profit of the Gestapo officials concerned.

The ships that carried the refugees from these Rumanian and Bulgarian ports were nearly all ancient coffin-ships, often Greek-owned: always small, insanitary, and unseaworthy. Not since the days of the slave trade has so much financial profit been extracted from so much human suffering. The British consul at Galati in Rumania protested at one ship that carried 900 refugees when it was hardly equipped to carry a tenth of that number. Frightened, sick, and dirty, often infested with vermin, the Jews crouched or lay in the dark-stinking holds of the transports.

They were short of food, of water; they had no medical attention. One refugee said:

You lost all sense of time. The voyage seemed to go on for ever. Conditions were terrible. Some of the older refugees travelling with us got so sick and feeble that they were unable to get up on deck, and were vomiting and defecating down in the hold, with what results can be imagined. The captain and the crew did not like us going up on deck in any case. They were angry and aggressive, and would not let us stay on deck more than a few minutes at a time. The crew seemed obsessed with the idea that all Jews were rich. They kept asking for money, wheedling and demanding alternatively.

One captain told his passengers that there would be no water unless more money was paid. Many of the refugees were almost penniless but a sum of money was collected and they were given water. Later the same technique was applied to food and more money was squeezed out of the wretched cargo.

But even the squalor and misery were less important than the physical dangers that confronted the refugees. Many of the ships employed on this traffic had actually been sold as scrap-iron. They had been bought by Black Sea or Mediterranean skippers as a grisly speculation from which huge profits were expected. The profits were made, but the casualty-rate was high. The Rumanian *Salvador* sank in the Sea of Marmora with a loss of 200 lives. In 1940, 1,700 refugees landed at Haifa without British permits for Palestine. They were instantly deported and put aboard the *Patria*. The *Patria* exploded in the harbour – it is said that a refugee, maddened by despair, was responsible – and 200 of the 1,700 Jews aboard were drowned. Seven hundred and sixty-nine Jewish refugees left Constanta in the *Struma* : all illegal immigrants who would attempt to land at Haifa. The ship was grossly overloaded, the hull leaked, and the engines were defective. It broke down off Istanbul. The Turks would not allow the passengers to land unless they could produce British entry permits for Palestine. Although the Jewish Agency made frantic representations, the British Government refused. The *Struma* remained off Istanbul for ten weeks. At last, despite the captain's protests, the Turks towed the wretched hulk out to sea. People on shore could read a large banner held up by the refugees. It said, 'Save us.' That was the last that was seen of the *Struma*, for it blew up six miles offshore. Seventy children, 269 women, and 428 men died. Two men swam to safety. When the British Government was criticized in the House of Commons for their unrelenting attitude, Lord Cranborne, Secretary of State for the Colonies, was comfortably pragmatic:

Under the present unhappy situation in the world it is ... inevitable that we should be hardened to horrors.

There were, of course, protests on liberal and humanitarian grounds in the House of Commons, spearheaded as usual by Josiah Wedgwood. He was outraged at the thought of the Royal Navy intercepting the refugee carriers. He described it as

conduct worthy of Hitler, conduct worthy of the Middle Ages ... carried on by the British Government.

and said that the policy would have the effect of sending the Jews back to the concentration camps.

Confronted with the British volte-face over Palestine immigration, it would have been easy for an American Jew to hate the smug, morning-coated stereotype of the British official, forgetting that the immigration policy of the State Department more liberally applied could have eliminated the need for much of this illegal immigration; and that the heartlessness of that policy was obscured by the urbane and evasive mask maintained by the Roosevelt administration all through the crucial years of Jewish emigration.

An ironical aspect of the whole question was that brutal enemies of the Jews like Heydrich and his Gestapo underlings actually saved large numbers of Jewish lives through their policy of forced emigration, whereas a 'moderate' like Hjalmar Schacht, who sought to solve the refugee problem by an elaborate long-term scheme, undoubtedly kept thousands of Jews in the Reich and, unwittingly, caused their deaths.

In the nine months following the Anschluss Heydrich squeezed enough foreign exchange from rich Austrian Jews to finance the exodus of 45,000 poorer Jews. This had drawn a remonstrance from Göring:

But children, just think. It doesn't help to extract your thousands from the Jewish rabble like this. We could lose so much foreign exchange that we may not be able to hold out.

LEAVING THE REICH

Heydrich had planned to try a similar operation with the 20,000 Jews who had been taken into 'protective custody' after Crystal Night.

Schacht's plan was more ambitious and complex. In December 1938 he went to London. He met Earl Winterton, Sir Frederick Leith-Ross, and Mr Rublee of the Intergovernmental Committee for refugees. Having been introduced to them by his friend Montagu Norman, the Germanophile Governor of the Bank of England, Schacht proceeded to outline a scheme which he said was acceptable to Göring and which was certainly worthy of his own talents for manipulation and persuasion.

The Schacht plan had a basic resemblance to the Haarvara agreement for emigration to Palestine, the only arrangement to facilitate Jewish emigration that had succeeded. The pivot of the Schacht plan was an international refugee loan. This loan was to be raised by 'International Jewry' and would remove what had always been the chief obstacle to Jewish emigration from the Reich: the penury of the intending emigrant. (The amount of money which he was allowed to take out of Germany had shrunk almost to vanishing-point as the years passed.) The Schacht plan would give every emigrant some 10,000 marks in an appropriate foreign currency. The loan would be guaranteed by a trust fund of one and a quarter billion marks, which Schacht considered would represent 25 per cent of the property remaining in Jewish hands. The loan would be financed through the export of German goods, the makers of which would be paid from the trust fund. This would ensure that no foreign exchange was lost to Germany through Jewish emigration. The transfer of Jewish assets to the host countries would be arranged through their increased purchase of German goods (as in the Havaara agreement with Palestine).

Schacht prophesied the emigration of two-thirds of the 600,000 Jews who still remained in the Reich. One hundred and fifty thousand of these – the able-bodied, those capable of earning a living – would go within three years. Their dependants, some 250,000 more, would follow when the wage-earners were settled (where, still remained to be decided). The 200,000 who would stay in Germany, mostly elderly and infirm, would be left in peace for what remained of their lives.

The reaction of Earl Winterton and Mr Rublee was favourable. Schacht returned to Germany. On 2 January 1939 he told Hitler at Berchtesgaden that the London delegates liked his scheme. Hitler was pleased and appointed Schacht as 'special delegate' for Jewish emigration. The German Foreign Office was told to no longer oppose George Rublee's coming to Berlin (this had been vetoed before) and it seemed certain that for the first time the Intergovernmental Committee would be able to negotiate directly with the German Government. Then, on 20 January, Hitler quarrelled with Schacht's refusal to put more notes in circulation and dismissed him from the presidency of the Reichbank. Later negotiations were carried out by Helmuth Wohlthat, head of the German Foreign Credits Control office.

Meanwhile in Britain and America the Schacht plan was meeting with criticism. It had come under the scrutiny of a committee of financial experts who concluded that although the plan had possibilities it would be hard to pin the Germans down to implementing it in any sincere or practical way. Moreover, leading British and American Jews were very opposed to the plan. They recognized in Schacht's 'International Jewry' Hitler's familiar phantasm and particularly resented Schacht's cool assumption that there existed Jewish billions merely waiting to be tapped. Both communities saw in this a huge extension of the Jews for ransom principle that had already been operated by Heydrich and the Gestapo. President Roosevelt described the plan as asking the world to 'barter human misery for increased exports'.

The door was not closed at once, however. Discussions continued with Helmuth Wohlthat. The three-year term envisaged for the emigration of the 150,000 able-bodied refugees was to be extended to five years; the trust fund was still to consist of 25 per cent of the remaining Jewish assets. Finance by 'International Jewry' would still be needed. Further details were worked out, such as allowing refugees to take personal possessions out of Germany (possible for the early refugees but impossible by 1938). The Haavara agreement would be allowed to continue.

This modified version of the Schacht plan scarcely had a chance. As the financial experts had predicted, it was impossible to pin the Germans down to any meaningful agreement. The trust fund would only finance the actual exodus from the Reich; the money needed by the Jews in the host countries would have to come from elsewhere. And the Germans wanted prior guarantees from the host countries themselves and, not surprisingly, these could not be obtained in view of the German Government's cynical vagueness as to how the Jews still in Germany would be treated while the plan was still awaiting fulfilment.

The Schacht plan had been doomed to failure from the beginning. The British and American Jewish communities had been right to see it as a cynical bid to hold hundreds of thousands of Jews to ransom and by doing so to solve Germany's foreign exchange problem. It is notable as almost the last attempt to dispose of the German Jews that did not involve killing them. ('Almost the last' because Hitler's fantastic suggestion of a Jewish settlement in Madagascar was still being talked of in February 1939.)

Now with the coming of war borders were closing all over Europe. In the late summer of 1939 the refugee organizations, already extended to breaking-point, decided that that they could accept financial responsibility for no more refugees. All the escape routes were gone; all the options exhausted for the German Jews. Such Jews as remained in the Reich lived from day to day, in a ghetto of the mind and spirit, from which most of them would escape only through death. Their story has been told many times; but the survivors, with whom we are concerned – those who had already escaped – would carry the sufferings of German Jewry within them for ever, however far they travelled.

Chapter Four

THE NEW ARRIVALS

As we have seen, leaving the Reich got more and more difficult from 1933 onwards. All the Jewish refugees who did leave had to go through what was basically the same procedure. They usually had to be sponsored by either a refugee organization or a private individual. They would then be examined by a British Consul in Germany; and, when they landed at a British port, by an immigration officer. Once in Britain, they would have to report and register with the local police.

Hugo Neher, as one of the first arrivals, should have found things easy, but in fact his passage was harder than other, later ones.

Since that Sunday afternoon, when he had to rush into the first house he came to because he could not endure the humiliation of standing in the gutter, an ignominious puppet sticking out his arm in a gesture he hated to propitiate a group of marching louts that he despised – ever since that afternoon Hugo had been determined to get out. For a time he was baffled; he did not know what to do and his parents had no advice to offer him. Then, after a week of brooding, restless and anxious – perhaps afraid that the edge of his resolution would get dulled because, after all, it is always easier to do nothing – he thought of Arthur Haley.

Arthur and he had met four years earlier in a youth hostel at Coblenz on the Rhine. Hugo had been nineteen then, Arthur twenty. As often happens with youthful encounters, their exchange had been at a wholly superficial level and yet, when they parted a week later, they thought of themselves as great friends. Through that week Hugo had taken immense pleasure in showing Arthur the picture-book beauties of the Rhine between Bingen and Coblenz, including the ancient castle of Ehrenbreitstein. Arthur had not visited Germany before, and Hugo had never been to England. Arthur was tall and fair. He did not talk much but smiled a great deal. Hugo was small and dark and he talked a lot — mostly in English. Arthur did not smile at Hugo's mistakes and, with Arthur, Hugo did not really mind making them, so that week he got quite fluent in English. Arthur had not come to Germany since — he was an articled clerk with his father, a solicitor in Bedford Row in London, and somehow his studies always got in the way — but he and Hugo had gone on corresponding, Hugo writing in English, Arthur in German, each commenting brightly on the externals of their life and each promising the other that he would come to the other's country, 'perhaps next year'.

Now Hugo wrote to Arthur, asking whether he thought it would be possible for him to come to England — not next year, but now, as soon as possible. Arthur replied immediately. He had spoken to his father, who would make some inquiries. A few days later Arthur Haley Senior wrote a careful letter of advice which he had been kind enough to have translated into German (although Hugo could read English very well by this time). He advised Hugo to get in touch with the Jewish Refugees' Committee and ask them to sponsor his entry into the United Kingdom. After careful thought he and his wife could not undertake the responsibility of doing this (Hugo had never even thought of asking them), although he would write a letter inviting Hugo to stay with them at their house in Wimbledon, and this letter would be so phrased as to constitute a reference or testimonial which could be shown to the immigration officer. He would also write to the Refugees' Committee, explaining that Hugo was an eminently suitable person to be admitted to Britain with their aid. Meanwhile Hugo had better see the British Consul in Berlin.

Hugo was delighted with the plan of action Mr Haley laid out for him. Already, in imagination, he had escaped; he was in England, breathing the air of freedom. Then, for the first time, he began to think of his parents. He had never really faced the fact that he would be leaving them; that he was selfishly planning to enjoy his new life without them, deprived of the ambience he had swum in, unthinking, since he was born.

His father thought Hugo's decision wrong, but it did not much worry him. Hugo was young and this kind of decision was a part of youth. Of course Hugo didn't like the Nazis – who in their senses did? – but this retreat to England could only be temporary. Hugo was a Jew but he was also a German: he would return.

His mother, Hugo knew, would never question his father's say, even though she might doubt its rightness in her heart. His father, of course, was the eternal liberal optimist. Even Hitler's coming to power had not damaged his hopefulness. If everything was not exactly working for the best in the best of all possible worlds, then life was still an impressive march forward – interrupted perhaps by setbacks and disappointments, but still a glorious progress towards distant shining peaks. Herr Neher rationalized Hitler's triumph as not really representing the will of the German people – after all, it had been Hindenburg's doing. However badly the Nazis might behave, the big industrialists were the real masters. When Hitler overreached himself – as he would – then they would take back the power. How? By cutting off his credit. And weren't all the big bankers Jews?

The arguments were all familiar. Even the youthful Hugo had heard them all again and again since Hitler came to power. He never argued with his father; he respected his father's intelligence, but he distrusted his bedrock optimism. If anything, his father's reasoning confirmed him in his decision to go, but for the first time he realized how much he was going to miss his parents.

Before he saw the British Consul, he received another letter from Mr Haley. He had been making further inquiries, and he was writing to advise Hugo not to advance political considerations as his reasons for wishing to enter Britain. Already a number of German Socialists and Communists had left Germany and some of them had tried to settle in Britain. Naturally they were not welcome. Some, believed to be Communists, had been turned back by immigration officers at their port of entry. Hugo must not risk being identified with these 'politicals'; much safer, especially as he was only twenty-three, to claim to be a student of English, anxious to gain experience of the British way of life. Even the Refugees' Committee would prefer him to give that reason.

After this Hugo rather feared his interview with the British Consul in Berlin, but it went smoothly. Jewish refugees were not yet the acute problem they were later to become. And the

German customs examination at the French border was still perfunctory; at that time outgoing German citizens were rarely searched.

Hugo first saw Harwich – and thus England – through a fine, insistent rain that soaked everyone on deck within a few minutes. Hugo was used to the harsh electric cold of Berlin and yet this sad English drizzle chilled him as he walked down the gangplank. The rain misted up his glasses: he could only see a cluster of roofs humped around a headland. But as he stepped down on to the oily concrete of the quay he tried to relish the moment, tried to fix it in his mind. This was England, the land of Shakespeare and Dickens, Hugo Neher's land of opportunity. This damp air – the air of a wet April morning in Essex – was yet the air of freedom he had so long wanted to breathe.

Hugo waited until most of the other passengers had gone, the English ones through the customs shed and then on to the train. He had seen other people entering a door marked 'Aliens' and he knew that this was where he had to go.

The office was small and, although it was early in the morning, already sour with cigarette smoke. Two men sat at a table. One was a good deal older than the other, almost sixty perhaps, with dark, peaked features. The other, much younger, perhaps thirty-five, was a heavy, muscular man with a complexion like underdone beef. Irrationally, Hugo couldn't help feeling that this man, humped over a table that looked too small for him, was really a German. He looked exactly like the kind of German businessman who orders dinner in a hotel and then creates an uproar, sending dishes back and cursing the waiters.

'You're very young, Mr Neher.' It was the 'German' who spoke. Was he the immigration officer? Were both men immigration officers?

'I'm twenty-three.' Hugo felt as if he had to apologize for his age.

'You speak English pretty well, Mr Neher.'

Evidently it was this 'German', the red-faced one, who was going to do all the talking.

'Yes, sir,' Hugo said.

'And yet,' the immigration officer cleared his throat, 'you claim that your reason for desiring to come to this country is a wish to learn English.'

Hugo didn't say anything. This man was hostile to him and he had not expected hostility in England. Then he said, 'Excuse me...'

'Yes!' the red-faced man spat out.

'I think you will find that I wrote that I desire to study English?'

'Yes! Well?'

'I know some English certainly... But I wish to know more. I wish to study English literature.'

'*You know English!*' The red-faced man brought the words out like hammer-blows. 'Don't you? Why are you coming here to learn something you know already?'

Hugo knew this immigration officer hated him. He knew the man was going to hand him over to the police. And the police would keep him locked up until there was another boat going to France and then they would put him on it and send him back to Germany.

'I said I desire to *study* English,' Hugo said. 'I think, sir... study is not the same as learn.'

'What does that mean?'

'Sir – I think an Englishman studies English... *Can* study English.'

The immigration officer was frowning.

'I mean,' Hugo persisted, 'an English student at Oxford – he can speak English, but he also studies English...' He broke off.

'It seems to me you speak it well enough to twist around with words,' the immigration officer grumbled.

There was a silence. The dark, older man leaned over and lit his cigarette from the one which lay smouldering in an ashtray in front of the big red-faced man.

'Mr Neher,' the big man said, 'I think you would save us all a lot of time if you were absolutely honest with us.'

'I am being honest, sir.'

'If instead of talking of studying English, you will admit that you are a political refugee?'

'No, sir. I have no particular politics.'

'You're a Jew, aren't you?' the immigration officer demanded. 'Do you think we don't know what's going on in Germany?'

Hugo did not answer. In an odd way he felt **comforted**

by the immigration officer's words. He was glad the English knew.

'They don't exactly like the Jews in Germany at the moment, do they?' the immigration officer said. 'It's not hard to see why a young Jew like you would want to get out.'

'I have wanted to come to England for a long time,' Hugo said.

'So have a lot of other people. It doesn't mean we're going to let them in,' the immigration officer said grimly. 'You still hold to this statement? That you've come here to study English? Eh?' He paused. 'Why didn't you just come over on holiday then? And what have the Refugee Committee got to do with you if you're not a political refugee?'

The dark man leaned over and said something Hugo could not catch. It was the first time the man had spoken. The red-faced man opened the letter from Mr Haley that Hugo had handed him when he first came into the office.

'This letter . . .' the immigration officer said. 'It doesn't say very much when you get down to brass tacks. Just what a nice chap you are and how he hopes you'll come and stay. He's a solicitor, I see. Why doesn't *he* sponsor you, eh? Why bother the Refugee Committee?'

Hugo had not spoken once during this series of questions and comments. He knew it was hopeless. He wished the immigration officer would let him go. Arrest him, if he liked; put him back on the ship; send him back to Germany. Anything rather than go on with this.

'Would you mind waiting in the other office?' the immigration officer asked.

The other office was piled high with dusty files. They filled every inch of the tiny room. Hugo could have sat down if he had moved some of them off the only chair, but he didn't care to and stood stiffly by the door.

After about ten minutes the immigration officer called him in again.

'One more question,' he said. 'You are not, and never have been, a member of the German Communist Party?'

'No, sir. Never.'

'We're not too happy about you,' the immigration officer said. He had Hugo's passport open in front of him. 'Four weeks . . . You can stay in this country for four weeks. On probation, you understand?' He was stamping Hugo's papers. 'Then you can apply to the Home Office for an extension if you wish. That doesn't mean you'll get it.' He had finished stamping. 'Probation means what it says. You'd better be careful.'

Neither man looked up when Hugo thanked them and left the office.

All the arrangements for Ilsa Geiss's departure for England had been made for her by Ludwig Mendl and by her cousin Walter Grunweg (who still carried on as an actuary in Berlin, even though his practice was being eroded still further by the ever-increasing pressure of Nazi measures against any Jewish professional or businessman who continued to function). She saw the British consular authorities and although by now, 1935, the situation had deteriorated considerably, Walter was able to gain the officials' respectful attention by pointing out Ilsa's standing as the widow of a professor and by emphasizing her comfortable financial status, which ensured that she would not have to be guaranteed financially by any refugee organization. Ludwig Mendl had arranged her sponsorship through a firm of merchant bankers in London with which his own firm had been associated for many years. In fact, as Mendl never seemed to tire of telling her, she was exchanging an enviable financial status for something like genteel poverty (although he did not use the phrase). But she was not to admit this to any British official at any time; she must rather exaggerate her means and imply that she was still comfortably off. By manipulation of a bank account in Holland, Mendl was transferring some more money from a trust account in Germany for the education of Kurt and Maria, so that Maria could finish at Dartington Hall and Kurt could go to a public school in England. While she was grateful to Mendl for the expertise he had used on her behalf, she still felt uneasy about the derisive remark she had overheard at the farewell party. Later she was to realize it had been self-defensive: he had been reassuring himself – against his own deeper judgement, perhaps – that he was right to stay in Germany.

The day before she left she had lunch with Walter at a café on the Kurfürstendamm. The café was small and expensive and the time – very early: hardly noon – carefully chosen because it was no longer easy for Jews to eat in public without being insulted. They had been discussing her forthcoming departure. Ilsa knew Walter probably agreed with Mendl's view of her action, although he was too polite to say so. Capital, to him as to Mendl, was a sacred concept; the thought of losing it, even as the price of safety, was almost intolerable. (Walter's rationalizations were to prove less costly than Mendl's; he was to survive the Final Solution after spending four years in a concentration camp in France.)

'I tell you what,' Walter said. 'I'd better give you some English money for when you arrive.' He had always been a great traveller; it was a matter of pride for him to know exacty what to give as a tip to a taxi-driver in, say, Budapest or the most fashionable place for morning coffee in Athens. He had already given her most elaborate instructions regarding her journey to Bremerhaven; from Bremerhaven to Southampton; and then from Southampton to Waterloo Station. He had even drawn a sketch-map showing her how to get to the firm of merchant bankers in Cornhill who were to handle Ilsa's affairs in England. This was all very helpful because her limited knowledge of English was her greatest handicap. 'Here's a pound-note,' he said now. 'That'll cover something to eat at Southampton and the taxi at Waterloo and anything else.' He was too tactful to say what she knew he was thinking: that she might find it hard to change her money on the crossing if the steward didn't know German. She thanked him. 'That's all right. I always bring back some local currency from any country I visit and it always comes in useful.' She put the pound-note away in her handbag. 'Don't forget,' he said, 'a taxi straight to Bayles in Cornhill. They'll take care of everything for you, I'm sure.'

Twenty-four hours later Ilsa and Kurt were standing in the customs shed at Bremerhaven. The customs examination for those leaving Germany was no longer perfunctory. All luggage was opened, and the contents of every bag examined in great detail. A couple ahead of them in the queue had been ordered into the offices behind the customs barrier. This meant they must be suspect: they would have to strip and submit to a search.

'They're looking for currency smugglers,' the woman in front of Ilsa said. 'They say these customs fellows get ten per cent on everything they find.'

'I wouldn't think that game would be worth it,' a man farther down the queue said. 'How many marks can they carry on them, after all? Even if they're not caught?... And if they are – what money can be worth a stay in a concentration camp?'

Ilsa was listening, but their words stayed on the surface of her mind, for she was plagued by doubt again. Now that she was about to step on a ship for England it was too late to turn back. But was she doing right? Kurt was a German boy: what violence would England do to his development?

Then she heard the man in the queue say, 'It's a long time since that couple went through the door. They must have found something. Those two are for the jump for sure.'

And then Ilsa remembered Walter's pound-note. It was in her handbag; she'd seen it there yesterday. Now she instinctively moved to open her bag and look again; then she stopped herself. It was still there; it must be. And she had never thought – Walter had such authority, somehow, that she had accepted the pound along with all his other instructions: never questioning it, never thinking about it. That was part of Walter's personality, his always knowing where to go and what to do in any place you were going to. That was something she had grown up with.

And now the pound-note was there, lying neatly folded in a purse along with a comb and her powder-compact. They were sure to find it; they must find it if they opened her bag. They very likely would; they often examined wallets and handbags, although not invariably (luggage was always opened and searched).

That single pound-note made her a currency smuggler. The newspapers were harping all the time on the attacks on the Reichsmark made by foreign speculators and enemies of National Socialism. Every piece of foreign currency – every pound and every dollar in particular – was of the greatest importance to the Reich. That was why currency smuggling was such a heinous crime. You were draining away the very life-blood of the New Germany.

And now Walter, quite unwittingly, full of brisk helpfulness and precision, had placed her in terrible danger. The customs men would pounce on that single pound-note: they would think she had others concealed about her and, even when they failed to find any others, they would still think her guilty. They would build up a case against her, look for her accomplices. She would be arrested and, as a Jewess, probably turned over to the Gestapo. And Kurt along with her. Nothing she said would be believed. They would both be sent to a concentration camp. Nothing could save them.

She looked along the queue. There was still no sign of the couple who had been taken into the office. There were four other people ahead of her now. Kurt caught his mother's glance and smiled, giving her a reassuring nudge.

They always said customs men went by instinct, that they always knew the ones to pounce on by their expression, the look in their eye. And even though these customs men were Nazis, they couldn't suspect *everyone* : they must go on the same system as customs men everywhere. And since she was really innocent, since she wasn't really a currency smuggler, there was no reason for them to suspect her. If only she *behaved* innocently : didn't blush or falter when they spoke to her. She *was* innocent. So if she kept telling herself, willing herself . . .

'Mummy.' Kurt nudged her again. 'Mummy – are you all right? You look awfully pale.'

Now she knew there was no hope. There were only two people in the queue before her – and she knew she was going to faint.

Ilsa had only fainted once in her life. She had been a young girl then, and she had fallen off a high stool in the kitchen of her father's house in Potsdam. She could not really remember what she had felt then, but she was certain she could recognize the symptoms in this drained, remote feeling, as if all her senses of hearing, seeing, and feeling were deadened, muffled, packed in cotton-wool. She closed her eyes for a moment : against the blankness of her closed lids she could see a red tide rising . . . She forced herself to open her eyes and, overbalancing slightly, put out her hand and steadied herself against the counter.

There was only one person ahead of her now, the woman who had first mentioned currency smuggling. There was only one customs man on duty : a young, sharp-looking fellow.

She must not faint. She must not. Her life depended on it – Kurt's too. She must think of something else. *Think of something else.* And suddenly she thought of that same kitchen at Potsdam, all those years ago, with the bright highly-polished warming pans ranged as ornaments on the walls. She remembered Gundl, the cook, with her rosy cheeks and her huge smile and how there always seemed to be something that Gundl had just made and which the little Ilsa wanted to eat...

She was there, facing the customs man, and she had not fainted. 'Well?' he demanded. He sounded cross. There were a lot of passengers and she was one of the last. She pushed her suitcases on to the counter in front of him, fumbling to open them. Kurt, beside her, was doing the same with the ones he was carrying.

The customs man looked through the contents of one of the suitcases, turning over clothes and shoes with perfunctory scorn; looked irritably at the other case; then marked them both with chalk. He took longer with Kurt's but by then Ilsa had moved away, going towards the end of the customs shed – extraordinarily, unbelievably safe, soon to be on the way to England with her son.

Lothar Kahlmann's parents had been *Ostjuden* from Poland. They had been in Germany long enough for Lothar not to have automatically become stateless under the laws the Nazis enacted regarding such immigrants; but the fact was important to him in another way. Whereas most of the long-established and completely assimilated German Jews had no relatives outside Germany, the children of the *Ostjuden* who had only come to Germany during the twentieth century often had uncles and aunts and cousins who had travelled farther in the same diaspora and had ended up in England or America. So, when Lothar made the decision to leave Germany, he thought at once of his cousin Mark, whose father, Lothar's uncle, had gone to London in 1909. There had been little communication between the brothers over thirty years, and yet the link between them, however tenuous, had never quite been severed. So Lothar had an address to write to in Stepney. He knew his uncle had lived there and had indeed died there ten years ago, but he had not heard from any of the other Kahlmanns since then. He wrote – in German, although he apologized for this, as Mark would hardly know the language – to Mark at that address.

He got a reply a few weeks later. He saw that Mark now spelt the name rather differently – 'Kaleman' – and the letter was written in English, so Lothar had to have it translated. Mark apologized in his turn; he knew no German and, although he might have written in Yiddish, he doubted if Lothar would be able to read that. He was glad, he said, to hear from his cousin, the son of the brother his father had loved. He understood very well how difficult things were in Germany for Jews and he would be glad to help Lothar if he could. He did not know what the rules and regulations were for Lothar to come to England from Germany, but he understood that if he, Mark, would undertake that Lothar would not be seeking any dole or public assistance, Lothar could come into England. Mark was prepared to do this for his cousin Lothar. Mark was about forty now; he had a wife and children, but the children were young; one of his brothers was dead, another was living in Manchester, and the third running a small button factory in Hackney. So Mark had no help with the clothing manufactury he had taken over from his father. Officially Lother could not be working in England but this was what he proposed. He, Mark, was a tailor; so was Lothar and he could be of great assistance to Mark with the refinements that were beyond the girls he employed. Lothar could live with the Kalemans over the work-rooms and who would know that Mark was paying him a salary?

Three weeks later Lothar was on his way to England.

In June 1933 Lord Reading told a meeting at the Queens Hall:

We have well in mind, in our duty as British citizens, that we must take care that we do not add to the great unemployment existing in this country.

These words, spoken not by a trade union leader fearful of job-losses but by a famous British Jew at the beginning of the German diaspora, indicate a very guarded welcome. Lord Reading's conquest of the British Establishment, if not as spectacular as Disraeli's, had been nearly as remarkable. Having triumphed at the Bar (not an area in which Jews commonly distinguished themselves then), he had gone on to become Viceroy of India, an office rich in power and encrusted symbolism. So his cautious words suggest the perennial attitude of the established Jew towards the *Ostjuden* – using *Ostjuden* in its widest sense – the attitude of the German Jews themselves to their fellows fleeing from Russia and Poland, of the Italian Jews to their brethren driven from Spain by the Inquisition, and of course of the Sephardim of Stuart times towards the Ashkenazi from Hamburg. Fortunately this was never an important factor and it seems ungracious to mention it in the face of the extraordinary work of the refugee organizations which were entirely the creation of the British Jewish community. But such an aspect cannot be absolutely ignored, especially when one remembers the strangely ineffectual pressure American Jewry brought to bear on President Roosevelt to alter his blandly indifferent attitude to the German Jewish refugees. And of course Lord Reading's words reflect the traditional objections to large-scale immigration into any country by any group.

In fact, as we have seen, the British Jewish community had responded to the plight of their German brethren immediately, and had given the British Government the guarantee that, pivotal as it was to immigration through the crucial years of 1933 to 1939, at the same time tended to underwrite official ambivalence and equivocation towards the refugee problem.

The oldest of the Jewish refugee organizations was the Jews' Temporary Shelter in the East End of London. This had looked after the first great wave of *Ostjuden* on their first arrival from Russia and Poland during the 1890s and after. In 1933 the Temporary Shelter prepared to welcome the German Jews. By May of that year, however, it seemed likely that this refugee problem was going to be of larger dimensions than anything ever encountered before. A secondary consideration was the fact that these German immigrants tended to go to north-west London rather than the East End.

After the Jewish community had given the British Government their historic guarantee, Jewish efforts for the refugees in Britain were coordinated in the organization known as the Central British Fund for German Jewry. The function of this body was both to raise funds and to direct policy. It formed subsidiaries in the shape of a Refugee Committee and a Professional Committee. The first functioned in London; the second dealt with the high proportion of refugee academics and professional men. The Central British Fund for German Jewry issued its first appeal in May 1933 and raised some £200,000. (The Central British Fund for German Jewry and its subsidiaries were roughly equivalent to the Joint Distribution Committee in America which since 1914 had been the chief body for the assistance of the Central and Eastern European Jews. In 1933 the Joint Distribution Committee included the Jews of Germany in its annual appeal to the people of the United States.) Subsequent appeals by the Central British Fund brought the total raised between 1933 and 1935 to nearly half a million pounds. It should be said that these sums represented not only the contributions of the rich Jews – the 'merchant princes' in the City and in industry – but also those of very poor Jews, some of them still working in the cramped sewing-rooms of Manchester and the East End of London. Nor must it be forgotten that the good-will the British Jewish community extended to the refugees was only partly represented by money: there were offers of hospitality and service so numerous that they can never be assessed.

And there was of course much help from non-Jewish sources. The most effective orator and perhaps the most baffling character among the Guilty Men, Lord Baldwin, launching a fund for the refugees that was to bear his name, asked his audience to come to the aid of the victims

not of earthquake nor of flood, nor of a famine, but of an explosion of man's inhumanity to man. Thousands of men, women, and children, despoiled of their goods, driven from their homes, are seeking asylum and sanctuary on our doorsteps, a hiding place from the wind and a cover from the tempest . . . They may not be our fellow-subjects but they are our fellow-men . . . I shall not attempt to depict to you what it means to be scorned and branded and isolated like a leper. The honour of our country is challenged. Our Christian charity is challenged and it is up to us to meet that challenge.

An outstanding figure in every enterprise on behalf of the refugees was himself of German Jewish origin: Otto M. Schiff, a partner in the City stockbroking firm of Bourke, Schiff and Company. Apart from his energy and devotion, Otto Schiff's long career of working for the refugees – he had started with those who had fled from Belgium in 1914 – had given him not only invaluable experience in dealing with the British immigration authorities but also a unique standing with the officials involved. His personal authority was to a great extent identified with the refugee organizations with which he was associated. This was to mean that refugees were often admitted to Britain on the recommendation of the organization alone and later (not through any desire of its own) the Refugee Committee was to acquire an almost life-or-death power in certain cases through the reliance placed on these recommendations by the aliens' tribunals.

By the outbreak of war 80 per cent of all the refugees in Britain had registered with the Jewish Refugees' Committee. A large portion of the funds collected by the Central British Fund for German Jewry (which was later to become known as the Council for German Jewry and, on the outbreak of war, to change its name yet again to the Central Council for Jewish Refugees) went to the Refugee Committee which dealt with individual cases, but there were many other calls on it by different groups, all deserving and all under-financed. These included agricultural and other training schemes, especially for the young refugees; the various organizations helping different categories like doctors, dentists, and academics; and, most important of all, the children.

In the years after 1933 these bodies proliferated into a network of organizations so complex and widespread that in 1938 all these independent strands were brought together under a Central Co-ordinating Committee (later to be re-named the Joint Consultative Committee on Refugees) under the chairmanship of Lord Hailey. In 1939 all these organizations under this committee were brought under one roof when they joined in buying the lease of a former hotel in Bloomsbury. This was named Bloomsbury House and, in the years that followed, it became famous as the essential ganglion for the welfare of the refugees. Everything came from here. Joint committees were set up to deal with the various aspects of the problem and to avoid duplication of effort in the areas that overlapped.

Assessing refugee testimony, it is impossible to overestimate the work done by these organizations. It was natural that individuals should come into conflict with them from time to time: it is always harder to deal with institutions than with people and many of the refugees – particularly the older refugees – were in a condition of near-breakdown when they arrived in England. But quarrels were rare. The work of the refugee organizations will stand for ever as a monument to the love and care and intelligence of the people who worked for them and made their success possible. The ideal before them never dimmed, was never in doubt.

The *Report for 1937* of the Council of German Jewry says:

It would be deplorable if, at this time, when the pressure in Germany is constantly aggravated, the tempo of ordered emigration should decline because of diminishing help from the Jewish organizations. The response of British Jewry to the need of German Jewry in its long-drawn crisis is the test of our people. The persistence of German persecution demands the persistence of Jewish solidarity.

The predominantly professional, even 'intellectual', character of so many of the German Jewish immigrants was, as we have seen, their greatest disadvantage. An often-heard story tells how a bus conductor whose route took him through Hampstead, Finchley, and Golders Green claimed he had only to lean out and shout 'Herr Doktor!' for a dozen erudite, bespectacled heads to pop out of as many windows in eager response. One of the most important sections of welfare activity was therefore concerned with helping those who had practised as doctors and lawyers; who had taught in schools or universities or conducted research.

As Leo Baeck said in his speech recalling Boycott Day, the Nazi assault on freedom and all the values that give scholarship its meaning did not evoke any significant protest from the German academic world.

A few brave men protested, but most of them were Jews themselves. Professor James Franck, the Nobel Prizewinner, resigned his university chair in 1933, although he would have been entitled to keep it (for the time being) under the 'Veterans Clause' of the Reconstruction of the Civil Service laws. He refused to be treated as an alien, he said, and 'an enemy of the Fatherland'. Mostly there was silence. Possibly there was an element of jealousy at work against the Jews. The Jews, barely one per cent of the population, had held one eighth of the professorships in the German universities. A quarter of the German Nobel Prizewinners had been Jews. A further cause of ill-feeling was the fact that many Jewish scholars and scientists from Eastern Europe had come to German universities. Another Nobel Prizewinner, the great physicist Max Planck, petitioned Hitler to stop the dismissals of scientists because they were Jews. He was told:

Our national policies will not be revoked . . . If the dismissal of Jewish scientists means the annihilation of contemporary German science, we shall do without scientists for a few years . . .

There was little the remaining Aryan scientists could do to prevent the virtual decapitation of German science, although few of them appear to have wanted to prevent it. 'Lie back in the mud and embrace the butcher,' as Brecht wrote in another connection. The Nazi physicist Lenard rationalized the pogrom with an attack on Einstein and the 'Jewish spirit' in science:

His [Einstein's] theories of relativity seek to revolutionize and dominate the whole of physics. In fact these theories . . . were never intended to be true . . . The Jew is strangely lacking in appreciation of Truth . . . The hasty characteristics of the Jewish spirit, to push forward with unproved ideas, has spread like a plague . . . The alien spirit is paralysing. All that is alien in race is detrimental to the German people.

In the light of such utterances, it is not surprising that the German academic world exhibited a mere simulacrum of scholarship, totally dominated by the State. But this attitude was to some extent rooted in history. The dependent nature of scholarship may have been inevitable in the time of the princeling and the *Hof-Jude*; but the University of Berlin had been founded in the spirit of the 'New Humanism' of Goethe and Humboldt. Unfortunately that tradition had not survived for long. German scholarship had never been equipped to meet state pressures. The historian Mommsen had been deprived of his professorship for his political views; and the dehumanizing process had continued over the intervening years. Under the Weimar Republic the theories of National Socialism had captured thousands of students. Under the Nazis themselves the universities became mere factories of propaganda. 'Applied science' meant designing bombs or testing poison gas. Each university senate became the microcosm of a 'parliament' in a Fascist country, with the Rector representing the Führer before an assembly of stooges.

The flood of academics from Germany during and after 1933 has been compared with the migration of the scholars from Constantinople in the fifteenth century. These refugees, at least, captured the imaginative sympathy of their professional colleagues in other countries. In Britain this mood gave birth to the Academic

THE NEW ARRIVALS

Assistance Council: a body that was to prove important not only to the refugee scientists but ultimately to the British war effort itself. Like nearly all the organizations connected with the refugees, the Academic Assistance Council later changed its name, becoming known as the Society for the Protection of Science and Learning. Its expressed aims were

> the relief of suffering and the defence of learning and science [and] assisting university teachers and other investigators of whatever country who on grounds of religion, political opinion or 'race' are unable to carry on their work in their own country.

The Academic Assistance Council did not merely attempt to get threatened German Jewish scholars and scientists out of Germany and Austria but went farther, seeking to find them university and other posts which would enable them to carry on the work that had been interrupted by Nazi persecution. One of the council's initiators was Sir William Beveridge (whose 'Beveridge Report' on social issues was one of the dominant themes in immediate post-war Britain). Involved with the Academic Assistance Council were several Nobel Prizewinners, including Lord Rutherford, as president, and Professor A. V. Hill; and a number of other members of the scientific and cultural Establishment like H.A.L. (later Lord) Fisher; Lord Cecil of Chelwood; Lord Lytton; and Professor S. Alexander, the philosopher. Walter Adams (now Sir Walter Adams, until recently head of the London School of Economics) acted as secretary.

The council set out to serve a high ideal: to assist and succour those whose devotion to knowledge was threatened by totalitarian brutality from whatever quarter it came (which at that time could only mean from the Nazis). As Lord Rutherford said:

> The universities form a kingdom of their own, whose intellectual autonomy must be preserved

and the Academic Assistance Council can claim to have preserved the spiritual and intellectual essence of the German universities, overwhelmed as they were by a new barbarism.

Having appealed for funds, the council set about compiling a register of displaced scholars and scientists (which included the names of some still in Germany) with a view to finding out where they could be placed, in lectureships, research posts, and special scholarships. In addition the council organized courses of lectures by distinguished refugees and provided its own scholarships and maintenance grants.

To attract popular support the council called a mass meeting in the Albert Hall, presided over by Lord Rutherford and addressed by Albert Einstein. It was rumoured that an attempt was to be made on Einstein's life by Nazi agents, and a number of plainclothes detectives were in evidence in the hall, but fortunately nothing happened.

An interesting footnote to the work undertaken by the Academic Assistance Council is provided by Lord Snow in his *Public Affairs* (1971), where he mentions the rescue activities of Professor Lindemann, Churchill's scientific adviser, the rather equivocal figure who later became Lord Cherwell and whose influence on war strategy is often considered to have been unfortunate. Lord Snow says that while Lindemann himself professed a 'rather silly antisemitism', he was responsible for bringing to Britain some of the best scientists in Europe (thus foreshadowing Lord Snow's own remarkable feat in getting refugee scientists freed from internment and then putting them to work for Britain). Lindemann brought Dr Nicholas Kürti and Professor Francis Simon to London; Professor Kurt Mendelssohn and Professor Heinrich Kuhn to Oxford. The introduction of Professor Mendelssohn and his colleague to Oxford meant that one of Lindemann's cherished institutions, the Clarendon Laboratory, was revivified. They worked there on 'superconductivity', studying the mobility of electrons in a conductor and thus the pattern of the smallest particles; and there the first equipment for liquifying helium was installed. Within a decade the Clarendon was known as one of the finest research establishments in Britain.

The Professional Committee of the Council for German Jewry had roughly similar aims to those of the Academic Assistance Council, but it dealt more with professional men – doctors and dentists and lawyers. These met with a kind of opposition that the academics, in the main, were fortunate enough not to encounter. One reason for this, of course, was that there were more German Jewish doctors seeking to re-establish themselves in Britain than there were academics of university lecturer status and above. Again, the field of purely academic studies had always had something of an international character. In the physical sciences at least Germany enjoyed a pre-eminence that was only slowly yielded to America. These German physicists and chemists were welcome anywhere for what they knew, the disciplines they could impart. For the German medical men seeking registration in England, the situation was very different.

The professions in England have been compared to the craft guilds in the Middle Ages in their wealth and authority and the privileges and benefits it is within their power to confer on those who win the right to enjoy them. It was hardly to be expected that the British medical profession would welcome an influx of German Jewish doctors without some resentment: these refugees were seeking to penetrate British middle-class society at its densest point. The medical profession in England was and is a highly organized enclave, jealously guarding its status and its deserved privileges. Through its representative body, the British Medical Association, it exerted a rigid discipline over its members – a discipline that as well as dealing with black sheep (doctors who performed abortions or went to bed with female patients) also created martyrs: doctors whose conduct was tantamount to 'self-advertisement' or who flirted with unorthodox methods of treatment. (It was about the doctors of this era, before the concept of Welfare Medicine had, however reluctantly, been accepted, that the best-seller *The Citadel* had been written.) Such a group, rigid, exclusive, embedded in the most conservative section of English society, could only regard these strange foreign doctors as a nuisance and something of a threat. The usual arguments about aliens grabbing British opportunities were advanced, but the question went deeper, although – as always when dealing with the refugees – one has to distinguish between widely differing attitudes within the same group. An eminent British practitioner, Samson Wright, headed the Professional Committee and did all he could to help the refugee doctors. Unfortunately a group called the Medical Practitioners' Union adopted a very different attitude and made several hostile pronouncements. These were seized on by one or two newspapers who tried to give the impression that the Medical Practitioners' Union was a body comparable with the British Medical Association. On 19 June 1938 the *Sunday Express* wrote:

There is a big influx of foreign Jews into Britain. They are overrunning the country. They are trying to enter the medical profession in great numbers ... Worst of all, many of them are holding themselves out to the public as psychoanalysts ... he [the psychoanalyst] often obtains an ascendancy over the patient of which he makes base use if he is a bad man.

This evocation of an evil Svengali of a psychoanalyst is the equivalent to the anti-semitic cartoons in Streicher's *Der Stürmer*. And the use of the word 'psychoanalyst' as a key to arouse fear and dislike was more relevant in 1938, when psychiatrists and their methods were much less widely understood than they are today. *Everybody's* of 17 September 1938 said:

Most of the alien doctors and dentists are Jews who are fleeing from Germany and Austria. And the methods these aliens are bringing into England are not always in accordance with the professional etiquette of this country.

Again, a note of fear and distrust is struck.

The British Medical Association naturally did not associate itself with these excesses, but its attitude was not friendly. Despite the assistance given to the refugees by the Professional Committee of the Council of German Jewry and such bodies as the Jewish Medical and Dental Emergency Association (supported by some Jewish doctors and dentists in England to help refugee members of their professions) the road to acceptance was long and hard. A number of the refugee doctors, particularly some of those who left Austria after the Anschluss, were famous and eminent enough to belong to that class of refugee whose acceptance, the British Cabinet had considered, would create 'a very favourable impression in the world'; but the British Medical Association regarded their talents and their sufferings with equal indifference. The then Home Secretary recalled that he himself would gladly have 'admitted the Austrian medical schools *en bloc*', and that he received an 'unpleasant shock' when he came up against the narrow chauvinism of the English medical Establishment. The British Medical Association did agree to set up a committee to advise the Home Secretary on the conditions under which refugee doctors might be allowed into Britain in the future. Later this committee was to report with satisfaction that the admission of refugee doctors was to be very severely limited; that each individual applicant would be carefully screened and would have to undergo at least two years of clinical study before being admitted to practise.

Some of the earlier medical immigrants like Professor Joachim had simply accepted the fact that the British Medical Association did not recognize their qualifications and then settled down to get a British degree. Georg Joachim has a clear picture of his father sitting down day after day, night after night (he hardly remembers him leaving the house, although he must have had to attend lectures and clinics), in the front room of the flat the family had taken in Edinburgh, poring over the English equivalents of the books he had studied at Göttingen nearly forty years before. It was not their contents that he found difficult – although the technical equipment of a specialist of many years' experience must differ greatly in orientation from that of a young student seeking to master first principles – but the language in which they were written. Professor Joachim had never spoken English well. He was not the kind of man who enjoys learning foreign languages and, as he said to Georg again and again, now he had to acquire an entirely new technical vocabulary. Georg remembers how his father would sometimes give up in momentary despair, although he never admitted this. The signal to the family would be the slamming of the door of the front room. Then a moment later his father would appear in the living-room, standing framed in the doorway – drawn, haggard, despondency incarnate, his son would think – before he ran into the room and collapsed on to the settee. Then his wife would make coffee and he would sip it, gradually recovering. He might even attempt a joke – but Georg found his father's attempted jokes more sad than funny. Then, after a time, he would boil a kettle on the gas-stove and shave. He never needed to do so – he had a very light beard – but he had great faith in the recuperative effect of a shave. Then he would go back into the front room and start all over again.

Georg Joachim considers that the struggle to re-qualify in Britain killed his father. Not perhaps directly, but by draining him of some vital essence that carries a man through into old age. As it was, he subjected his mind and body to a severe strain at a time when, for many men, retirement is ceasing to be a remote fantasy and is becoming an agreeable and not-too-distant reality. He was fifty-seven when he qualified in Britain. For two years he carried on a general practice in Kilburn, mainly among Irish immigrants and fellow German refugees. (The idea of pursuing his speciality again seemed too remote.) Then, two days after his fifty-ninth birthday and two months before war broke out, he died of a heart attack.

Georg considers that his father was probably happier during the blinding, obsessive years of study in Edinburgh than he was later on in London. In Edinburgh he was aiming at a single goal; in London he was oppressed with money worries and with concern for the future of his wife and children in the face of the war he knew was impending.

Younger refugee doctors found the Britain of the pre-war years a frustrating place. (Later, when the war really got going, their services were welcomed.) One young doctor had qualified at the University of Vienna two years before the Anschluss. He had been lucky enough to be on holiday in France when the Germans marched into his country and he never returned to Austria. He thought of going to America but England seemed easier. He says:

I always think I came at a bad time. If I had been earlier, I suppose I might have set about re-qualifying at an English university. I would have been young enough to do that. If I'd been later – but not too late of course, not after war broke out – I wouldn't have had to wait so long for my qualifications to be recognized. As it was ... I kept going to the Medical Department of the Council for German Jewry – it had only been started a month and I must have been one of the first to register. At first they were quite optimistic; apparently the British Government were being co-operative and then – bang! – all of a sudden it was all off. The B.M.A. [British Medical Association] was being bloody-minded. I understand that the row really concerned the psychoanalysts who were literally streaming out of Vienna at that time ... Small fry like me weren't relevant to it – a young man who'd just qualified and wanted to do orthapaedics. But I think there was an element of jealousy in the B.M.A. attitude to the Austrian medical schools. I heard later that the government would have permitted 500 German and Austrian doctors in but that the B.M.A. cut it to 50. I can well believe that.

At that time I didn't have any money at all and I didn't know

THE NEW ARRIVALS

anyone in England. I used to have to queue up at the refugee office for a hand-out. Many of the others waiting were old and sick people: I felt pretty useless . . . Then one day a man approached me as I was going away . . . He was quite old, about fifty – which I considered old then – and I thought at once he wasn't an Englishman. He introduced himself as Dr K—. He said he was in practice in the Mile End Road in East London. He invited me to have a cup of coffee with him and we went to one of those underground ABC teashops there used to be all over London. He bought me a cup of coffee. The way things were, you can imagine – I was glad to get that. As I say, I guessed he wasn't an Englishman and I knew he wasn't German or Austrian. Actually, he was Russian. He'd been brought to England with his parents when he was a baby. He must have been Jewish – of course – but strangely enough he would never actually say so . . . Anyway, he said he had a proposition to make to me. He said he understood the difficulties we refugees were having in getting our qualifications accepted and he'd seen me going to the committee office day after day (I realized later that he must have been hanging around on the look out for someone like me). Would I like to come and work for him as a kind of medical secretary? My keep and pocket-money. A completely unofficial arrangement of course . . . It would have to be, of course, because apart from not being able to practise medicine I had no labour permit to do any job at all . . . Dr K— kept stressing that the B.M.A. would be sure to recognize the refugees' qualifications soon and then – he kept hinting – there would be a chance of a partnership . . . I don't think I believed that part of it but of course I agreed to go. What had I to lose? . . .

He had two surgeries, one in the Mile End Road, one in a sidestreet – both ordinary shop-fronts with the main window blacked out: I'd never seen anything like them before . . . He had a big practice: mostly very poor people, some Irish, but mostly Russian and Polish immigrants who'd come here thirty or forty years ago and their children – some of the older ones still couldn't speak much English after being here all these years . . . Anyway, I soon realized that he'd picked a refugee in order to get an assistant on the cheap . . . Not that he did anything actually illegal. I couldn't actually examine patients, obviously, or go out on visits alone – but he gave me a white coat and had me marshal the patients and he got a snap diagnosis from me on every one and this saved him time. He wasn't so much a bad doctor as a machine . . . A machine for getting through a queue as quickly as possible, grabbing their few bob, and getting them out into the street again. He never had anything in writing from me, of course, and no doubt if there'd been any trouble with the B.M.A. he would simply have denied everything, and said he'd just given me a roof out of charity. What he did do and what surprised me was that he supplied medicines he himself prescribed for his patients – although I've heard that other doctors in England did this at that time. But of course after I arrived I did all his dispensing – that was another thing he got, a dispenser for free . . .

I stuck it all for three months, and I didn't leave because I had to sleep in a damp attic or because the food was bad or my 'pocket-money' would hardly buy cigarettes . . . I don't think I left him because of the way he treated his patients either – half-bullying, half-flattering – awful! No, I think I went because I didn't trust him and I had the feeling that if I stayed he might involve me in something that would mean I would *never* be recognized by the B.M.A. And also because I knew I was being exploited – and so many refugees were, I think. Not refugee doctors so much – but refugees generally, especially those who had no particular skills, and I think they were often exploited by the very people who should have helped them most.

This Austrian doctor subsequently got a labour permit and was working as a machinist in a factory when war broke out. In 1941 by a special Emergency Order refugee doctors who had not re-qualified in Britain were put on a temporary medical register on the strength of their German or Austrian qualifications. This young doctor joined the R.A.M.C. and served in North Africa and Italy. In 1947 the Medical Practitioners and Pharmacists Act was passed, making these temporary registrations permanent, and he had by then specialized in orthopaedics as it had been his original ambition to do.

The refugee dentists found things even harder than the doctors. Those who arrived before 1937 managed in some cases to get admitted to the Foreign Dentists Register, but those who came later found their German and Austrian qualifications rejected.

The professional group that suffered most in their exile were the lawyers. The legal profession in Britain confronted the refugee with a complex pattern of social and craft rituals. The English Bar, with its Inns of Court, where young barristers had to eat a certain number of 'dinners' before they could be admitted; the cult of personality reflected in 'taking silk' (becoming a King's

Counsel) and in the 'star' system that made the names of advocates like Patrick Hastings and Marshall Hall household words – all this must have baffled the sober doctors of law from Munich or Frankfurt. Even the more mundane half of the profession, the solicitors, functioned in a kind of dusty Dickensian tradition that was far removed from anything on the Continent. But worse than these externals, however confusing, was the fact that in Britain the law itself was different. The British system was based on the common law: a great maze of decisions and precedents extending far back in time, whereas the German stemmed broadly from Roman law. And the work of a lawyer is in any case far more concerned with social and economic facts peculiar to the country he is practising in than is that of a doctor. Medicine is international. So the plight of the refugee lawyer was much worse than that of the refugee doctor. However dog-in-the-manger the British Medical Association might be at the moment, the doctor knew that ultimately his skills would be needed. Not so the lawyer. Many abandoned their profession entirely. Martin Beradt told the story of the refugee lawyer who locked himself in his room, took out his gown from his trunk and, standing before the mirror, proceeded to address an imaginary jury. A few were able to establish themselves in the comparatively narrow field of international law. Some were determined to enter the British legal profession; and oddly enough found it was easier to penetrate the narrow alleys and gracious lawns of the Inns of Court than the High Street office of the suburban solicitor. A solicitor had to be a British subject; a barrister did not. (Later, having gained British nationality, a number of these barristers became solicitors.) A few refugee lawyers found posts in the academic world; and in the years following the war there was a good deal of work for refugee lawyers in the claims made against the German Government. More lawyers returned to Germany after the war than members of any other category of refugee.

A number of those who abandoned the law and entered industry made more substantial progress than would have been possible in their own profession – at least in Britain. A lawyer from Mainz came to England in 1939 and, finding it impossible to practise law, got a job in a factory early in 1940. After his release from internment later that year he went back to the same chemical firm and eventually rose to be managing director through a series of marketing posts. He doubts whether the law, in Germany or England, would have offered him a comparable success.

An important aspect of the work of the Council for Germany Jewry was *Aliyah* (Hebrew for 'emigration'), which was carried out among the younger refugees. This was essentially an extension of the training plan which the Reichsvertretung had attempted to carry out in Germany: the training of young Jews between seventeen and thirty and school-leavers of sixteen and over, mainly in agriculture and in certain manual skills, with a view to their eventual emigration to Palestine. While this work of *Aliyah* continued to meet with ever-increasing difficulties in Germany itself, it was organized by the Council of German Jewry among young German Jewish immigrants to Britain up to the outbreak of war.

As in Germany, the greatest stress was laid on agricultural training, but a variety of other skills was taught. Up to the limitation placed on Jewish immigration by the British Government in 1937, Palestine was able to absorb these immigrants; thereafter, up to the outbreak of war, the situation was difficult. The larger part of the quota allowed was filled by agricultural settlers direct from Germany and Austria. A special Agricultural Committee was formed under the chairmanship of Colonel Waley Cohen (later his place was taken by Mrs Rebecca Sieff). The committee placed some 1,400 young Jewish trainees with farmers and in hostels.

Aliyah was of course a noble conception in itself and some years later when the state of Israel was at last a reality, the practical value of these years of planning and training was apparent. But more importantly, *Aliyah* crystallized and kept alive the sense of racial identity that might otherwise have been lost to many young Jews, displaced, stateless, deprived of all the props to self-esteem furnished by an upbringing in a stable society. The decision to lay the stress of *Aliyah* training on agriculture and other manual skills was of course a very practical one and reflects – again – the predominantly middle-class nature of the German and Austrian refugees. Despite the many young agriculturists who came to Palestine before 1937, there were so many immigrants from the professional classes, especially doctors, that the authorities set up the cry: 'No more doctors! Please send us some patients!'

It is not surprising, then, that the training-plans for *Aliyah* should sometimes have run counter to the preferences and ambitions of individuals. While admitting the principle of the greatest good of the greatest number, some young refugees felt like conscripts of an ideal. What of the son of a doctor, coming to England as a young refugee, who did not want to be a farmer – but a doctor? Or a historian whom the concept of *Aliyah* decreed should mend typewriters?

Not that Hugo Neher, at twenty-three, cherished such a large ambition. If he had known anyone well enough to confide the fact, he would have said he was interested in certain aspects of history and hoped some day to write of them. 'Historian' would have seemed too grandiose a phrase. But to be a typewriter mechanic? Hugo had no mechanical aptitudes. When he was eleven, his Aunt Lotte had given him a huge Meccano set – which had given his father infinite pleasure. After a time, Hugo had abandoned all pretence of playing with it. Mechanical things worried Hugo: he had only to look at any kind of machine, he suspected, for it to go wrong. His emotions can be imagined, therefore, when he was handed a list of possible trades with every alternative crossed off except 'Typewriters: Assembly/ Repair'.

Hugo had never thought of himself as a candidate for *Aliyah*. He had walked away from the immigration office at Harwich possessed by an incredulous sense of freedom. During his time with the immigration officer – how long had he been in that office – ten minutes? half an hour? an hour? – he had lost all hope; his world had narrowed to a single despairing question: what was he going to do? How could he go back to Germany now?

All through the journey across the dismal Essex flatlands he felt dazed with joy. His mood persisted through the long wait in the bottleneck of tracks and signals outside Liverpool Street. Then, as the train moved into the dark, echoing steam-wreathed station, he reached a point of exultation that, recalled, still brings a tear to Hugo's eyes. Lining the platform, there stood a row of grave-faced, sturdy men. Each of them wore a white armband with the emblem of Magen David. They were there to offer the homeless comfort and to succour their fellow Jews who had fled homeless to a foreign land.

Hugo himself had gone to stay with the Haleys. He had reported to the local police at Wimbledon and been reminded of what the immigration officer had marked on his papers: he was not to take a job. He had very little money. The euphoria of the first few days drained away from him. Then he was summoned to the Refugee Committee. He was interviewed by one of its members, a middle-aged stockbroker whose family (Hugo heard later) could trace their roots back to the Sephardim who were allowed back to Britain by Cromwell. This committee member spoke in mild, almost muted tones and Hugo's youthful optimism was reproved by his gloom. 'You wish to *stay* in England?' the committee member probed gently. 'Really?' He shook his head. 'Most of the young people – and indeed the not-so-young – whom we are helping are proposing to re-emigrate.'

'I hadn't thought about that,' Hugo said.

'Ah . . .' the committee member sighed. 'Then you should. You must. There's nothing here for you in this country. Nothing at all.'

Hugo didn't know what to say. The committee member spoke with such finality that no comment seemed possible. Hugo tried to explain that he had always admired Britain, its literature and institutions. So indeed had his father before him. And surely everyone must admire the British attitude towards the Jews: the opportunities they had been granted in this country. When you thought of Disraeli . . .

Hugo stopped, aware that he was not saying the right things.

'America,' the committee member said. 'I suppose you don't have relatives in America who could sponsor you?'

'I don't want to go to America.'

'Want?' the committee member echoed. 'What we want and what we get . . .' He left the sentence unfinished. 'I can only repeat that there are no prospects before you in Great Britain. In fact,' he added deprecatingly, 'the prospects don't look too bright for any of us anywhere.'

His gloom and his mildness together anaesthetized Hugo. If the committee member had been less mild, if he had tried to impose his will, Hugo would have argued back. As it was, he listened. Zionism, the committee member said. Hugo was a Jew; he must

THE NEW ARRIVALS

have some attitude to the concept of a National Home. Hugo admitted that he was – unlike his father – a Zionist. Yes: he believed in the Zionist ideal.

But not for himself? the committee member had asked gently. A merely theoretical Zionist in fact? Had he never thought of going to Palestine and helping to build up a wholly Jewish society? Had he heard of *Aliyah*? The training of young people who, in God's good time, would create a new Israel?

Listening, Hugo was stirred by a kind of guilt. His personal dream of England, his dream of becoming a writer, even an historian, was in conflict with the other dream this gentle man was reviving now. He went on listening. *Aliyah* might be the answer to his dilemma, the committee member suggested. The terms which the immigration officer had set for Hugo's admission to Britain had been such that it would be difficult for him to remain unless the committee could promise that he would re-emigrate. He was young enough to go on *Aliyah* training. He would become skilled and then in due course he would go to Palestine and make a new life there.

Hugo felt confused. He thanked the committee member and asked whether he could consider the suggestion. Certainly, but perhaps he could come back tomorrow? There wasn't a great deal of time.

That afternoon Hugo went for a long walk on Wimbledon Common. The committee member's proposal had fired him with a certain enthusiasm – and yet he felt doubtful. Was he being asked to sacrifice himself for an ideal? He had read that there were too many professional people going to Palestine; that what they wanted was farmers, and after that artisans, mechanics, people who could use their hands. Well – anything to do with machines was out of the question. Agriculture? To farm under the blazing sun of Judaea? Well . . . perhaps. Almost at once he found himself building another dream: that of himself as a farmer in Palestine and, at the same time, the historian and chronicler of the New Israel. His farm a place of pilgrimage for cultured Jews from all over the world. They would come to seek him out. The details were vague . . .

It was ridiculous, but it comforted him. Otherwise, he felt he was sacrificing everything.

The next day he went back and told the committee member

that he would undertake training for *Aliyah*. The committee member said he was very glad to hear it.

But agriculture? Unfortunately the three farm settlements which took trainees from among newly arrived refugees were all full up. It would have to be industrial training. That was, if anything, still more important. The committee member now seemed to have got more decisive: he did not even ask Hugo if he liked the idea. Then he handed Hugo the list with its single remaining alternative of typewriter mechanic. He would go to Bolton in Lancashire for three months' training.

Hugo dumbly accepted. What else could he do? The committee member had made it clear that, if he did not accept this proposal, the Refugee Committee could do nothing for him. By now his four weeks' 'probation' was nearly up. The committee member congratulated him on the chance he was getting: his passport would be sent to the Home Office for the necessary approval, but that, Hugo was assured, would only be a formality as he was going on a training-course sponsored by the committee.

The next ten months were a time of misery for Hugo. Not that the workers in the factory were not kind to him: they were. He got to like the Lancashire people and their pawky, quacking accent. And the other Jews on the course were nice lads, most of them younger than he was, in their late teens. But far from conquering his innate resistance to machines – or, as he sometimes thought of it, their resistance to *him* – he found it grew worse. He made some progress, but it was grim, tortuous work. To think of spending his life doing this! In Palestine or anywhere else. Even when he had acquired a fumbling minimum of competence with the hateful machines, he had to fight hard to overcome his total boredom with what he was doing. He tried to outflank it by chopping each day into sections: arrival to morning tea-break; morning tea-break to the wash before lunch; lunch to the cigarette smoked in the factory-yard at three o'clock; and so on.

After ten months had passed like this, an important member of the Refugees' Committee arrived in Bolton to visit the trainees. Having looked at the factory and talked with the management, this committee man, a member of another long-established English Jewish family of great wealth and connections, interviewed the trainees one by one. It was clear that his visit to Bolton was in the nature of a 'passing-out' parade in the Army. 'Well,' the committee man said genially to Hugo, 'it's nearly time for you lads to go off to Palestine.' Suddenly Hugo was stricken with panic. The factory routine, dull and hateful as it was, had contrived to deaden his awareness of what he had let himself in for. All he could manage to do was stammer out that he didn't think he was quite ready to go yet. He needed a bit more training. The committee member was clearly not pleased, but more baffled; no trainee had ever sought delay before; they were usually only too keen to leave. 'I need more time,' Hugo repeated. 'I must be fully skilled before I get to Palestine.' The committee man said he would see what he could do, and did in fact arrange for Hugo to have a further six months' training. He didn't think the authorities would have any objection. (In fact, they did not: Hugo's passport continued to travel between Bolton and the Home Office; by the time an extension of time was granted, another was almost due.)

At the end of his further period of training Hugo returned to London. He felt extremely confused: divided by the claims of the ideal – *Aliyah* in Palestine or what he owed to himself, his own destiny? What good would a reluctant and hardly competent mechanic be to the National Home? On the other hand, had he the right to waste the training he had received? But he knew that if he had been tough enough to reject the Refugee Committee's proposal and told them that he would stay in London and fend for himself – as some other young refugees had done – the British Government would not have sent him back to Germany.

Not long after that Hugo Neher compared the attitude of established Jewry to that of a respectable and prosperous family on whom is suddenly thrust a number of recently impoverished relations. The family does its duty by them – as family piety demands – but it does not ask the poor relations to linger in the house longer than may be absolutely necessary. And so, according to Hugo, the (often unconscious) attitude of many people involved with the refugees was, 'So you're here? Well, we've got to help you: that's our duty, but be a good boy, learn a trade and get away to Palestine.'

Now, many years later, Hugo feels this may sound harsh, but he is still convinced of its underlying truth.

After several weeks of hanging around London, living on the little money he had managed to save from his sparse wages as a trainee, Hugo answered an advertisement for a job that specified French and German as necessary qualifications. He had no labour permit and at this time had no hope of getting one. But this was a problem that faced him whatever job he took. The alternative was to go to Palestine.

His application was answered and he went to see the proprietor of a one-room concern called the Garvas Agency: a tiny, miniscule version of the huge news agencies like Reuter's and United Press. The owner, a Mr Carlmann, hired Hugo at once. They would 'get round' the question of the labour permit. Mr Carlmann – Hugo never found out his Christian name – made a living by selecting tit-bits from the newspapers of the world about matters that had escaped the attention of the larger agencies. He then peddled them around Fleet Street. It was difficult to see how Carlmann made this pay; his basic equipment was only a table, a telephone, and a sheaf of newspapers from every corner of the world. But Carlmann did get an occasional scoop. He knew a great many languages – Hugo never knew how many – Dutch, Hungarian, Swedish. Carlmann managed to communicate a sense of mystery in whatever he did; even his nationality was a mystery, although Hugo thought he was probably a Hungarian. But Hugo enjoyed working with him; it was his first experience of what are nowadays called 'communications' and, despite his worries about his parents being still in Germany and the war that seemed certain to come, he felt he had a right to be happy at last.

The work of the Domestic Bureau of the Council of German Jewry was of wider importance than its name might suggest. As domestic service was for a long time the only form of work available for refugees, unless they were being trained for re-emigration, many women sought to become domestic servants. The backgrounds of these women were as diverse as those of the Jewish 'farmers' who had tried to emigrate to South America. Those who registered at the Domestic Bureau included doctors, nurses, teachers, radiologists: women of almost every occupation and temperament. Those without previous experience as servants – the majority – were given a short course before being registered.

THE NEW ARRIVALS

As domestic service represented almost the only escape route from Germany, it was sometimes abused by refugees who persuaded people in Britain to offer them employment simply to get them out of Germany. But even if the authorities were persuaded, the refugee would be in the position of an illegal immigrant and would find it almost impossible to make a living.

Up to 1939 over 14,000 people were admitted with domestic permits, accompanied by nearly 1,000 children. There were also several hundred married couples. Moreover a further 7,000 women were admitted under permits directly from the Ministry of Labour without passing through the Bureau.

A married couple who entered Britain as domestics through the Domestic Bureau of the Council were Marcus Sachs and his wife. It had been originally intended that their children Leah and Paul should go to Britain first under one of the children's schemes, but in the event they all left Vienna together.

By what seemed extraordinary good fortune, Marcus and Ann Sachs had been accepted as gardener and cook-general in the household of a chartered accountant and company director called Rayner. He lived in stockbroker territory in the Home Counties and Mr Sachs was assured by the secretary of the Domestic Bureau that he would prove a considerate employer. There was good accommodation provided for the Sachs family: an old converted coach-house encrusted with ivy and with a small garden in front of it. Ann Sachs thought it had charm even though it was a good deal smaller than the flat near the Belvedere Palace. She felt she could do a lot with the place, and the children loved it. They had settled very well, and started going to local schools.

From the beginning Ann Sachs was a great success with the Rayners. She had always been a good cook and there was a young German refugee girl as additional help (there were cynics who suggested that the Refugee Problem had helped solve the servant problem that had been a talking point with the British *haute bourgeoisie* ever since the First World War, but Mrs Sachs always maintained that the Rayners, at least, had acted out of pure good-will). Almost at once she established a good relationship with Mrs Rayner – neither subservient nor uneasily familiar – and this was to continue for as long as she remained with them.

Marcus Sachs, however, started off with his employer on a doubtful note. In Mr Rayner's world, every man was a gardener – if only an evening and weekend potterer on suburban lawns. He didn't give much for so-called 'professional' gardeners. They were often lazy devils: specimens of his *bête noire*, the British Working Man. He had felt he could not go wrong engaging a middle-class fellow of solid background like Sachs. Such a fellow would surely know something about gardening; in fact a man who'd been tied to an office all his life would probably welcome a pleasant job in the open air. ('I wouldn't mind having the chance myself,' as Mr Rayner had said jovially to his wife when the idea first occurred to them of employing a refugee couple after the death of Martin, their gardener for twenty years, and the retirement of his wife to live with her married daughter.) But Mr Rayner had not reckoned with Marcus Sachs, a sedentary man who had lived, from childhood to middle age, in flats without a garden.

Mr Rayner had taken Mr Sachs round the gardens and the orchards on the first day and had been disappointed at his lack of response. (Marcus was, of course, rendered blank: what was there to say to all these neatly clipped hedges, these billiard-table lawns?) But as the days passed and all Mr Sachs could do was wander around, occasionally clipping something that did not need clipping, Mr Rayner grew worried. He was a very good-natured man, but he felt an irritated sense of perhaps having foolishly given way to that good nature in sponsoring this fellow for this job without checking that he could do it – although it was all for a good cause, of course. He tried to establish some kind of employer-employee relationship with Mr Sachs but, as he complained to his wife, 'One doesn't know how to treat the fellow exactly . . . and he doesn't give you much of a lead.' On one occasion he asked him, 'What did you say you did in Vienna, Sachs?' Mr Sachs eagerly began to explain how he had been chief accountant in the largest shoe-manufacturing firm in Vienna; and, mistaking Mr Rayner's embarrassed murmur for encouragement, he said, 'We share the same profession, I believe, Mr Rayner? You yourself are an accountant, are you not?'

Mr Rayner agreed that yes, indeed he was; but as soon as politeness allowed he made an excuse and went back into the house. He felt embarrassed. Not only for employing a member of his own profession in a manual job, but also a deeper embarrassment at Mr Sachs's tactlessness in having reminded him of the fact. Meanwhile the garden and Mr Sachs's activities in it continued to be a source of worry to Mr Rayner.

Helga Zinn was a student of art-history in the University of Munich. Her mother was dead and her father had been arrested by the Gestapo in the round-up following Crystal Night. She succeeded in getting to Britain through the Domestic Bureau and arrived in London the week before her twentieth birthday. The lady at the Domestic Bureau seemed a little concerned as to whether Helga would find Mrs Willis a suitable employer – thus reversing the usual attitude, although Helga was too tired and too fearful to see any humour in it. 'She's a nice lady – of course she's a gentile lady, you understand? A little excitable possibly, but I'm sure you'll get on very well with her.' Helga knew that gentiles sometimes criticized Jews for being excitable; here again the usual values were reversed and this only made her feel more apprehensive. Then, on top of the bus that was taking her from the bureau to the hostel in West Hampstead, she heard a woman with a German accent having a furious row with the conductor. Helgo looked away, out of the window, but she winced as she heard the woman raging and spluttering, living up to the worst anti-semite's image of the frantic, gesticulating Jewess. And then Helga heard a woman behind her say to her companion, 'Listen to that! Got no self-control, have they? Get a bit excited and they're jabbering like monkeys!'

Mrs Willis lived in a village ten miles outside Norwich. Helga had been given precise instructions about changing buses at a village halfway between Norwich and where Mrs Willis lived. Once there, she had to make several inquiries before she found the house. Fortunately her English was quite good.

Mrs Willis turned out to be a small blonde lady with a determined expression. She embraced Helga feverently. 'Oh, you poor creature! When I think what you and your people have suffered.' She did not suggest giving Helga a cup of tea or any sort of refreshment after her journey from London. Instead, she took her on a conducted tour of the house. Helga was drooping with exhaustion as they trailed from room to room. 'That belongs to my Les,' was a frequent comment of Mrs Willis as they passed water skis or boxing gloves, pinned to walls with the air of trophies. That Les was Mrs Willis's son was clear but Mrs Willis did not say where he was at the moment. At last Helga got a meal, eaten unrelaxedly while Mrs Willis talked of the various girls of different nationalities she had employed. 'But you Jewish refugees,' she said, 'you deserve to be helped. And I believe in helping people. I've had help myself in my life and where would I have been without it?'

Helga was to learn that many of these remarks of Mrs Willis's were rhetorical questions which did not require answers. Mrs Willis was not unkind, but she was devouring, with her hungry, fixed smile. She never left Helga alone, except when she went to the bathroom, or when she was asleep. Helga was not exactly overworked, but leisure was unknown. She often told Helga how attractive she was: 'You natural blondes: you're so *clean*-looking.'

Helga had read a good deal about the class distinctions that dominate English life and she wondered where in that complex strata Mrs Willis belonged. She wasn't 'working-class'; equally well, she wasn't a 'lady'.

The first weeks in Norfolk weren't exactly unhappy. Helga got enough to eat; the Nazis were a long way away, although she longed for news of her father – although not the ultimate, terrible news (she was to receive that four years later). But she wondered how long she could stick Mrs Willis.

When he came to Stepney in 1937, Lothar Kahlmann was entering a more 'Jewish' environment than anything he had known in Germany. Everything had combined to keep this part of the East End of London a ghetto-type society. The bombing of London by the Luftwaffe was to erase this close-knit enclave, but in 1937 it was still peopled largely by the Russian and Polish immigrants who had come from 1880 onwards. They, their children and grandchildren, suffered little pressure towards assimilation into any English way of life. In the East End of London then, as in New York's East Side during the earlier years of the century, it was possible to live in an ethnic Pale, speaking only Yiddish, eating Kosher food, and never having any real contact with the gentiles one passed in the Mile End Road. There were a certain number of Irish immigrants in Stepney; but although there were a few clashes between the two communities they remained isolated from each other.

Lothar Kahlmann had been apprehensive about everything connected with his coming in England – the journey, the interview with the immigration officer, the registration with the English police, and, in a curious way, perhaps most of all afraid of the meeting with Mark Kaleman and his wife Judith.

But everything had gone well. He had got out of Germany without incident; the immigration officer had seemed to lose interest when Lothar explained that he was going to relatives who were sponsoring him; the police at Stepney were polite and considerate. Mark and his family had welcomed him with a warmth that had surprised and touched him. German Jews, Lothar suspected, did not let their feelings go so unguarded; they were not anxious, even among themselves, to be seen to be acting like sentimental, excitable Jews. Mark laughed and cried and gesticulated all the time. Lothar had felt almost embarrassed for him at first. And he had been a little shocked when he saw and heard the rows between Mark and his wife: so noisy and unrestrained that you would think they would come to blows. They never did, though; and they wallowed in sentimentality in the course of what they called 'making up'. Lothar remembered his own parents who, although Eastern Jews by birth and culture, had tried to be disciplined and 'German' in most things.

Mark was just as excitable with the girls in the work-room, but they took no notice. Lothar was irrationally surprised to find that they were all Jewish: it took him a little time to get used to the fact that he was now living in a Jewish world, where he was not always walking alone, aware that he was being classified as a Jew, judged as a Jew, and possibly hated as a Jew.

He had not been at Mark's long before he became aware of the tension among the Jews of the East End. The enclosed nature of their society made this sense stronger for the Kalemans than it had been for Lothar in Berlin, working away in his room in the alley through the archway. No doubt this was due to the isolated kind of life Lothar had lived; it was also due perhaps to the greater identification of the German Jews with the German people, that made them less conscious of their identity as Jews – at least in the beginning, before Hitler had declared them pariahs. Now the Jews in the East End were being threatened in the same ugly terms as the Nazis had used to the German Jews before they seized power in 1933.

Mosley's blackshirts were all over the East End. Jews could see the slogans painted on the walls: 'Fuck the Yids', and the Mosley sign, which people unkindly described as a flash in the pan, beside them. (There were swastikas painted too.) At street corners they saw posters for the Fascist paper, *The Blackshirt*: 'Mosley warns Jewish Finance.' Loudspeaker vans would park in the street opposite Mark's work-rooms and his wife Judith would find it impossible to get the children to sleep against the harsh, distorted voice shouting menace through the hot summer evenings. And in the streets where the Irish lived they could hear the same hideous voice ranting away: 'The Jews have got the money. And how d'you think they've got it? From you, of course! Jewish sweat-shops! The Yids drive in big cars on the money they make out of you . . .'

The Jewish Board of Guardians started a Jewish Defence Committee which provided speakers to counter the stream of propaganda; the Jewish ex-Servicemen's Association mustered vigilantes to protect Jewish districts. In October 1936, a few months before Lothar arrived in London, the Battle of Cable Street took place. For months both the Communists and the Fascists had used the East End streets as a venue for their spasmodic, brawling warfare: Cable Street was really less of a pitched battle than the confrontation of opposing armies. The occasion was a provocative march by the Fascists through the streets where they were most hated. The Communists rallied under the slogan that had become famous in the Spanish Civil War, 'They shall not pass', while the Fascists were equally determined to show themselves masters of the East End. The police waited anxiously on the sidelines and on the day mustered 6,000 constables – a third of the force. The trouble reached its climax not far from Mark Kaleman's tiny clothing factory, in Cable Street, Stepney, where a huge crowd of Communists, Jews, and other East Enders waited for the blackshirts. The police tried to force a passage through the mob and failed. Seeing the danger of serious bloodshed, Sir Philip Game, Metropolitan Police Commissioner, consulted the Home Secretary, Sir John Simon. Mosley was ordered to disperse the blackshirts. He was furious and accused the government of 'surrendering to Red violence and Jewish corruption'. A week later the Fascists took their revenge in a savage outburst of violence in the Mile End Road. They smashed the windows of Jewish shops and houses and beat up anyone in sight who looked Jewish. A young man was thrown through a plate-glass window and then the blackshirts threw a four-year-old girl after him. This brutal attack became known as 'the Mile End pogrom' and was still much talked of when Lothar Kahlmann arrived in Stepney.

After these events, mass violence tended to diminish in the East End, but the community in which the Kalemans lived was still locked in tension and anxiety. There were still streets which no Jew dared to walk at any time. One night Mark and Lothar did not leave the work-room until after nine o'clock. The girls had gone home an hour earlier. It had been a hot day and the narrow streets seemed to store the heat against an even hotter day tomorrow. Everything was quiet; there were no blackshirt loudspeaker vans around tonight. Judith had asked Mark to buy some bread. He had suggested that Lothar should come with him to try to get a breath of fresh air. They walked to the corner of Salmon Lane; then stayed talking with the shopkeeper for a few minutes.

They decided to walk home in a big half-circle: along Salmon Lane in the other direction till they came to the railway line; then back into the Commercial Road and up White Horse Street and back to the work-room.

It was still light; the sky was blue with the rare, drained blueness of a perfect summer's evening; but the railway arches beside the bridge were dark and neither Lothar nor Mark saw the two blackshirts till they were well clear of the arch and out in the street. Both carried broken beer bottles.

Mark shouted a warning to Lothar. Instinctively, they drew together and, turning, started to run back the way they had come. One of the blackshirts soon caught up with them; the other hardly pretended to chase them but wobbled along drunkenly for a few yards and then gave up, his head slumping forward.

But his companion came on, drawing level with Lothar and, as he did so, lifting his arm with the jagged bottle-edge to tear Lothar's face. But Mark, younger and more agile than Lothar, wheeled sideways and charged, rugger-scrum fashion, butting the blackshirt in the stomach with his head. The intended slashing cut with the bottle-edge was deflected and the rough edge of the glass caught Lothar on the wrist as Mark's charging head sent the blackshirt spinning to one side. They heard the bottle crash on the pavement and the blackshirt cursing and retching and then they were running away as fast as they could.

They ran all the way home, but neither of the blackshirts pursued them any farther. Their attackers had been drunk: that was obvious. Otherwise two middle-aged Jewish tailors would never have got away from two young Fascists. The two blackshirts must have been out on the booze and, the pubs having closed, then decided to wait in the railway arch until a couple of Yids came along. Mark had heard of something like this happening before.

Mark was apparently much more upset than Lothar. He went upstairs to the bathroom and was violently sick. He was glad he had acted promptly to save Lothar and yet he felt a revulsion from the act itself. 'It's not right for a Jew,' he said. 'We do not do things like this. It is not our way.' His wife reminded him that the East End Jews had provided Britain with some of her best boxers. He only shook his head. 'Boxing? It's not the same thing.'

Judith bound up Lothar's wrist and said he ought to go along to the London Hospital to make sure the cut wasn't infected. But the cut wasn't the serious part of the incident for Lothar. Naturally he couldn't help comparing it with what happened that night in Berlin when, like a coward, he had turned from the Jew struck down by the brownshirts. How would he have behaved tonight if there had been more blackshirts? If Mark had been knocked down and was having his head kicked in? How would he have behaved?

He kept thinking about it, and wondering if the situation in the East End of London with Communists fighting Fascists and Fascists savaging Jews wasn't exactly like the situation in Germany just before 1933.

To consider the Nazi persecution of the Jews and the sufferings of the refugees who fled from that persecution is to risk inoculating oneself against feeling, for this was a torment so great that the imagination fails before it. And if this is true in general, then how much more true of the refugee children: innocent, helpless, their lives smashed almost before they began.

THE NEW ARRIVALS 149

As the situation in Germany grew worse and the fathers and mothers of children began to disappear into concentration camps, more and more children became homeless or orphaned, vulnerable to all the evil forces that were set loose in the Third Reich. From the beginning efforts were made to help these children, but for reasons that have already become familiar in a larger context – the indifference of individuals, the evasion and legalism of governments – again, too little was done, too late. Many children were rescued, but many more died, simply because not enough people cared enough about them to save them.

Certainly the most important of the organizations founded to deal with the problem was the Children's Inter-Aid Committee which was founded in 1936. It dealt with both Jewish and Christian 'non-Ayran' children and by 1937 it had placed 150 children in Britain, mostly in private homes. At this time a number of children were sent out of Germany to be educated abroad (although the German Government was to frown on this). Special schools were established for pupils from Germany. The great increase in refugees after the Anschluss and the pogroms in Germany was reflected in the much greater number of refugee children coming to Britain in 1938. That year the Inter-Aid Committee brought over 1,500 children, again many going to individual homes. Later the committee (which had become the Movement for the Care of Children from Germany) increased its work still further (a good deal of the funds raised by Lord Baldwin's appeal went to the Children's Movement). The movement was organized on a regional basis, with twelve district headquarters. In November 1938, after Crystal Night and the intensified persecution that followed, it was decided to attempt to rescue the children on a mass scale. (But even in the case of these children the British Government stuck rigidly to the proviso of a financial guarantee by the organization responsible and insisted that the children re-emigrate before they attained the age of eighteen or when their training was finished.) There was a public appeal for funds and for homes for the children. As soon as the news of this extension of the Children's Movement became known in Germany and Austria, the headquarters of the movement received many thousands of letters and photographs of children. Many were from parents who were prepared to give up their children to save their lives. The children who were to come to

Britain were chosen by the central committees of the Jewish and Christian non-Aryan communities in Germany and Austria. The first shipload of these arrived in December 1938; the last on the day war was declared. Up to the outbreak of war 10,000 children were brought into Britain.

These statistics are impressive and they reflect the greatest credit on the humanity and devotion of the organizers and workers of the Movement for the Care of Children from Germany. Unfortunately the total number of children saved is only a tiny speck of the total lost. If the measures adopted in November 1938 had been adopted three years earlier; if the government had relaxed their condition of financial sponsorship in the case of children; if more people had been willing to take a refugee child into their home – but it is futile to speculate what might have happened if only one of these conditions had been fulfilled. None were fulfilled – and so these other children had to die. The workers for the movement will never forget the faces of that gallery of lost children whose photographs arrived in their offices – often accompanied by letters of heartrending appeal by their parents. Although there were many who offered to take children in, many more would offer financial assistance but not a home. Most pathetic of all, potential sponsors were able to exercise their aesthetic preferences in terms of life and death. Fair-haired girls of seven to ten had a better chance of escaping the gas-chamber than a boy of twelve or over.

Ilsa Geiss, who was now settled in a cottage in Essex, not far from the Borley Rectory of hypnotic memory, was able to arrange sponsorship for many German Jewish children. She had become friendly with the local vicar and they evolved a partnership. Ilsa corresponded with the children's organizations or with the parents in Germany and Austria; the vicar arranged for homes for the children throughout that part of Essex. But the number they could place was tiny compared to the number who wrote, asking, pleading, beseeching: 'This is Heidi, who is twelve. She is lame, but very cheerful . . .' 'Martin is nine. He has a gentle nature and I know you would like him . . .' She, too, is haunted by these lost innocents. She will never forget their names or their faces, and today her eyes fill with tears when she speaks of them.

Chapter Five

ENEMY ALIENS

'Will my Right Honourable Friend bear in mind that you cannot trust any Boche at any time?'

Lieutenant Colonel Acland-Troyte, c.m.g., d.s.o., Tory Member for Tiverton, shouted these words after Anthony Eden had explained to Parliament that certain selected men, 'enemy aliens', were going to be released from internment and allowed to enlist in the British Army. The date of the debate was 23 July 1940: one is thus anticipating, overruling chronology, but the Member for Totnes' words are worth quoting, if only to establish a mood; to show how little right-wing attitudes had changed in forty years. His angry intervention could stand for hundreds of similar utterances in Parliament when the subject of enemy aliens was discussed.

By the middle of 1939 the whole situation was intensely confused. The question of money remained at the heart of the dilemma. The refugee organizations were tortured by their impotence in the face of the thousands of Jews still trapped in the Reich but, still prisoners of the financial guarantee they had given the British Government in April 1933, they found themselves forced to impose ever harsher conditions on potential refugees. The sponsor of a child had to deposit £50 to meet the cost of its re-emigration; the skills and qualifications of refugees seeking labour permits were to be more rigorously examined; sponsors of refugees over sixty had to undertake to support them for the rest of their lives. The unsinkable Josiah Wedgwood protested at the fatal implications of this last condition in particular; he pleaded that children at least should not be forced to re-emigrate; that trainees be allowed to finish their courses without interference. Above all, he demanded that the refugees be released from the straitjacket they had unwittingly imposed on themselves when they offered their guarantee in 1933. The Home Secretary, Sir Samuel Hoare, made a small concession in 'considering' the admission of certain categories of skilled refugee workers. Wedgwood persisted, suggesting that the Home Secretary might tell the refugee organizations that less stringent guarantees might be acceptable to the government. Hoare would not agree to this, but it was clear that the situation was fast becoming intolerable.

Around the same time, various suggestions were being put forward for the settlement of the refugees on an international basis. The Intergovernmental Committee suggested that the governments who had been represented at Evian should contribute to an international fund, private individuals also contributing an agreed proportion to this fund. Louis de Rothschild had another proposal: an international loan for refugee settlement. Interested governments and private sources would contribute in equal parts; this loan, it was hoped, might reach £20 million. British Government reactions to these suggestions were not actually unfavourable; official circles saw in these plans a chance to obtain the elusive cooperation of the State Deparment. (The White House indulged freely in idealistic rhetoric on the refugees' behalf, but never relaxed its regulations for a moment.)

By July the British Cabinet was at last considering whether to modify the 'no admission without guarantee' proviso on which it had stood for so long. A debate in Parliament was impending at which this question would certainly be raised; the Intergovernmental Committee were to meet at the end of July. Reluctantly, almost tortuously, it was agreed in principle that the British Government could participate on an even money basis with other governments in any acceptable scheme for refugee settlement.

Before the government could take any firm decision, however, or even discuss the matter in full cabinet, the matter was raised in the House of Lords. Diverse but influential voices were raised on behalf of the refugees, including those of the Bishop of Chichester, Lord Cecil, and the Marquess of Reading. They all stressed the impossible position of the refugee organizations and demanded that the government give financial aid. But as things stood Lord Dufferin and Ava, the government spokesman in the

Lords, had not option but to reiterate the old line of no admission without financial guarantee.

As he was doing so, Sir Samuel Hoare was explaining why the British Government was being forced to change its policy. He laid particular stress on the difficulties of re-emigration. This had been delayed in many cases and the refugee organizations could no longer provide for many of the re-emigrants for whom they had given guarantees. These transients delayed in Britain were the most acute part of the problem (and indeed a large proportion of the German refugees who eventually settled in Britain were originally transients). It was feared that these people, if their re-emigration were delayed long enough, might become a 'public charge'.

There was an element of the lesser evil about the government's change of attitude. Eventually the decision emerged that financial assistance should relate only to emigration overseas (so that re-emigration as a condition of entry to Britain was retained); and, more significantly, that the British Government would only contribute if other governments did the same.

The grudging nature of this proposed reversal of policy is apparent. The government was afraid that the refugee organizations might collapse altogether; but the hope of inducing American co-operation was also important. The British Government was not going to move in the matter unless the Americans did too. Washington was informed through the American ambassador that the British Government proposed to make a statement on the matter at the next meeting of the Intergovernmental Committee. The ambassador, Joseph Kennedy, pointed out in reply that there were negotiations still in progress between the German official, Helmuth Wohlthat, and George Rublee of the Intergovernmental Committee. (It will be remembered that these negotiations succeeded Dr Schacht's plan after Schacht himself had fallen out with Hitler.) It was hoped that the outcome of the Wohlthat–Rublee talks would be a foundation (sponsored of course by 'International Jewry') that would undertake the settlement of many thousands of Jewish refugees. While the White House professed to believe in the possibility of establishing this foundation, the British were sceptical. Moreover, British Jews naturally distrusted the Germans and deeply resented the blackmail implicit in the plan. (The foundation was actually to enjoy a brief existence, headed by a former Prime Minister of Belgium, but the war killed it.)

Noting the American attitude, Earl Winterton duly put the British proposal before the Intergovernmental Committee. Cautiously presented, it met with a more than cautious reception. In fact the meeting exhibited the recurrent syndrome that marks all the international conferences held to discuss the refugee problem: a shuffling-off of all decision into a decision to hold yet another conference. This time it was to be a conference chaired by President Roosevelt at the White House in the autumn.

Meanwhile, Chamberlain told Parliament that the government was considering participating in financial arrangements to solve the refugee problem. Press reactions to this were predictable: the *Daily Mail* regretted that Britain was taking on a burden that was really Germany's; equally predictably, the *Daily Express* did not approve. *The Times* and the *Daily Telegraph* gave qualified approval; the *Manchester Guardian* welcomed an important change in government policy.

It is useless to wonder how many lives might have been saved if the British Government had changed its mind sooner. But since the decision to aid Jewish emigration was still hedged around with conditions, so contingent on similar aid from other countries, particularly America, such speculation is more than usually academic. In any case, by the time the government made this announcement, almost all the escape routes were closed. Such German Jews as were to survive had mostly left Germany.

The mood of that English summer of 1939 had changed from that of the previous autumn. Gone was the Munich mood that had coalesced in a bubble of frantic relief when Chamberlain returned with his historic inanity, 'Peace in our time'. By now, most people knew what they were in for. Some were calm, expressing a 'things have got to get worse before they're better' attitude, a 'we've got to show this here Herr Hitler' attitude. With others, the mood of fear that had bred the euphoria of Munich gave way to a ghoulish, masochistic wallowing. For years journalists had been indulging in fantasies about the effects of aerial attack on British cities. The Germans had a gas that caused everyone's eyes to drop out within a radius of twenty miles.

Imagine the effect on London, on Birmingham . . . The gas-mask became an obsessive symbol of horrors to come. There weren't enough of them. Photographs appeared of babies being fitted with them. A doctor wrote of the necessity to provide an adequate supply of coffins for those victims whose remains were still worth burying.

What of the refugees? What was their mood? At the beginning of the war there were some 50,000 refugees from Germany and Austria and some 6,000 from Czechoslovakia in Britain. Apart from having in common an obvious joy in having escaped at all, the attitudes of individuals naturally varied. On the whole, the refugees seem to have experienced a general sense of relief that was summed up by Ilsa Geiss: 'Now we can permit ourselves to hope.' Hugo Neher, now established in a little office off Fleet Street, with typewriters no more than a memory, thought with a mixture of excitement and anxiety of the possibility of joining the British Army. Georg Joachim, at school near Oxford, already, with the flexibility of his fifteen years, felt himself sufficiently English to think of the Germans as 'the enemy', although his mother wept at the prospect of war and his sister, still pinioned by her thick German accent and her inability to better her English, half-tearfully, half-angrily, spoke of herself as an 'enemy alien'. She wondered if it would be safe to go shopping in Hampstead now that war had started. Lothar Kahlmann felt glad that someone was saying 'No' to the Nazis at last. It was the first time anyone had opposed them: in Europe, in the world. All the same, he remembered Cable Street and the time the black-shirts had waylaid Mark and himself near the work-room. Would Mosley get more powerful during a war?

With some exceptions, hopeful attitudes were less common among the older refugees. The writer, Stefan Zweig, settled in a beautiful house on Lyncombe Hill in Bath, fell a victim to a mood of fatalistic despair as he compared the brilliant August of 1939 in England with the blazing July of 1914 in Austria. Listening to 'Run, Rabbit, run' and 'We're going to hang out the washing on the Siegfried Line' bawled out by truckloads of young soldiers as they rattled past his house, he reacted with irritated pessimism to British complacency – which, he grudgingly admitted, was itself an obtuse kind of courage. But it did not console him. The Nazis would come here too, he told his gardener and confidant. 'They'll come,' he said again and again. 'Nothing can stop them now. Nothing...'

The strongest and perhaps the most generous reaction came from some of the Jews – not necessarily refugees themselves – who were committed to the Zionist cause. One of these was that brilliant and complex figure, Professor Lewis Namier, who had sacrificed many years of his academic career to act as liaison between the restless Zionist groups and the British Establishment, which he had penetrated and understood to a degree that recalled the great Disraeli himself. In her biography of her husband Lady Namier describes how he telephoned Walter Elliott, then Minister of Health, at the end of August 1939. He asked for an interview. Namier told Elliott that he was taking on himself the responsibility of speaking for his fellow Jews (he meant in the first instance the Jewish Agency). The Jews would stand by Britain. They would wish to immediately raise a Jewish army recruited from all countries. He, Namier, was out of touch with the Zionist congress at present in session in Geneva but in view of the implications of the German-Soviet Pact he had no doubt that the congress would enable key Jews everywhere to begin organizing this. If the British Government made up its mind quickly enough, he would fly to Geneva at once and set things in motion. Walter Elliott listened politely and promised to set these proposals before the Cabinet. A day or two later Namier recorded in his diary that Moshe Shertok (later Sharrett) of the Jewish Agency had told him that he, Shertok, now had definite instructions from Geneva to do what Namier had already proposed.

The reaction of the British Government was, of course, entirely negative. Thanks were conveyed; but the spontaneous gesture was first chilled and then dissipated by polite evasions. It is not hard to imagine what the Tory Cabinet thought of the prospect of an army of foreign Jews. That was certainly something to be considered some time in the future – if at all. The hope was stiffly expressed that 'suitable individuals' would do their duty.

It seems probable that Namier's patriotic and generous intervention was actually resented. (Particularly generous when one recalls the British turnabout on Jewish immigration into Palestine.) Some years earlier Namier's efforts on behalf of the refugees had drawn an angry outburst from Lord Cranborne who had called him 'tiresome' and not to be trusted. In fact, Lewis

ENEMY ALIENS

Namier's whole life reflects the paradox of the brilliant Jew or foreigner who conquers an Establishment but always remains vulnerable to covert prejudice and resentment within it.

When they had recovered from their first exaltation that Hitler was to be challenged at last, many of the refugees were possessed by a comforting sense of solidarity with the British, feeling that they were in the same boat as their hosts – whom they certainly liked, but who were after all very different from the Germans.

The most immediate and important effect of the war was to bring re-emigration to an end. This affected thousands of refugees, since so many of them had come to Britain on the understanding that they would in due course proceed from there to America or Palestine. Of the German and Austrian refugees in Britain some 27,000 had definite arrangements to go to America sooner or later. It is hard to exaggerate the sense of insecurity induced by thus finding themselves caught in a country which they had hitherto regarded as a mere stopping-off place or halfway house. (Some did adjust and, acquiring a sense of solidarity with the British, chose to remain; others never did and fulfilled their original intention of going to America, even after several years.) The practical results of the cancellation of thousands of re-emigration plans were certainly harsh and immediate. The refugee organizations were faced with the prospect of maintaining a multitude of people who had never intended to stay in Britain at all. Those who had been able to bring some money out of Germany and were still living on it might soon find themselves destitute; the employment position of the refugees was unchanged; the young and fit could not join the Services and civilian employment remained severely restricted. In theory, of course, one could still go to the United States, but shipping was disrupted by the outbreak of war. Thousands of refugees held steamship tickets which had been bought with German marks and were therefore useless now.

But most important of all was the fact that from the moment war broke out every German and Austrian refugee was an enemy alien. The very phrase was traumatic to men and women who had already suffered anguish and insult before they escaped, often to find themselves penniless and dependent on the charity of others in a foreign country. Worse, from the beginning of war all enemy aliens had to go before a tribunal that would examine them and decide whether they were 'genuine' refugees or not.

There were 120 of these one-man tribunals, usually composed of a King's Counsel or county court judge with a police secretary in attendance. Their duty was to classify each refugee who came before them according to whether he or she could be considered a threat to national security. The tribunal could order the internment of anyone who aroused their suspicions – Category A – or exempt from all restrictions (except those that applied to all foreigners whatever their origin) – Category C. Those refugees who did not fall into either of these categories – those whose credentials did not win them complete freedom from restrictions and at the same time did not arouse serious doubts in the tribunal – were put into a third, intermediate group: Category B. Those in this B class could not travel more than five miles, except in the London area, without first getting police permission.

A further distinction to be made by the tribunals – one which cut across the A, B, and C categories – was between 'refugees from Nazi oppression' and non-refugees. With a few exceptions – mostly people who were ill or about to re-emigrate – practically all refugees came before the tribunals. Of 71,600 refugees examined, men and women, 600 were put in Category A; 6,800 in Category B; and 64,200 in Category C. One hundred and sixty of the 600 placed in Category A, 4,100 of the 6,800 in Category B, and 51,200 of the 64,200 in Category C were deemed 'refugees from Nazi oppression'.

It will be noticed that out of a total of 71,600 examined, only 55,460 were thus described. What of the other 16,140 persons examined and classified who were not considered to be refugees from Nazi oppression? Few sets of statistics are wholly consistent, but there seems no doubt that most of the discrepancy can be attributed to the varying attitudes of different tribunals. Like any other assembly of individuals, they varied widely in orientation and approach. Some were primarily legalistic; others were clearly not free from chauvinistic prejudice. On the whole, the refugees praise the tribunals for their fairness and objectivity, although it is worth recording at this point that here – as in most refugee testimony – there is an inherent tendency to speak gratefully of British institutions and to praise the fairness of British officials. No doubt this reflects the refugees' experience; but no doubt it also reflects a feeling of gratitude towards the country that had taken them in.

Ilsa Geiss speaks of her interview with the tribunal at Colchester. The presiding official was an agreeable red-faced gentleman. By now Ilsa was familiar enough with British stereotypes to describe him as looking like a 'typical colonel', although he was actually an eminent King's Counsel. Still remembering the advice she had been given, she was careful to rather exaggerate her financial affluence when the colonel skirted around the question – displaying a tact that aroused her admiration. He remarked that it was unusual to find a refugee lady living alone in a remote part of Essex. He asked about her children: Kurt at school in Cambridge; Maria in her last year at Dartington Hall. When she mentioned this, she was amused to see an almost imperceptible frown crease his brow as he murmured, 'Dartington Hall?' He must have heard of it as one of those new-fangled 'progressive' schools where the children were allowed to get up to God-knows-what. Ilsa was duly put into Category C and deemed a refugee from Nazi oppression.

Hugo Neher seemed at first to be unlucky with his tribunal. It sat in a drab council school off the Bow Road. The interrogator here was a local stipendary magistrate: a small, clerkly-looking man who wore the black coat and striped trousers of the traditional bureaucrat. Again, Hugo got the impression that he offended by being too young. And a refugee who had been here six years? Clearly it struck a suspicious note. While the immigration officer had been bluff and blunt-speaking, a bit of a bully, this interlocutor was coldly polite.

'You describe yourself as a refugee from Nazi oppression?' he asked.

'Yes, sir,' Hugo said. He knew it was better to say too little rather than too much.

'And yet you've been here since . . .' the interlocutor looked down at the form, 'April 1933?'

'That is so.'

'Yes . . . You were a refugee *then*?'

Hugo paused before answering.

'A refugee from what? At that time?' the little man persisted.

'The Nazis,' Hugo said.

'*Then*?'

Hugo noticed that the interlocutor's nose was like a sharp predatory beak; his questions came sharp as beak-blows on wood.

'Hitler came to power early in 1933,' Hugo explained quietly. 'He had made his intentions towards the Jews quite clear before that.' He paused. 'And I am a Jew.'

'You claim here' – the interlocutor tapped the form in front of him – 'to be a refugee from "persecution".' His cold voice clothed the word in sceptical quotation marks. 'Has anyone claimed that the German Government took any action against the Jews *before* April 1933?'

'They instituted a boycott of Jewish shops on 1 April 1933,' Hugo said.

'Would you really define that as persecution?'

'It began a long and calculated policy of persecution,' Hugo said. 'You will accept that, sir?'

'We have to accept that, I suppose,' the interlocutor said. 'But we're concerned with you and your background, Mr Neher.' He paused. 'I think you will agree that you personally are not the victim of persecution?'

'But I am a Jew – '

'Quite so, Mr Neher. And therefore' – the chairman permitted himself a smile – 'a probable object of discrimination in the present circumstances in Germany.'

Hugo shrugged. 'Obviously.'

'What I am saying is that you were not actually persecuted. You anticipated persecution. A different thing, Mr Neher.'

There was a silence. Then, 'What are your political views, Mr Neher?'

'I haven't any.'

Hugo knew this was the wrong answer but he felt exasperated. He knew what the man had in mind. Because Hugo had come to Britain so early – before the real persecution began – he was suspect. That first exodus from the Reich had included many Communists and this bureaucrat thought he, Hugo, might have fled because he was a Communist, not because he was a Jew.

But now the interlocutor seemed to lose interest. He followed with a few routine questions. Then he seized on Hugo's work-record.

'You were being trained as a typewriter mechanic with a view to eventual re-emigration to Palestine?'

'That is correct.'

'And yet now, five years later, we find you working at . . .' the little man looked up. 'The Garvas Agency . . . It's described as a news service?'

'Translations too.'

'It seems very different. What's happened to the typewriters, Mr Neher?'

'I don't like them.'

'You don't like them!' the interlocutor repeated. 'And yet this career was the considered choice of the Jewish Refugees' Committee?'

'Not exactly. I chose that out of several alternatives.'

'Your own choice then!'

'I didn't feel very enthusiastic about any of them.'

'Indeed? Nevertheless these occupations were no doubt put forward as a result of a careful evaluation of the labour situation and of a realistic assessment of your own abilities.'

'I suppose so,' Hugo said. Then he added, 'I'm quite good at my present job.'

'Your language qualifications, no doubt . . .'

The little man shuffled his papers. Then he whispered to the heavy, bleak-faced man who sat beside him. (This, Hugo learned later, was the police secretary who attended all these tribunals; as an extra check, it was said, against spies masquerading as refugees.) Hugo was asked to withdraw for a few minutes. He went outside, to pace up and down the asphalt-covered playground. He tried to fasten his attention on the legends scrawled on the walls: 'Tom Beesley is a silly-bogs.' 'Ann Mason has big titties.' He did not succeed. For the first time since he had walked away from the immigration officer at Harwich, he felt frightened. The 'English' persona he had laboriously created was about to be shattered: how thin was the crust of habit and acceptance men set up against disaster. They would arrest him, he felt certain: call him a dirty little Jewish Communist; drag him off to some hideous, wind-swept camp on an island off the coast.

After five or six minutes – he wasn't sure how long – he was called in again. He had been placed in Category C and accorded the status of a refugee from Nazi oppression.

In comparison, Lothar Kahlmann's experience at an East End tribunal seems to have been almost perfunctory. Again, what

English he had almost deserted him, but this did not seem to matter. The presiding lawyer relied wholly on the information provided by the Central Council for Jewish Refugees. He did not seem interested in Lothar in any personal way. Lothar, too, was classified as Category C.

But while the total achievement of the tribunals has been praised, many of their decisions seem to have been of a distinctly arbitrary nature. Most of the judges and lawyers who functioned in them came, after all, from the same section of middle-class and upper-middle-class society; they were sustained by a high ideal of professional duty but were naturally vulnerable to the prejudices and insular attitudes that occur in any group. A particular complaint against the tribunals was that there was no consistency about putting people into the intermediate Category B. Some tribunals made all domestic servants Category B, which created many difficulties for them, particularly when they were employed in country districts as many of them were. The five-mile limitation on their movements often made them virtual prisoners. Other tribunals put unemployed refugees or all those living in refugee hostels into Category B. (When they got jobs, they were told, they would be promoted to Category C.) This, of course, created a vicious circle. Restricted as they were by their Category B label, they found work much harder to get.

Incidentally many non-Jewish refugees found their gentile blood a disadvantage. Some tribunals put non-Jewish refugees into Category B because they found it hard to believe that they could be opponents of Hitler on ideological grounds.

A letter in the *New Statesman and Nation* in December 1939 gives an instance of this.

Question : What is your race and what are your political views?
Answer : I am an Aryan and a Social Democrat.
Question : Then why did you leave Austria in 1938? You could have safely stayed. Hitler only persecutes Communists and Jews.

The letter, which is an attack on the one-man tribunal system, goes on to give other examples of judicial obtuseness on the tribunals. A refugee doctor was asked, 'So you are a Jew and a well-known doctor in Berlin. Why did you leave your practice, Doctor?'

The writer of the letter attributes a traditional clubman's

attitude to certain backwoodsmen tribunals, a mental stagnation that 'one had devoutly hoped [was] safely buried beneath mountains of periodicals and surrounded by a haze of cigar smoke and an aroma of Napoleon brandy'.

The letter goes on to make the point that the comparatively small number of refugees interned in 1939 (this was of course written before the large-scale, indiscriminate internment of refugees in 1940) were in many cases merely the victims of insular prejudice. The writer cites the cases of an Aryan Austrian Socialist vouched for by the Secretary of the Civil Service Clerical Association and a member of the Austrian anti-Nazi Ostmaerkische Sturmscharen. The letter suggests that in many cases the suspicions of the employers of refugee domestics had been aroused by the official restrictions imposed on them and the servants had been sacked as a result.

The financial and social standing of the person interviewed is usually a relevant factor in any confrontation where an individual offers himself to be judged by an authority with significant power over his destiny. Obviously the nearer the judged approximates – socially, educationally, financially – to the position of the man who is judging him, the better he will do, if only because he will express himself with more confidence. In the case of the German and Austrian refugees this did not always follow. Their overwhelmingly middle-class origin won them sympathy, but sometimes previous professional eminence aroused antagonism in the official confronting them. (A 'What do I care what he was in Berlin? He's in England now' attitude that was sometimes also apparent among the employers of refugees.) Any hostility in the interviewing authority – however slight and well-masked – would of course be seized on and magnified by the refugee, keyed as he was to a hair-trigger sensitivity. Expressions of overt anti-semitism were almost unknown, but certain strands of anti-semitic thinking and feeling do lie buried beneath the surface of British life and these must have been occasional, often unconscious influences.

More obvious was the anti-Bolshevik syndrome. Some tribunals interned men whose crime had been to fight the Fascists in Spain. And any infringement of the technicalities of immigration – such as overstaying the period of a visitor's permit – often meant classification in Category A and consequent internment. Sometimes men were put in Category A for the most trivial reasons. One young Austrian was described as 'difficult' by his employer and interned 'to teach him a lesson'.

The majority in Category A who were interned at the beginning of the war were of course of Nazi sympathies; and the minority of anti-Nazis among them, such as Aryan German Socialists or veterans of the Spanish International Brigade, suffered terribly. The refugees' lobby, headed by Eleanor Rathbone and Colonel Wedgwood, continually agitated for the release of these anti-Nazis; eventually new tribunals in the shape of Regional Committees began to review all doubtful Category B cases and they were still doing this when mass-internment was ordered in 1940.

The new Minister of Home Security and the man responsible for all these measures was Sir John Anderson, later Viscount Waverley. His greatest preoccupation was civil defence and he is perhaps best remembered for the Anderson Shelter, a humped steel creation that crouched in a million suburban gardens. One of those Scots who seem to enter into the very marrow of the English Establishment, he had had a career as a colonial administrator in India and Ireland. He was undoubtedly a man of high principles, but there may have been a certain lack of imagination behind the severe proconsular mask. It would be unfair to suggest that he was unduly influenced by the anti-alien forces that were gathering in Parliament, in Fleet Street, and elsewhere. He had no prejudice against the refugees as such, but simply 'administered' them as he had administered other subject peoples of the Crown on behalf of the government he served.

The long months of the 'phoney war' actually produced a lessening of tension for most refugees. The state of being at war with Hitler and the Nazis naturally made the majority of English people more sympathetic towards the Jews who were Hitler's victims. Many of the refugees wanted to join Air Raid Precautions and other civil defence organizations but were not permitted to do so. Then in November 1939 Sir John Anderson issued an Order in Council that modified certain existing regulations on the employment of aliens. They were excluded from various defined categories of employment: work of national importance – armament works; power stations; civilian employment in military establishments; factories producing directly for the war effort. But with these exceptions, an alien could register at an employment exchange and be given any job for which no British worker could be found. (The employment exchange would issue a labour permit on the proviso that the working conditions of the refugee would not be inferior to those of a British worker.) In fact, it was even possible for an alien to get a job in one of the industries of national importance if he got a permit from the Auxiliary War Service Department, which would in theory carefully screen the applicant. But Anderson's Order in Council defined the areas of prohibited employment rather loosely and much depended on the Auxiliary War Service Department's interpretation.

This Order in Council, for the moment at least, proved a turning-point for the refugees. The almost totally blank wall that had confronted them was now seen to offer a certain number of doors. For many refugees the prospect of being free to go and seek employment was an intoxicating release.

Helga Zinn could hardly believe that she was free to end her hateful incarnation as a domestic. If only she could get a job in a factory! But she had been put in Category B because she was a domestic, so she had first to obtain Mrs Willis's permission to absent herself for a day; if and when that was granted, she had to clear the ten-mile journey to Norwich with the local police. That accomplished and arrived in Norwich, she had to go to the employment exchange and then, if they had any job that suited her, she would have to go to it and be interviewed. All this in the space of one day . . . She felt sick at the complexity of it. She registered the promise of action in her mind; she would do it but not immediately; it was too difficult. Three weeks passed before she could bring herself to approach Mrs Willis.

Helga had intended to make her request obliquely, to skate around it by degrees; but when the moment came disgust overtook her and she bluntly asked for a day off.

'Of course, dear. You're entitled to it,' Mrs Willis said. 'Naturally. Why didn't you ask me before? What day would you like, dear? Sunday?'

'If you do not mind, Mrs Willis' – Helga carefully enunciated each word: she remembered the lady on the top of the bus and her 'jabbering like monkeys' – 'Sunday is not a suitable day.'

'Isn't it, dear? I should have thought it the most suitable day.

"Six days shalt thou labour and do all that thou hast to do.". . . . Isn't that right, dear?'

'I do not think Sunday, Mrs Willis,' Helga said.

'Oh, well . . .' Helga knew Mrs Willis was not pleased. 'I thought you might be wanting to go to church, dear – although you never do, do you?' She was staring at Helga, the half-smile she always wore, fixed and mask-like, almost malign. 'Mind you, I won't ask you what you do want to do. I know you're a girl who likes to keep her little secrets. Not that there's any harm in that. I understand young girls. They like to keep their little secrets.' She paused. 'Got some shopping to do, dear? You won't get much in the village.'

'I wish to go into Norwich, Mrs Willis.'

'Norwich?' It might have been fourteen hundred miles away and not fourteen, Helga thought. Mrs Willis went on, 'You haven't forgotten you have to go to the police and get their permission before you go outside the five-mile limit? It's a nuisance, dear, but of course we've got to be careful. Some of these enemy aliens aren't harmless young girls like you. They're dangerous men. Enemies of Britain. So we've got to be careful. We've got to go on preserving our British way of life!'

At last Mrs Willis promised to let Helga off the following Tuesday. She didn't question Helga any further but made a few covert references to Helga's non-existent boyfriends: 'No, you don't have to tell me, dear, if you don't want to. I'm not one to pry.' Helga never understood when she was supposed to see these boyfriends since she rarely left the house. 'If my girls had suitable followers I never objected. It wouldn't have been fair and I've always been fair to the girls I've had in service here. Good food, easy hours – a home from home and a damn sight better than most of the homes they come from, I can tell you, my dear!'

To Helga's surprise, Mrs Willis did not overload her with work during the intervening days. On the Monday evening Helga actually had time to work at her English, to write a letter to Leonore, and to wash her hair.

On Tuesday Helga had to take Mrs Willis her breakfast as usual; then she would catch the nine o'clock bus to the village where the police station was; then, assuming the police gave their assent, she would catch another bus to Norwich.

At half past eight Helga tapped on Mrs Willis's bedroom door and took in her breakfast tray. To her surprise the curtains were already drawn back and Mrs Willis was sitting up in bed, staring towards the door, her small features clamped into a mask of rage.

'You think I don't know why you want to go into Norwich?' she demanded. 'You want to go and get a job in a factory where you'll meet a lot of *men* . . . That's it – don't think I don't understand you, my dear. You're just like the rest! . . . Miss-Helga-Zinn' – she mimicked Helga's accent – 'I vas a student of ze history of art!' Her voice had become harsh and strident, overlaid with a glottal cockney Helga had not heard there before. 'I don't mind telling you – you looked like a bloody skiv the first time I saw you and how right I was, Miss-Helga-Zinn! I could tell what you were thinking about . . . I could tell what you were thinking about . . .' She paused for breath; she was almost spluttering with rage. 'If my Les'd been home, do you think I'd have kept you here for a second? *Man mad* – you dirty Jew bitch!'

Helga stood paralysed with shock and disgust. Her hands were trembling and she nearly dropped the breakfast tray, but she managed to lower it safely on to the table beside the bed.

Mrs Willis had stopped speaking. She lay back on the pillows, her eyes closed. Then she turned her head inwards, against the pillows and Helga saw she was crying.

'Mrs Willis . . .'

Mrs Willis turned and looked up at Helga. Tears had mingled with mascara to hideous effect. She looked not only old, but grotesque. Helga realized that Mrs Willis must have made herself up in readiness for Helga's entering the room.

'I knew you wanted to leave me,' she said. 'I knew you didn't like it here. I knew you must be bored. A beautiful young girl like you should have fun and gaiety . . . An educated girl too, a cultured girl. You shouldn't be here, waiting hand and foot on an ignorant old woman.' Her voice was choked, bleary with tears. 'And now you're going into Norwich to get away from me. You're going to Norwich to get a job – to get away from me. You're going to leave me all alone and you know I won't be able to get anyone else. After all I've done for you too. "Ye were hungry and I took ye in." That's in the Bible too.' Her voice changed; she grew aggressive again. 'But then you're not a Christian, are you? You're a Jew. You don't like Christ. You've got your own teachings . . . Eastern teachings . . .'

Helga stood listening to her. She did not attempt to defend herself. What could she say? And anyway Mrs Willis was really talking to herself out of a bitterness with which she, Helga had no concern.

She put the tray down and murmured, 'Excuse me, Mrs Willis,' and she left the room.

Ten minutes later she caught the bus to the next village, saw a police sergeant who checked her papers in a perfunctory way, and then got on the bus to Norwich. There, after a cup of tea and a cake in a café, she went to the labour exchange. The fact that Helga was employed as a domestic servant did not much interest the prim young woman who sat at the hutch labelled 'Women R-Z'. The fact that Helga's surname began with 'Z' did interest her. 'Don't get many Zs here. Got a few Xs recently, but they were all Greeks. Cypriots really, I suppose . . .' She sent Helga to a small dress factory on the outskirts of Norwich where machinists were required. Helga presented her card of introduction to the owner, a man called Spiegel who was in his fifties and obviously Jewish. Despite his name he spoke with what Helga now recognized as the distinctive Norfolk accent. He looked at the card. 'You're a refugee,' he said, as a statement not a question.

'Yes.'

'German of course,' he said.

'Yes.'

He started to pace up and down. This was a tiny office. Helga thought how untidy and comfortless it was, with the faded patterns tacked to the walls and travellers' samples of cotton and rayon tumbled across the table.

After a moment he said, 'I'm sorry, Miss Zinn, but I don't see how I can do it. You see – this concern is one hundred per cent English. I'm English; my girls are English. And well – let's be frank, Miss Zinn, you're a foreigner, a German. It's not so much myself – I've got my girls to consider. Let's be frank – they might not like it: working with a German . . .' He stretched out his hands, palms outwards, in what struck Helga as a gross parody of a stock Jewish gesture.

She got back to the employment exchange a few minutes before it closed. The prim girl at the hutch gave her another card of introduction. This time she got the job; painting gold lines on glassware in a small factory in the city centre. That night she gave notice to a sullen, frozen Mrs Willis. The local police were very helpful, arranging things for her. The sergeant suggested that she might apply to go before the regional tribunal at their next sitting so that, now she was no longer a domestic, she could be re-classified as Category C.

A long time afterwards, the mother of children, married to an Englishman, Helga was able to distil certain patterns of thinking and feeling from her experience as a frightened young girl in a foreign land. Her encounter with Mr Spiegel showed her the ambiguous welcome the long-established Jew sometimes extends to the immigrant. Her uneasy relationship with Mrs Willis was a classic instance of a neurotic's attempt to exploit a person in a dependent and subservient position. Those German Jews who, like Helga, had obtained jobs as cooks or maids or gardeners – jobs that brought them into intimate contact with their employers – were particularly vulnerable before people like Mrs Willis, especially as many of them already carried within them an explosive insecurity, an obsessive fear that the Nazis were going to catch them in the end.

Marcus Sachs found himself in a situation that, while it did not resemble Helga's *vis-à-vis* Mrs Willis, still stemmed from an unresolved and unacknowledged conflict between him and his employer. Mr Sachs was a humiliating failure as a gardener. So bad indeed that Mr Rayner's trees and lawns were at risk through his labours. Everyone realized this: Marcus's wife and certainly his employers, the Rayners. But as kindly and fair-minded members of the English upper middle class, the inheritors of a benign and liberal tradition, the Rayners could not bring themselves to dismiss Mr Sachs. What would happen to him if they did? He couldn't be sent back to Germany but he might be sent to an internment camp in England. That would be rather hard on the old boy. Anyway, they had sponsored the Sachses and felt responsible. And what about his wife, Ann Sachs? *She* was invaluable. A tremendous success. If she'd been British and had worn a muslin apron and starched cuffs, you'd have called her a Treasure. One didn't want to part with her, especially with a war on and any domestic staff an absolute impossibility. On the other hand, the garden couldn't be allowed to go to the devil like this.

Obviously Mr Rayner's alternatives were to either dismiss Mr Sachs or else let him go on drawing his wages and get a local lad to do the actual work. Unfortunately, Mr Rayner could not accept either alternative. His principles prevented him from firing Mr Sachs; at the same time they also prevented him from allowing Mr Sachs to draw his wages in return for such a disgraceful performance as a gardener. So he continually nagged Mr Sachs, but always in an apologetic and ineffectual way. Not that his relationship with his gardener had ever been anything but equivocal. He could not treat Sachs as an equal – he had been careful to forget the man's timid overtures to him as one accountant to another – nor could he enjoy with him the brisk master-and-man interchange he'd had with old Martin, who had been his gardener for twenty years.

Ann Sachs knew all this and was unhappy about it. She herself was perfectly prepared to leave, although Mrs Rayner treated her with almost gushing consideration; she was only concerned about Marcus. Since employment had now got a little easier for the refugees, it seemed to her possible that Marcus might get work in his own field, as an accountant. But when she suggested this to him, he only shook his head. She persisted; they were both Category C; if she got another job as a housekeeper, perhaps in London, then they would have enough to live on until he got a post that would enable him to use the skill and experience of a lifetime. He could not want to go on in his present humiliating situation. He had to do his own work again, feel pride in his own achievement again.

But Marcus didn't respond. He made excuses and she knew them for excuses. He seemed apathetic. Ann tried to argue with him; then she realized that his natural pessimism had crystallized into a masochistic despair that made Mr Rayner's disapproval in some way necessary to him.

Of course he was not alone in displaying such an unnatural passivity. Other middle-aged and elderly refugees accepted similarly hopeless situations. Like Marcus Sachs, they had given up; they had lost their nerve. Helga Zinn was young when her troubles overtook her; she had not forgotten how to hope.

Everyone agrees that up to May 1940 at least the refugees' new-found feeling of solidarity, of being in the same boat as their hosts, was shared by most British people. The atmosphere was friendly and there is no reason to suppose that this was much altered by the newspaper attacks which began in late January 1940 and which can now be seen as early symptoms of the eruption of xenophobic feeling that was to bring about mass internment in the summer of the same year. The *Daily Sketch* and the *Sunday Express* led the attack. Abandoning the earlier line that refugee workers would grab badly needed jobs, snatch the bread out of English mouths, they seized on a theme at least as old and still more certain: the refugee as spy. The tribunals were denounced for being half-hearted, for only having interned a few hundred of these dangerous men. It was even suggested that enemy agents masquerading as refugees had caused the explosion at the Royal Gunpowder Factory at Waltham Cross. The stock alarmist tricks were exploited, including the old but effective device of pretending to give the opinions of the police themselves. Faceless 'police spokesmen' were quoted to such effect that the London police commissioner had to issue a statement denying that Scotland Yard was 'gravely concerned' at the leniency shown by the Aliens Tribunals. Such reports, he said, were quite without foundation.

Despite the energy with which it was conducted, this newspaper campaign does not appear to have altered the climate of feeling to any appreciable extent: evidence that, although there are xenophobic and anti-semitic strands running through the British consciousness, they are deep-buried and hard to arouse. Throughout this period – February to April 1940 – the authorities as represented by Sir John Anderson and the various chief constables remained unperturbed. When members of the anti-alien lobby mounted a scare about German refugee domestics in the Aldershot area being a threat to security, Anderson reassured the Commons. Neither he nor the chief constables were in the least worried. He added that he saw nothing to justify a policy under which all enemy aliens would be treated alike and interned. The majority of them were bitter enemies of Hitler and the Nazis.

This was said in March. By the beginning of May the policy of the British Government had changed: mass internment had begun. What had happened to bring about such a complete reversal of policy? Up to April the newspaper campaign had apparently had little effect; during May more newspapers joined in and the government decided to introduce internment. What had happened, of course, was what has been called the Six Weeks' War from 10 May to 25 June 1940, although the Germans had really established a pattern of victory in the first five days. Fear – or more truly shock – was the catalyst. In such an atmosphere rumours proliferate; a hostile *Zeitgeist* began to haunt against the refugees.

The German conquest of Holland was of particular importance to the refugees. It was achieved by a classic blitzkrieg lasting only five days, conducted largely by parachutists and troops landed from transport planes behind the flooded lines the Dutch had hoped would delay the invaders. It was the first time that a country had been largely conquered through airborne attack. An important ancillary factor in the German victory was the so-called Fifth Column – a title that was to ring through the world in the succeeding weeks and months and was to be used with great effect in propaganda against the German and Austrian refugees in Britain.

The Fifth Column in Holland consisted of thousands of German men and women who had entered the country as the result of an agreement between the Dutch and German Governments by which any German citizen who wished could enter Holland. The Dutch were to suffer bitterly for this act of appeasement towards Germany. It meant in effect that thousands of guerrillas and saboteurs were already in Holland before Germany attacked. They waited quietly, unsuspected, in a variety of guises – as clergy, academics, tourists, students, domestics, even nuns. Once the Germans invaded, they threw off their disguises and went into action, guiding and supporting the invading troops through the five days of war. They had infiltrated everywhere : they made the German victory certain. No wonder the concept of the 'Fifth Column' filled the British people with fascination and alarm.

Through those hot and anxious days in May stories began to filter through to England of the extraordinary feats of the Nazi Fifth Columnists, of the bizarre disguises they had adopted, of the frightening way they had overrun all Holland. More significantly for the refugees in Britain, S.S. men were said to have posed as orthodox Jews in wigs and false beards. A spy was alleged to have been found among a group of Jewish refugees from Holland.

A link, slight and tenuous at first, between 'Jew' and 'Fifth Columnist' sprang into being. Guilt by association is a common psychological mechanism. A fateful sequence was established: German-Jew-Fifth Columnist. Such an identification may have been instinctive at first; it was soon to be deliberately exaggerated and fostered and spread through the media. Overnight, German Jews became objects of fear and suspicion. Overnight, the campaign against the refugees acquired weight and credibility; its sponsors saw their chance and began to talk about the potential Fifth Column in Britain – the German and Austrian refugees.

It was useless for Colonel Wedgwood and Eleanor Rathbone to point out that comparisons between the Fifth Columnists in Holland and the German Jewish refugees in Britain had no validity; to argue that the Dutch Fifth Columnists had been patriotic German citizens and not despised refugees from a Germany that had hunted and persecuted them. The unreasoning identification had been made: every day it found expression in some new quarter. It was useless to plead that no refugees anywhere had as yet been unmasked as spies. After the invasion of Holland more and more voices were heard to echo Colonel Henry Burton who had demanded in Parliament, 'Would it not be better ... to intern the lot?'

But how spontaneous was the reaction against the refugees? To what extent was this clamour to 'intern the lot' a conditioned, a manufactured thing? It was of course said that the government had yielded to 'public opinion' in acting against the refugees ('public opinion' is always an intangible), but genuine mass opinion rarely moves governments. Mass Observation reports in April 1940 indicated that there was little feeling against the German and Austrian refugees among the bulk of British people. The little disapproval there was stemmed from the familiar economic reasons: the fear that they (the refugees) 'would take British jobs'. Tom Harrisson, head of Mass Observation, writing in the *New Statesman and Nation*, pointed out that these observations had been made in April. By July the process of conditioning had gone farther and the voices of various impressive upper-class figures had been added to the newspaper uproar. This had had the desired effect. He noted, of course, the shock effect of the fall of France and of the vulnerable position in which Britain found herself but he considered this of secondary importance. The anti-refugee mood, he believed, was a manufactured one, created by certain newspaper groups with the acquiescence of the government.

The papers of the Rothermere group were the most hostile to the refugees, followed by some of the Kemsley group (and, of course, in a rather different sector, by *Truth*).

Professor Lafitte has argued in his *Internment of Aliens* (1940) that the newspapers most hostile to the refugees were precisely those that had been most friendly to Nazi Germany in pre-war years, and that they were engaged in purging their guilt by setting up the refugees as scapegoats against the public remembering this. This is no doubt true but the argument has wider implications: it opens up again the question of the ambivalent attitude of the Tory Establishment to Germany and the mixture of fear and self-interest that made the British Right so obstinately pro-German throughout the thirties. To suggest – as some of the pro-alien lobby did at the time – that there was any concerted plot against the aliens is to over-simplify. The hostile climate of May and June 1940 grew out of a combination of factors.

Lord Rothermere, the owner of the *Daily Mail* (the most consistent of the anti-refugee papers), had flirted with Mosley's Blackshirts. The plodding financial *alter ego* of his brother, the ebullient manic Lord Northcliffe, Rothermere called 'Hats off to the Blackshirts' because he presumably saw in them a protection against the Communists he dreaded. Rothermere did not support the Blackshirts for long, but the *Daily Mail* consistently backed Nazi ambitions in Europe. Their correspondent Ward Price celebrated the Nazi takeover of Austria and Czechoslovakia. Shortly before the Anschluss, Lord Rothermere wrote an article justifying it on racial grounds. More than any other group, the Rothermere papers reflected the mind of the appeasing, pro-German Establishment. In April 1940 the *Daily Mail* demanded that the police round up 'every doubtful alien in the country'. On 24 May it said:

The rounding-up of enemy agents must be taken out of the fumbling hands of local tribunals. All refugees from Austria, Germany and

Czechoslovakia, men and women alike, should be drafted without delay to a remote part of the country and kept under strict supervision . . . As the head of a Balkan State said to me last month: 'In Britain you fail to realize that *every* German is an agent. All of them have both the duty and the means to communicate information to Berlin.'

On 12 July 1940 an article was published called 'Canada is out to win'.

In Montreal a shopkeeper told me that he is convinced that Hitler drove out the Jews . . . with the express purpose of sending Gestapo agents among them to the Christian countries that took them in . . . 'Poor refugees! Huh! All they have to do is say Hitler was mean to them and we take them in and feed them and half of them are spies!'

The note struck by the Kemsley papers was equally consistent. The *Daily Sketch* always pursued the pro-German, appeasing line. The *Sunday Chronicle* published a series of articles in which the catch-cry 'Intern the Lot' was not only echoed but embellished:

'The Fifth Column.' And what about the spies here? . . . I have German friends but I would very willingly indeed see them all . . . behind bars and I have told them so to their faces. Why should we be blown up as we are walking over a bridge, unless it is strictly necessary? Or poisoned by contaminated water, or hit on the head by the local gasworks as it descends to earth? No, sir. The letters readers send about Germans who are going free in their own district would make your hair stand on end. Particularly the women. There is no dirty trick that Hitler would not do, and there is a very considerable amount of evidence to suggest that some of the women – who are very pretty – are not above offering their charms to any young man who may care to take them, particularly if he works in a munition factory or the Public Works.

Enough has been quoted to show the determined nature of this propaganda. Certain key-themes are emphasized and repeated. The wolf in sheep's clothing motif was continually presented: the apparently harmless refugee cynically fooling the good-natured Britisher who had taken him in. The 'very pretty' refugee women are in the best 'Olga the Beautiful Spy' tradition, while the suggested blowing up of the local gasworks and the poisoning by contaminated water are calculated to make the reader's flesh creep enjoyably. Most telling of all are the references to the Fifth Column. There is no doubt that this was the most potent of the influences leading to mass internment; and it was given what must have seemed like an official endorsement in a broadcast by Sir Neville Bland, British Minister in Holland, on 30 May 1940.

> It is not the German or Austrian who is found out who is the danger [he said]. It is the ... man or woman who is too clever to be found out. That was apparent in Holland, where, as I have already said, many of the obvious Fifth Columnists were interned at the outbreak of war – but where there still remained a dreadful number at large to carry out the instructions they had from Germany ... I hate to have to say this to you but ... say it I will: Be careful at this moment how you put complete trust in any person of German or Austrian connections. If you know people of this kind who are still at large, keep your eye on them; they may be perfectly all right – but they may not and today we can't afford to take risks ... We have many lessons to learn from Holland ... there may still be some devilish surprise in store for us.

The first step towards mass internment was taken, as Mr Osbert Peake of the Home Office was later to explain in Parliament, because the Germans were now in possession of ports very close to Britain. Therefore the military authorities insisted that

> the whole of the coastal belt on the east and south-east coasts of England must be made into a protected area. Not only did they press upon us that enemy aliens, about whom we know so much, should be turned out, but they pressed upon us also that neutral aliens, about whom we knew much less, should be removed. It was, in my view, quite impossible when a policy of this kind was put forward by those responsible for the defence of this country against invasion to refuse to accept it under those circumstances.

The decision to evacuate aliens from the coastal belt certainly seems logical enough, but internment is another step again. According to Mr Peake the reason for this was:

> The result of declaring the whole of the eastern and south-eastern coastal belts a protected area was that large numbers of aliens were torn up from the shallow roots which they had been able to acquire since they came here and had to remove. They had no jobs and had to proceed, with public feeling what it was **at that** time, in the face of suspicion and mistrust ... The only practical

method of dealing with the situation was, in fact, to intern the males.

The logic of this is not so clear. The Army authorities said 'Get them out'; they did not say 'Intern them'. It is apparent that a considerable element of rationalization must have entered into the government's decision. As we have seen, a newspaper campaign of great intensity had been mounted against the refugees for over three months; and the government had no doubt also been exposed to subtler but even stronger pressure from the right-wing elements who had dominated the era that had culminated in Munich. These groups were no doubt discomfited to find Britain at war with the Germany they had admired and sought to propitiate for so long. Some of them reacted (like the newspapers that had backed Hitler) by making scapegoats of the refugees, but a minority certainly hoped that an accommodation with Nazi Germany was still somehow possible. (Of course it was these influential, faceless people – whether one sees them at Cliveden, in a club in Pall Mall, or in a City boardroom – who would have provided the real Fifth Column if Hitler had invaded Britain. Even in that tense summer of 1940 Viscount Elibank could argue in the House of Lords that Laval and Petain had been justified in embracing the Nazis because it was the only way they could save themselves from the Communists.) In May 1940 these diverse but inherently xenophobic and anti-semitic groups still exerted great power. This was, after all, still their government: the government of the guilty men, the hollow men. Sir John Anderson was immediately responsible for policies towards the refugees but his temperament and background would tend to make him follow the line the Cabinet laid down. The first steps to implement the new 'enemy aliens' policy were taken on Sunday, 12 May when Churchill had only been prime minister for two days. (He had succeeded Chamberlain on the evening of 10 May.)

The coastal belt declared to be 'protected' took in a wide sweep from Inverness to Dorset. All male German and Austrians between the ages of sixteen and sixty were rounded up (excluding the 'invalid and infirm') for what was described as 'temporary internment'. Male foreigners of the same ages (sixteen to sixty) were only allowed to remain in this protected area on the condition that they reported daily to the police; that they obeyed a curfew lasting from eight in the evening to six in the morning; that they used no motor vehicle – other than public transport – or bicycle for travelling.

The Home Office made an announcement. Regret was expressed: it was acknowledged that 'for the time being' the new measures would involve great hardships for individuals, but the vital interests of the country overruled such considerations. The rigours of these measures would be mitigated as soon as circumstances permitted.

This first announcement presented the first anti-refugee actions as purely a matter of military exigency; it was phrased in a mild and conciliatory tone. But once initiated the new policy developed with a rapidity that matched the speed and magnitude of the collapse in Europe. The first round-up in the coastal belt took place on Sunday night, 12 May; by Thursday, 16 May, Holland had surrendered and fierce fighting was going on in Belgium. On that day all male Germans and Austrians – between sixteen and sixty, again – in Category B were taken in. The total number arrested was about 2,200 and this became a major security operation, involving a fleet of cars and the mobilization of police throughout Britain. According to *The Times*, the internees in Sheffield filled two motor-coaches and were guarded by a detachment of soldiers.

Quite apart from whether these measures were justified or not, protests soon arose at the manner in which they were put into effect. It was said that the arrests had been carried out with a suddenness and a secrecy more typical of the Gestapo or the Ogpu than the British police. Was it necessary for the arrests to have taken place at night, without prior warning? It was not, after all, as if these people had committed any offence. There was no reason to suppose that they would try to run away – where to? – and they had all submitted themselves to investigation by the aliens tribunals. In some cases, indeed, they had already been re-examined before the new Aliens Advisory Committees. (These had already started on the men in Category B; the women remained to be dealt with.) On Friday, 17 May, the Christian Council for Refugees from Germany issued a statement signed by a number of clergy of various denominations. They expressed the fear that an atmosphere was being created that might foster a witch-hunting attitude towards people of German origin : particularly cruel and unjust because the refugees were themselves the victims of persecution by the Nazis.

Each grim new development in Europe brought an intensification of the anti-refugee measures. On Monday, 27 May, as the German sweep westward continued, fighting on the Somme began. On the same day 3,000 German and Austrian women in Category B were interned. According to *The Times*, in many cases the police had to wait until the women got dressed. (Again, most of the arrests had taken place at night and in the early hours of the morning.) The Home Office kept repeating that internment was only temporary.

And still each defeat on the Continent brought a new stroke against the refugees. One could argue that the authorities chose them as scapegoats for those other Germans who were at this moment roaring towards the Channel Ports; more probably officialdom was gripped by an understandable mixture of muddle and panic and found in these measures a comforting illusion of action. On Monday, 3 June, King Leopold of Belgium surrendered and the Dunkirk withdrawals were in full swing. A day or two later the net was extended to include a further 300 aliens in Category B, this time aged between sixty and seventy; the 'protected' coastal areas were enlarged; foreigners everywhere over the age of sixteen were subject to a curfew from 10.30 p.m. (midnight in the London area) to 6 a.m.

By now – mid-June 1940 – it was estimated that some 7,000 men and nearly 4,000 women were in internment camps. And on 20 June, with France defeated and Churchill preparing Britain to stand like an outpost under siege, the government's attitude to internment changed. Official announcements were no longer mild and apologetic; there was no more talk of internment as merely temporary. Sir John Anderson said in Parliament that he had authorized chief constables to intern any German or Austrian person in Category C about whom there appeared to be any doubt. This of course gave the chief constables immense power over any refugee who came within their jurisdiction, and was immediately challenged in Parliament. Anderson admitted that refugees could be – in fact were being – interned without any reason being given. It had to be this way, he said : it was a matter of military necessity. He gave the impression that only those who attracted the hostile attention of the chief constables would be interned. But on 25 June all Category C males under seventy were ordered to be interned. (There were certain exceptions, such as invalids and those in jobs of national importance.) On 11 July Anderson clarified the degree of power the chief constables were to enjoy. They had not, he said, discretion to exempt enemy aliens from internment: they did have the power to hold those whom they considered should be interned on security grounds.

In practice their powers seem to have been exerted in a largely negative way. A majority of males in Category C were interned, including a number of those in the exempted class who were considered 'suspicious' by the authorities. The extent to which 'suspicious' information was fairly assessed must have varied with individual chief constables. Certainly they were generally criticized for not consulting the groups most able to give them information: the refugee organizations, who had exhaustive dossiers on those who had passed through their hands. In fact, individual officials arrived at more or less arbitrary decisions, with generally unfortunate results for the refugees.

With the exception of between four and five thousand who had enlisted in the Auxiliary Military Pioneer Corps (the government had allowed selected men to do so from the previous November onwards and had stopped recruiting in May) and the few thousands in the exempted classes who had not excited the suspicion of the chief constables, the majority of the male refugees were interned by the middle of July. Then, towards the end of the month, it was announced that some of them were being shipped to Canada and Australia, along with enemy prisoners of war. On 22 August, Sir John Anderson said that 2,358 German and Austrian refugees of Category A and 4,206 refugees of Categories B and C had been deported. (It will be noticed that the number given for Category A was much greater than the number so classified by the original tribunals: the explanation given was that this figure also included German merchant navy personnel, classed as civilians, who had been taken prisoner on ships seized by the British Navy. For some reason Sir John Anderson was unable to break down the figure of 4,206 between Categories B and C.)

If the months of newspaper agitation, followed by the flurry of panic decisions taken in May and June 1940, did succeed in arousing distrust or hostility towards the refugees, such a mood was short-lived. Already, by July, the unimaginative, blanket nature of the internment measures had provoked a reaction. The lumping together of captured Nazis and refugees from the Nazis appeared particularly unjust. The swing against government policy coalesced in the Commons debates of 10 July and 22 August when the refugees were championed not only by the faithful Josh Wedgwood and Eleanor Rathbone but by a much wider spectrum of Parliamentary opinion.

That bare framework of dates and decisions is soon established; but the world of suffering that lies behind those sparse facts can scarcely be suggested, let alone conveyed. Every refugee suffered to some degree, for the fact of exile is itself a wound, but some, naturally, had to endure more than others. Clearly their suffering bore some relation to the freshness of their alienation from their native, German environment; a refugee like Hugo Neher, who had come in 1933, had grown a carapace of habit with which to face life in a new country. (Although he, and many like him, saw themselves threatened during that summer of 1940.) But generally speaking, the later the refugee had arrived, the more frightening he or she found the anti-alien measures of May and June 1940. Those who had escaped from Germany in 1937 or 1938 – particularly those who had come after Crystal Night or even later – had already sweated on a rack of pain and insult that the earlier refugees had escaped. Few men and women, however well balanced they might have been when Hitler first came to power, could avoid being infected with a sense of persecution if they had suffered from the systematic isolation the Nazis had imposed on the Jew in German society and from the continual presence of the Gestapo – a presence that grew ever more pervasive and menacing as the net drew tighter and tighter on Jews who sought to escape from the Reich. These refugees had escaped that net, but usually with ravaged nerves and a paranoid awareness that, under the mask of order and stability, the modern state is always ready to bully and destroy its citizens.

In any case, apart from the uncertainty of their position as refugees, these Germans and Austrians, like all Jews in Britain of whatever nationality, were wondering what lay before them as they somehow endured that hot, uneasy summer of 1940. They were experiencing not only the common shock and anxiety at the savage, cataclysmic breakthrough of Hitler's panzers across the Channel, but they pondered another question, much more precise and terrible: What would be their fate if Hitler invaded Britain? A refugee speaks of this as

the awareness of the final option. You knew it was there, confronting you. If Hitler did come – and somehow it was hard to believe that he would, for England looked so solid and *usual*, despite the air-raids and the fact of our being so ill-prepared – a Jew had to kill himself. There was nothing else for it. That's why I call it the final option. I didn't actually carry poison. I didn't get that far, but I know those who did.

One representative figure always carried a phial. This was Victor Gollancz, founder of the Left Book Club and publisher of the books in bright canary-coloured jackets with the accusing, minatory titles that spearheaded the reaction against the Guilty Men (title of a Gollancz book about them). Another who was aware of the final option was Chaim Weizmann, the Zionist leader. When the battle in Europe was entering its last phase, his wife Vera, who was a doctor, went around chemists' shops accumulating lethal doses of veronal. One was for her husband, one for herself, and one for Lewis Namier, another man who knew exactly what to expect from the Nazis. In his beautiful house in Bath Stefan Zweig waited, no doubt meditating the suicide he was afterwards to accomplish, but meanwhile hypnotized by the nightmare exactitude with which his fantasies of the ultimate Nazi triumph were being fulfilled. His biographer describes the strange trance-like gloom of those days, with the calm beauty of Bath (which Zweig thought resembled Salzburg) contrasting with the phantasmagoria of violence and hatred the news from Europe conjured up in his mind.

But these were famous Jews. Weizmann was of international importance; Gollancz and Namier were respected, if unorthodox, figures in English life; Zweig was one of those distinguished refugees the British Government had wished to attract. The basic day-to-day problems would be unknown to them. The externals of money and communication would never bother Stefan Zweig: he would never feel himself insulted by a post-office clerk who did not understand his broken English; never scuttle down a side-street because he saw a policeman's helmet in the distance.

If these assured, eminent men suffered, saw their final option as a phial of poison, then how much worse the situation of the average refugee, bewildered, penniless, hardly knowing the language, a shrinking interloper in a foreign country. And of course the great majority of refugees were like this: penniless and bewildered and, because they expected hostility, inviting it.

Most of the later refugees were entirely dependent on the various organizations that had sponsored their entry and in many cases supported them after they had reached Britain. These later refugees tended to be more dependent on the aid organizations because, as we have seen, they had been able to take hardly any money out of the Reich. In the first six months of the war the battered morale of these men and women had been soothed by at least the distant prospect of order and security. Some of them had found jobs, even if these were not the jobs their training and background equipped them to do. Later, if the war went well, they might be able to get back to their own businesses and professions. If these latest arrivals were not able to share the 'senior' refugees' sense of identification with their English hosts, they knew that someone was fighting Hitler at last and that they could 'permit themselves to hope'.

Then came the measures of May 1940, shattering the world of all the refugees, no matter how well established they might be.

Individual responses were, of course, as varied as individual circumstances; but few refugees who were interned escaped some shock and disillusion. They had seen the Gestapo at work; they had dealt with the German police, who had inevitably had to play a subservient role before the Nazis; and then they had come to Britain, to be confronted by the familiar stereotype of the British Bobby – heavy-handed, perhaps even slightly comic, but cosy and reassuring, helping blind men across the road, the magnet for lost children and stray dogs. Few refugees made the mistake of sentimentalizing the English character, but after some months or years in the country and despite misunderstandings and occasional anti-semitic gestures, most of them had come to accept the essential decency of British officials and institutions. Now came internment, to make the most sober-minded of refugees wonder if this cosy decency had all been a mask.

Most refugees were careful to emphasize that the British police and military had treated them well, but nevertheless the nightmare was real while it lasted. Individual soldiers behaved with kindness and courtesy; but a general complaint was that the arrests were conducted as if the refugees were criminals and the blame for this must lie with the chief constables, who in many cases arranged for midnight arrests, Gestapo-style, and sent lorry-loads of soldiers to accompany the police vans. There was an unexpected ruthlessness about snatching the internees away without giving them time to arrange anything, even to communicate with relatives. (In some cases nothing was heard from the internees until many months later, and then a card would arrive from Canada or Australia.)

Not all arrests were made at night. On 13 July several detectives walked into Hampstead Public Library at around 1.30 p.m. The exits were barred and the detective in charge announced that all Germans and Austrians present were being taken into custody. The British subjects present having established their identity to the officers' satisfaction, the refugees were escorted to their homes by detectives, given a stay of minutes in which to pack and to say goodbye to their relatives (assuming they were at home) and then taken away. An elderly refugee describes a similar round-up which took place in Hampstead High Street:

It was about twenty to one and I'd been doing some shopping for my wife who wasn't well – I remember she'd been to the dentist the day before but she still had an abscess and was in great pain. I was just about to turn up Heath Street when I noticed a group of people in front of me: not really a group – three men and a woman. The woman moved away, rather as if she'd been asking directions from the men or the other way round, and then one of the men came up to me. He said, 'You're a German!' Not a question: a statement, just like that . . . I was amazed. I didn't say anything, I was so amazed. How did he know? We didn't wear the Yellow Badge in England . . . I think he showed me some kind of police identity card – very quickly, just a glimpse of it – and then he said, 'I have reason to believe you are an enemy alien, to wit a German national and a holder of a German passport and therefore subject to an order under the Aliens Act . . .' Those may not have been the exact words, but it was something like that. He wanted to take me straight away in a police car but I kept saying about my wife being ill at home. I got so upset I was shouting and I think that was why they allowed me to go home and see my wife. One of the detectives came with me; the others stayed and they were stopping other people and taking some of them in. They had a van parked in a side street. They let me see my wife for about twenty minutes – I remember she was still in a lot of pain – and then they took me away in the van.

This refugee's wife next heard from him months later when he was in Canada.

Almost all the refugees agree that they were hustled away into internment as if every moment counted. In some cases the police took the internees home and allowed them more or less adequate time to make their farewells; in others, this was only granted after furious protests on the internee's part. But whatever time was granted, the refugee never had time to arrange his affairs. Almost invariably he left behind him unpaid bills; a suspicious and possibly angry employer (if he'd had a job); and worst of all – especially if he was leaving behind a wife who did not understand English – usually an unsolved accommodation problem: either a flat at a rent his wife could not afford to pay or a rented room whose landlady was appalled to see her tenant in trouble with the police.

To his surprise, Hugo Neher was not interned at all. His job with the Garvas Agency had abruptly ceased. Early the previous November Mr Carlmann had come into the office one morning at ten instead of eleven. For almost an hour he had moved uneasily about, opening drawers and shuffling papers; then he had announced, 'Er . . . Hugo. There is something to tell you. I shall have to ask you to take a week's notice. I shall be closing this business.' There had followed many hints and elliptical allusions. Hugo had been left with the impression that Mr Carlmann was going off to, at the very least, run the British Secret Service. 'Work of . . . national importance, Hugo, I can only say . . .' Although the Garvas Agency had seemed like success when he had first got the job, he found he was not as upset as he might have expected. He had been disappointed at his rejection by the Pioneer Corps, but now he thought of a way in which the frustrations of the typewriter years could be put to positive advantage. He applied at the labour exchange in Long Acre for a job he had seen advertised: as a factory machinist. As he had expected, the 'technical qualifications' that had been so undervalued in Bolton now proved an advantage. He was granted a permit and by December 1939 he was at work in a factory in Sheffield, making a spring attachment for the sighting of anti-aircraft guns. What he had not expected was that his early arrival in Britain – which had apparently aroused the suspicions of the immigration officer and the aliens tribunal – would now prove an advantage. In May 1940, although he had expected to be interned as so many Category C refugees were, as an immigrant of long standing he was left alone and continued to work in the factory until the middle of 1944.

Helga Zinn was not so fortunate. Norwich was in the 'protected' coastal belt. All male enemy aliens in the area were, of course, rounded up and sent into internment on 12 May. Helga, as a woman in Category B awaiting re-classification by the regional committee, was arrested on Monday, 27 May. She had finished work about six o'clock and was drinking a cup of tea after her evening meal when the police called at her lodgings. There were two detectives, a sergeant and a constable, and they seemed embarrassed at having to arrest a young woman. 'That's all right, Miss; you take your time, Miss,' they kept assuring her in the Norfolk accent she had at first found strange but had now grown to like. She was taken to the police station and given cups of tea and ham sandwiches, although she protested that she'd just had her tea.

Helga was kept in a small, apparently disused office behind the charge-room for several hours. Later that evening she was joined by two other women who were to be interned. One was a Jewess, an Austrian, considerably older than Helga. She was a teacher at a girls' school in Norwich; she seemed overwhelmed with shock and horror at being arrested and kept bursting into tears. The other woman was young, about Helga's own age: blonde and attractive, not Jewish as far as Helga could judge. She was distinctly unfriendly; she would hardly speak to the other women. From her accent she came from southern Germany. She did mention, in her tight-lipped way, 'my husband' and Helga got the smell of a moneyed arrogance from her. Much later, around midnight, the three women were taken by car to the outskirts of Huntingdon. There they were lodged in a school that had been taken over as a reception-centre for women internees. Conditions there were bad: nearly a hundred women of all ages were crammed into four classrooms, sleeping on straw palliasses (there were not enough of these to go round and some of the later arrivals tried to sleep huddled up around the dead radiators in the biggest classroom). There were two lavatories, but one of them had clearly been out of order for a long time. The day after Helga and her companions arrived the other one got obscenely blocked, the floor swimming in water and urine. After that the women had to be escorted in relays to a public lavatory a quarter of a mile away. Their escort consisted of three sullen policewomen, who looked as if they blamed the unfortunate female internees for the war itself. Meals were brought in heat-proof containers from a nearby anti-aircraft site; unfortunately, by the time they arrived the food was nearly cold: an *olla podrida* of swedes, potato, and greasy mutton. Helga felt despairing: how could she possibly endure such conditions; above all, the lack of privacy that made her suddenly conscious of her own body as an embarrassment, a cumbersome machine for producing dirt and sweat that demanded baths and soap and clean linen – things that, once taken for granted, now seemed like a dream. She kept telling herself that this wasn't a Nazi concentration camp; she should be thankful for that. These were British soldiers guarding her; these men weren't going to kill her. But her present discomforts stifled her imagination; whatever a concentration camp was like, this was awful, this was intolerable. She couldn't stand it. Fortunately, at the end of the fourth day at the centre, a number of army lorries drew up. The weeping, protesting women were herded into the lorries by embarrassed soldiers and the sullen, irritable policewomen. It was rumoured that they were being taken to Liverpool and this proved correct. A day later Helga sailed with several hundred other women for internment in the Isle of Man.

Marcus Sachs had been placed in Category C and yet he was taken into custody on 16 July. In theory this must have been because the chief constable had reason to suspect him, but to anyone who knew Marcus Sachs this was such a ludicrous supposition that neither his employer, Mr Rayner, nor the Jewish Refugee Committee believed in it for a moment. Presumably the chief constable worked on some blanket assumption of German Jewish guilt, or possibly he had been given false information. Mr Rayner, perhaps compensating for his criticism of Mr Sachs as a gardener, was tireless in his efforts to get him released from internment, lobbying his local M.P., with whom he had business connections. The M.P. was put out at first but, after the debate of 22 August, was less embarrassed at finding himself making common cause with such an eccentric as Josh Wedgwood.

Marcus Sachs had been taken first to an 'aliens' collection station' on Kempton Park Racecourse, about thirty miles from the Rayners' house. Here the internees were under military guard, living under conditions of some discomfort, especially considering that a majority of the men interned were relatively elderly. Mr Sachs was billeted in a section of the offices formerly used by the Tote; he slept in a corner of a room divided by glass partitions. The wind blew stonily through the pigeon-holes through which, not so long ago, eager punters had passed their choices and, if they were lucky, later collected their money. But Mr Sachs was fortunate: there were only nine other men sleeping on the office floor with him. In some of the larger rooms as many as a hundred men lay sardine-like on a stone floor, shivering – although it was mid-summer – under two thin blankets. Worse than the physical discomforts – and this complaint appears again and again in the refugees' accounts of internment – was an inability to fill the void each day presented. There was nowhere to go; no common-room or recreation area where the internees could rest, read, talk, write letters. All Marcus Sachs could do was lie on his narrow straw palliasse (the contents of which never ceased to creak uncomfortably beneath him) or sit on the huge empty grandstand and, if he felt imaginative enough, try to people the blank expanse of the deserted course with the grey toppers and gay parasols of a summer meeting (something which Marcus Sachs, of course, had never seen). Often meals were eaten standing up. A staple item was 'Irish stew' – a mockery of its name for it contained hardly any meat – and, everlastingly, dry bread and black tea.

Mr Sachs remained at Kempton Park for three weeks. Then he was transferred to the Isle of Man.

Lothar Kahlmann hoped he might escape internment. He was Category C: Mark had told him that Sir John Anderson had announced that only those Category C refugees about whom chief constables had definite suspicions would be interned. So he, Lothar Kahlmann, had no need to worry. And he had the irrational hope he might escape because there were comparatively few refugees in the East End. Most of the German and Austrian Jews had gone to north-west London, to districts like Hampstead and Willesden Green. Then, at the beginning of June, the police began a sweep through Whitechapel, Shadwell, and Stepney. It was the most disturbing affront to the East End Jews since the Mosley riots. Dr Mallon, Warden of Toynbee Hall, protested in a letter to *The Times* of 23 July 1940 :

It is hard to write with composure about the present treatment of friendly aliens in East London. How can one explain or excuse the internment of elderly men, many of them invalids who have lived blamelessly for forty or fifty years? Men who have not been away from London for twenty years; men who have occupied a single residence for half a century; men who are ailing or have ailing wives; obscure and helpless men about whom the synagogue and their neighbours know all that can be known; men of whom it is not even pretended that there is any suspicion, are being interned or have been interned in scores . . . Nothing seems to weigh with the authorities except that men are alien and not over seventy. Such men are taken at short notice, often inconsiderately and harshly, and apparently without leave to communicate with their families . . . Surely in the interests of sanity and humanity and of the national cause the government will intervene.

Dr Mallon was describing severities that were occurring all over Britain; but anti-alien policy in the East End was being pushed to peculiar lengths, for many of the 'enemy aliens' seized there were *Ostjuden* who had fled from persecution in Russia thirty or forty years before. If they were dragged off to internment, it is not surprising that such a newcomer as Lothar Kahlmann should be swept into the net. He was taken one hot Sunday afternoon from the work-room and brought on foot to the police station. An hour or two later he was taken to Brixton Prison in a black maria. He remembers the police as neither agreeable nor particularly harsh. He was not told he was being taken to Brixton jail and the journey in the dark closed van seemed endless as they swayed and twisted across London, sometimes braking so hard that Lothar and the other men in the van were thrown against each other and on to the floor.

Conditions in Brixton were unpleasant enough, although probably superior to those in the many inprovised reception-centres and camps throughout the country. Lothar had to share a cell with two other internees. One was a short, dark man called Max Lang. He had the harsh accent and quick *Galgenhumor* of the street-corner Berliner. He might or might not have been Jewish: Lothar thought probably not. He suspected Lang of being a Communist – not because he proclaimed himself one but because he talked continually of the brawls and street-fights in Berlin in the years before the Nazis achieved power. 'Two million votes!' he would say. 'That's what the Nazis lost in 1932. Just a year before Hindenburg handed them Germany on a plate ... Two million votes – and the Reds got a hundred seats in the Reichstag. Do you doubt that Germany was betrayed, Herr Kahlmann? Do you think Thalmann and the other capitalists didn't sell out Germany to the Nazis?'

The other man in the cell was an Italian: a big, pasty-faced man who, on the rare occasions he did speak, never did so above a whisper. He gave the impression of being too frightened to say anything. He was an ice-cream seller who had lived in Stepney for twenty years. He had been interned on 11 June, the day after Mussolini had brought Italy into the war. Lang enjoyed making needling remarks about 'Il Duce', but Valachi only turned his gentle, cow-like gaze towards them, saying nothing. Unlike Lothar or Max Lang, who appeared to have no human ties, Valachi was a family man. He would sit in a corner of the cell, apparently insulating himself from his surroundings, and then take out a number of snapshots from his pocket, holding them out, fan-wise, like a hand at cards. Then – the ritual never varied – he would gaze at each photograph in turn for minutes at a time, finally sliding each one behind its fellows until he was left gazing at the one on top of the pile. As he looked, his eyes would fill with tears and by the time he had reached the last snapshot he would be weeping aloud. According to Max Lang, who had once looked over Valachi's shoulder, these were photographs of his wife and children.

The food in Brixton might have been acceptable if it had been well prepared; but the prison cooks contrived to make everything swim in greasy water. Lothar found the exercise periods the hardest to endure. The men detained in Brixton were by no means all refugees from Nazism; the old prison contained a number of Fascists – including the British detainees under Regulation 18B: Fascist and Nazi sympathizers from every social level. There were also Germans; and the instinctive policy of all these Fascists – not only in Brixton but everywhere they found themselves imprisoned with refugees – was to cultivate aggression as part of their morale; to be as tough and offensive as possible; to show that they were not daunted by imprisonment and were delighted by the opportunity it gave them to torment the Jews they hated.

In Brixton, perhaps because the internees were not, after all, convicted criminals, supervision of exercise tended to be lax. This gave a small group of Fascists a chance to indulge in some quiet Jew-baiting. These three Fascists were all English : blackshirts, Mosley-men. Two of them were small, chunky and tough; the third, tall and broad, a mountain of a man. They used to hang around the entrance to the block from which their chosen victim would emerge. They had a roster of victims : all Germans. There was an elderly jeweller from Prague; a language teacher from Berlin who had been in England for twenty-five years; a frail, pale-faced young student of not more than twenty (the favourite victim); and Lothar himself. The Fascists would wait until the victim was halfway across the prison yard and then move towards him in a kind of pincer movement, closing in as they drew level with him. Then – at first in complete silence – they would station themselves in exact formation : one at each side of him and one behind. They would walk so close to him that they were likely to kick his ankles – apparently accidentally – and if he tried to escape they would trip him up. Once the victim had accepted the inevitability of their presence and was walking in painful step with them, they would start to mutter in unison, one voice overlapping another, continuously : 'Fucking-yid-fucking-yid-fucking-yid-kick-his-shitting-balls-in-fucking-yid-fucking-yid-fucking-yid-fucking-yid-kick-his-balls-in-fucking-yid . . .' This would continue throughout the exercise period, never ceasing for a second. In addition, the victim would be kicked from time to time and tripped up at least once. Sometimes the whole exercise would be carried out in silence; and Lothar could never decide whether this was not really worse than the continual, hypnotic mumble of abuse, because one's nerves cracked wondering when the abuse was going to start. An occasional variant of the technique was to walk up to the victim and stand facing him, head pushed forward to within an inch of his head, snarling and making faces.

Protests to the prison authorities were no use – not because they condoned this behaviour but because the blackshirts invariably played dumb and accused the Jews of having persecution mania.

One fact emerges from all these accounts of internment: an almost anarchical lack of organization. The worst feature of this was the obtuseness (or callousness) that set Nazis and Jews down together in the same prisons and internment camps.

Ironically enough, those aliens whom the tribunals had considered the greatest security risk often enjoyed the best conditions in internment. These were the people who had been placed in Category A. (A number of them were, of course, Nazi and Fascist sympathizers and suspects.) Their relative good fortune consisted in being sent to 'civilian' prisoner-of-war camps, which meant that they enjoyed the legal status of prisoners of war. This meant that their conditions were governed by an international convention signed by Britain and Germany. Thus they were assured of better treatment than obtained in the chaos of improvised camps to which most Category B and C internees were sent. But while food, bedding, sanitary conditions – the physical amenities – might be better for such Jewish refugees as were sent to prisoner-of-war camps, this was more than offset by the fact that Nazis and Nazi sympathizers were likely to predominate in these camps.

In one such a camp a measure of self-government was allowed to the prisoners but at least half of them were Nazi sympathizers and this led to a clash between the two groups. The Nazis behaved with their usual arrogance, singing the 'Horst Wessel Song', and sometimes ganging up on the Jews and even physically assaulting them.

Women who were interned as civilian prisoners of war encountered a similar situation. They were sent to various prisons for women including the ancient Holloway jail in north London. There, the fact that they were not subject to the usual prison discipline aroused the jealousy of the other prisoners. Antisemitism proliferated behind the dank and mouldering walls. When the air-raids started, some of the other prisoners would shout, 'That's the stuff! Blow the dirty yids out of their rat holes!' At exercise the other women prisoners would dance around the internees, shouting, 'The yids! The yids! We've got to get rid of the yids!'

The brief accounts of internment already given could stand for refugee testimony in general. They reflect the physical discomforts, the psychological malaise suffered by thousands in prisons and camps throughout Britain. The refugees in Categories B and C were not treated as civilian prisoners of war and therefore not guaranteed specific conditions under any international convention. They had one advantage: they were less likely to find themselves interned with Nazis.

The War Office was responsible for general internment through the crucial three months from May to July 1940, although the Home Office remained in charge of women internees. When considering the disorder and inefficiency that caused so much suffering, it is only fair to remember that the War Office was at that time subject to pressures and difficulties unique in its history. These were the weeks of agony on the beaches of Normandy and Dunkirk. The Army had to re-group and, so far as the wretched supply position allowed, be re-equipped. From the point of view of logistics alone, the situation was desperate. From that of morale, it might have seemed hopeless. In the event, the British Army survived; was re-equipped; reorganized; fought again and won. But amid the shock and confusion of May 1940 the organization of some twenty camps for enemy aliens must have seemed an intolerable extra. The work was often delegated to junior officers who did the best they could with inadequate supplies and personnel.

Many of the refugees understood the difficulties the Army might have in feeding and housing them, but complained bitterly about the iron shutter that had descended and cut them off from all news of the outside world, denied them letters from their wives and children, and kept those wives and children in agonized doubt as to the fate of many refugees. If the logistics of internment were bad, communications were even worse. Not only were personal letters denied, but there was a blackout of all news that included magazines, newspapers and radio sets. The refugees who had been taken in at the beginning, in early May, hung in torment as to what was happening in France. Holland and Belgium had been overrun before they had been arrested; there were rumours that France had fallen. A number of the refugees had relatives there – it will be remembered that many German Jews had felt drawn towards France and had gone there when the Nazis first came to power: what was going to happen to them? The fall of France coincided with a further big haul of internees and these brought into the camps the knowledge that the French police were handing over Jewish refugees to the Gestapo. There was a clause in the Compiègne Armistice terms that specified that all German subjects found on French territory were to be sent back to Germany. And what about Britain? The Germans might invade any day. The internees were subject to all the fear and uncertainty that affected everyone else – as we have seen, men like Chaim Weizmann and Victor Gollancz carried phials of poison against the Germans' coming – but in a hysterically magnified form. Herded together, deprived, often intimidated, scarred by their earlier sufferings, these men and women were the prey to morbid rumours of destruction and defeat. Would the British Government come to terms with Germany? Would the internees be handed over, like the German Jews in France? In one camp the internees heard that the invasion had already taken place and that this was why food was so short. In another – because transport to and from the camp had, for some reason, been interrupted – it was believed that rail and road communications all over Britain had been disorganized, again as the result of a successful German invasion.

In the cramped discomfort of the camps, a rumour would burgeon and spread from one tent or hut to another. And of course the morbid suggestibility of the internees was aggravated by the enforced silence between them and their relatives. However hard-pressed the military authorities may have been, this is something that can hardly be excused. For the first few weeks the silence was absolute. Then field service postcards were issued to the internees, so that they could write to their relatives telling them where they were. They were also permitted to write a maximum of 24 lines every week on a special letter-form. But there was no certainty of delivery: a letter or card might take up to six weeks to arrive. And postal services from the outside world to the internees were even worse. Letters would be sent back from the camps marked 'Not known' or 'Gone away'. Food parcels would be opened and their contents pilfered. The censorship was a great cause of delay. In one camp letters posted on 3 July were not examined by the censor until 15 July. On 19 July the letters were returned to the internees who had written them; the censor objected to some remarks in the letters. It was later explained in Parliament that some 100,000 letters from internees had been held up in the censorship office in Liverpool for nearly a month. It is impossible to exaggerate what these failures and delays must have meant in sheer despair to the internees and their relatives.

A further cause of hardship was the apparent inability of the authorities to keep adequate records or file documents properly. This derived from the ham-fisted methods of the Army itself. When an internee arrived at an 'aliens collection station' his money and papers would usually be taken from him. A note would be made of the amount of money and his papers put in an envelope bearing his name. Unfortunately, a large proportion of the money disappeared; and in many cases the documents were treated by the authorities as little better than waste paper. They were tied up in bundles; then lost, destroyed, in one case dispatched to Canada by mistake. A number of refugees suffered great inconvenience when they were eventually released through the loss of their papers. Transfers from one camp to another compounded the confusion, especially as a number of camps appear to have kept no proper records. When one man was being transferred, it was discovered that his documents had been lost. An identity card had to be improvised in the shape of a piece of cardboard bearing the internee's fingerprints and franked by the camp commandant's office.

Visits to the internees by relatives were often difficult to arrange: sometimes impossible. Apart from the distances sometimes involved, official objections had to be overcome. The total effect on the refugees of their being delivered over to a vast blind machine, arbitrary in its decisions, anarchical in its workings, was a Kafkaesque sense of disorientation, a numbing loss of identity.

A clear line of development is apparent in government policy. At the beginning, according to official statements, internment was intended as a temporary measure. By the middle of June, France having fallen, the idea of internment as a temporary measure had been abandoned. The mass of internees were being moved, generally, towards Liverpool; it would appear that it was intended that most internees should either be housed on the Isle of Man or transported to Canada and Australia. In fact, many internees remained on the Isle of Man and a considerable number were transported – with tragic results, particularly in the case of the *Arandora Star* – before public opinion, which had already begun to make itself felt in the Commons debate of 10 July, began to check the whole process in the debate of 22 August.

Although the mass of internees eventually found themselves on the Isle of Man or, if they were very unfortunate, on a ship bound for Canada or Australia, the names of two other camps recur in refugee testimony.

One of them is always spoken of with particular disgust: Wharf Mills, a derelict cotton mill at Bury in Lancashire. Here the internees suffered every possible humiliation. The place was rat-infested; the windows were broken; the rain beat in through the many holes in the shattered glass roof. The interior was littered with remnants of belts and pulleys; the shafts that had driven the looms still remained. The floors were rotten, and covered with oil and grease. Holes in the floor would fill with water when it rained through the roof. The lavatories consisted of buckets in the factory yard. Two thousand internees had to wash from eighteen taps. At the beginning there was no bedding, only old planks; no tables and no chairs. The blankets issued were often verminous. At Wharf Mills the conditions were so bad that the normally docile internees were reduced to a state of near-mutiny. They told the camp commandant that they wouldn't be treated like criminals and demanded better sanitary facilities and proper bedding for the sick among them. The officers in charge, it was said, entirely disregarded these complaints.

The other principal camp outside the Isle of Man was at Huyton in Lancashire. Here some 3,000 internees were held in an unfinished housing estate. The internees lived in the houses without furniture or any bedding except straw sacks. Each house had four rooms and, later, after a new commandant had been appointed, certain basic furniture was provided. The younger internees were kept in tents during the first weeks and suffered great hardship owing to the bad weather. Medical facilities were particularly bad and, had the refugee doctors not offered the single Army medical officer their services, would have broken down completely. The situation was made much worse by the fact that – as in most of the camps – a large proportion of the internees were elderly men. There was no first-aid equipment. A great number of the internees developed depressive illnesses, particularly after they heard of the loss of the *Arandora Star*.

The camps on the Isle of Man represented the greatest concentration of enemy aliens in Britain. Generally speaking, conditions were a good deal better than those at Huyton or the notorious Wharf Mills. The 'camps' on the Isle of Man were in face groups of houses – normally used as seaside boarding-houses – cut off by barbed wire fences. They had been stripped of all their normal furnishings, although a few essential pieces had been left in each house. There were beds, but not enough for all the internees; many of them slept on straw palliasses on the floor. There were no chairs or tables in the bedrooms and there were never enough blankets to go round. Catering arrangements were not centralized, as they were elsewhere; food was issued to each house and the internees were responsible for cooking it, so a good deal depended on the abilities of individuals. The sick – always a fairly high percentage of such an elderly group as the refugees on the Isle of Man – were able to get some extras, like milk. The camp canteen, which was manned by internees, sold such necessities as razor-blades and toothpaste.

Internee life on the Isle of Man would appear to have been endured on something like the physical level of an army training unit in Britain, except that the internees were not expected to undergo the violent physical exercise prescribed for army recruits; nor were they sustained by the kind of group morale that can emerge among the most unpromising bunch of recruits. Most of the internees were tired men; they had been asked to suffer too much already and internment had come as the last straw.

In theory each of the camps on the Isle of Man was a democracy governed by officials appointed from among the refugees themselves: house-leaders, group-leaders, camp-supervisors, who were answerable to the military authorities. In some camps the internees who offered themselves for office were not necessarily those most fitted for it, but were moved by a desire to salvage their own *amour-propre*, bruised and diminished by the fact of internment. These were the house-leaders and camp-supervisors who tended to come into conflict with their fellow-internees and who were described as 'acting like typical petty bureaucrats'.

In other camps this limited form of self-government was in the hands of the more politically aware among the inmates on a committee basis and this resulted in something like democracy although, again, there were always individuals who complained that these selected representatives in fact represented only themselves. Relations between the internees and the army authorities naturally differed from camp to camp. In some there existed a considerable degree of cooperation; in others an unresponsive commandant could take up a stance that varied from a merely unimaginative interpretation of regulations to downright obstruction.

As the weeks passed and some kind of pattern of life in internment emerged, the more intellectually active among the refugees sought to create an atmosphere that would take them beyond the mere necessities of eating, drinking, and sleeping and help them to overcome the brutish sequence of the dead dull days. Now, for once, the predominance of professional men, even of 'intellectuals', among the refugees was of some advantage. Each of the camps was full of academics who were eager to talk and teach, to pass on their particular disciplines to their fellows behind the wire. In several camps 'People's Universities' were founded. Usually lacking any textbooks or works of reference, the refugee academics offered classes in English, German, French, and Spanish; lectures on psychology, biology, music, mathematics, physics, and many other things – the range as wide as or wider than that offered by many real universities. In another camp which contained a higher proportion than usual of young internees (under twenty-five) a 'Youth University' was started; and a school was organized for the numerous boys who had come into the net because they were sixteen or over.

The camps were equally rich in literary and journalistic talent and by July a number of camp journals had begun to appear. These were mostly slim, duplicated affairs, but there were also several wall newspapers. There was the *Mooragh Times* (Mooragh was the district in which the camp was situated) whose contributors included the exiled novelist Robert Neumann; another similar paper was the *Onchan Pioneer*. Marcus Sachs remembers with pleasure some of the entertainments mounted by his fellow internees on the Isle of Man, including a revue with satirical sketches that featured a cabaret star he had often seen in Vienna. In contrast to his time at Kempton Park, he thinks of Mooragh almost with affection. Not only were physical conditions easier but the livelier atmosphere prevented him from sinking into the mood he had suffered at Kempton Park: a depression that surfaced in an obsessive concern with small discomforts, with petty deprivations that assumed enormous proportions. And on the Isle of Man he had made some new friends for the first time since he left Vienna. (He was only to remain at Mooragh four weeks; then Mr Rayner's efforts on his behalf were successful. He was released towards the end of July and sent to do a job in the accounts department of a chemical plant in the West of England.)

Indeed, many of the internees found life in the Isle of Man at least tolerable. Eugen Speir, a Jew who had been long resident in Britain, found compensation in the cultural activities the internees created for themselves. Three members of the celebrated Amadeus Quartet met for the first time in the Isle of Man: they said that the long empty hours gave them a chance to plan and rehearse which they might never have found anywhere else. Heinrich Fraenkel, the author and journalist (an authority on the Nazi Establishment and later the biographer of Himmler and Göring) actually wrote a book while interned on the Isle of Man: *Help us Germans to beat the Nazis*. He was granted permission to do this by the Home Office and was given every facility by his camp commandant. He was even allowed to receive recent copies of the Gestapo journal *Das Schwarze Korps* and Streicher's *Der Stürmer*. Dr Fraenkel considers that the internment camp was the ideal background against which to write this particular book, surrounded as he was by a wide variety of Germans who were alike only in their opposition to the Hitler régime.

The women internees on the Isle of Man perhaps enjoyed more physical comfort than the men – they were billeted with private landladies in boarding houses, first at Port Erin and then, when accommodation overflowed, at Port St Mary – but they seem to have adapted themselves less successfully to exile. This may have been because less attempt was made to give the women any sense of community; they were not allowed to organize their own administration to the extent the men were. They naturally felt isolated and were even more prone to loneliness and depression. The multiplicity of interests available to the male internees were almost wholly lacking among the women. And of course they were emotionally more vulnerable than the male internees. Many of them were separated from husbands and children; their sense of uncertainty and deprivation was even keener than that of the men.

Helga Zinn was lodged in a house at Port St Mary, and she says of her time there :

The atmosphere was never pleasant, not for a moment. It was like being left at school over the holidays when all the girls are bored and unhappy ... At first I was sharing a room with Maria Seeghers and Marta Geilart [the middle-aged teacher and the snooty blonde who had been arrested with Helga] and that was not too pleasant. Maria was always miserable, always weeping and saying she had been born under an evil star. Geilart wouldn't talk at all. I didn't know anything about her for a long time, even though we were living in the same room. I think she may have talked a little more to Maria than to me because, although she hated and despised all Jews, she naturally despised a Jew who was only in a factory – like me – more than a Jew who taught in a school – like Maria. Maria said Geilart was married to a German engineer who had been working in Norwich and that he'd been over in Holland when the war started so he'd been able to get back to Germany while she was still in England and so got caught. She'd been put in Category B – I can't think why because she was a real Nazi, but probably because she had friends among the rich English milords ...

Anyway, it got much worse when they kept sending more women in – these women were older too, and it was harder for them. They put three more in our room and then of course there wasn't enough beds or blankets and we were told we must share. Two of the new women were quite old and one a young girl – all German Jewesses – and of course Geilart was furious when it was suggested that she should share a bed with one of us ... She chose to spend one whole night in the corridor and then the next night she was exhausted and she tried to force one of us out so she could get a bed to herself. She stood in the middle of the floor and spoke in a loud voice so even the old deaf woman would hear : 'I'd rather sleep with a dog or a pig than a Jewess! A dog or a pig! Better than a Jewess!' We just lay there and pretended not to hear her and she kept repeating 'A dog or a pig!' rocking herself from side to side. Then, after a time, she just stood there. She must have been dying with exhaustion. Not long before morning – it was getting light – she pushed into bed with Maria Seeghers. She didn't say anything and Maria didn't say anything. I suppose Geilart thought it would be less demeaning to share a bed with a Jewess who was a teacher than with a Jewess who painted glass in a factory. The funny thing was, Geilart herself snored terribly – and we none of us ever said a word to her – imagine! But although she accepted defeat over the bed, it didn't make any difference. She was just as arrogant; treated us like dirt. There were quite a number like her among the women internees; they formed a kind of clique. Maria always said the landladies gave the Nazis more food because they were anti-semitic and because some of these Nazi women had money and paid them. I don't know about that, but certainly the camp authorities didn't make any distinction between the Nazi women and the Jewesses – if anything they treated the Nazis better.

This may be tinged with a natural resentment, but it does reflect the claustrophobic nature of the life of the women internees on the Isle of Man. The stories of the women internees have a sour note that is lacking in the men's. While the men speak with pleasure of the divisions they made for themselves – the lectures, the evening discussions, the plays and revues – the women have no comparable memories. One speaks of the smartly dressed contingent of German women who arrived from Brighton and Hove; another of the unfortunate group of nuns who came from the German Hospital in London and whom an imaginative chief constable had evidently decided were a threat to security. Another internee recalls that, despite the chronic shortage of medical facilities, women refugee doctors found it hard to get their qualifications acknowledged by the authorities. Another hardship was the higher proportion of Nazi sympathizers among the women than among the men. Others remember the queueing for the five shillings a week they were allowed to draw from their own money. 'Queueing! Always queueing! And everyone gets hysterical and angry with each other . . .' There are stories of tyrannical landladies; of intense hatreds generated over the gas-stove in the cramped kitchens of Port Erin; of a Lesbian relationship between a young Jewess and a big blonde sergeant-major of a woman, the wife of a German naval officer, who had been caught in Britain when war broke out.

There is no point in multiplying anecdotes which duplicate each other. All memory – and certainly memories of events more than thirty years past – is highly selective. Most of the internees, men or women, looking back on their days at Kempton Park or Huyton or the Isle of Man, recall the same kind of happenings, emphasize the same hardships or the same small but vital pleasures. And nearly all of them apologize for any implied criticism of Britain with phrases like, 'But of course it wasn't as if we'd been prisoners of the Nazis. These were British soldiers guarding us. We knew we were safe.' Heinrich Fraenkel is actually generous enough to defend internment on the grounds that the British were fighting the Nazis and therefore could afford to take no chances.

If internment was a harsh and traumatic experience for the refugees, then deportation was a dangerous and frightening one. And if internment was badly organized, with little regard for the individual, then deportation was conducted with a callous and haphazard disregard for all human values.

On 2 July 1940 the liner *Arandora Star* was torpedoed and sunk by a German U-boat in the Atlantic. It carried some 1,500 German and Italian deportees from Britain who were being taken to Canada. *The Times* of 4 July 1940 said:

When a rescue vessel arrived at a Scottish west coast port yesterday with survivors of the Blue Star liner *Arandora Star* it was learned that many interned Germans and Italians had been the victims of Germany's latest act of ruthless submarine warfare. The survivors had terrible stories to tell of struggles between German and Italian prisoners to reach the safety of the lifeboats. In striking contrast was the description of how the captain of the liner and many of the ship's officers were last seen standing on the bridge and on the decks as the vessel went down ... The passengers on the *Arandora Star* were mostly enemy aliens trading in this country who had been interned on the outbreak of war. They were being sent to Canada for internment to avoid possible complications in the event of enemy parachute troops being landed in this country. The liner had on board some 2,000 souls, 1,500 of whom were Germans and Italians. The remainder were mostly British troops providing a guard for the aliens, and members of the crew ... there have been some losses among some British troops and the crew. The heaviest sufferers, however, appear to have been the Italians. According to survivors, a torpedo struck the liner but it must have ripped her open because she did not take long to sink ... The

liner was attacked without warning about six in the morning in
broad daylight. The scenes on board were indescribable as the
Germans and Italians fought to get to the lifeboats. The Germans,
'great hulking brutes', said one survivor, swept everyone aside in
their rush to the boats. The poor Italians stood no chance against
them and the hostility between the two nationalities was bitter, both
on board the liner and in the rescue vessel, and British troops had
to keep them apart. The ship sank so rapidly that it was a case
of everyone for himself and the Germans made it clear that they
intended to let nothing stand in the way of their safety . . . An
Army Sergeant said that only a fortnight ago he had had the
experience of being bombed while returning from France but this
was a more frightful experience because of the conduct of the
aliens . . . [another] survivor said that the aliens fought one another
in a mad scramble for the boats. At one stage he saw thirty men
fighting for the chance to slide down a rope to the boats . . . He
paid high tribute to the expeditious manner in which the survivors,
clinging to the rafts and in the lifeboats, were picked up by the
rescue ships. The *Arandora Star*'s lighting system was put out of
action and the engine room staff had to scramble through the darkness to the decks . . .

This *Times* report has been quoted at length, partly because
it gives the essential facts of a disaster that had great influence on
British public opinion and thus, ultimately, on British Government policy; but also because it is illuminating to compare this
account with those of German Jewish refugee survivors from the
Arandora Star. Reading *The Times* report, one is not aware
that there were any refugees aboard the *Arandora Star* at all.
There is the reference to 'enemy aliens trading in this country'
but there is a curious vagueness as to who these Germans and
Italians were. It is hard to escape the impression that *The Times*
writer is presenting everything in terms of 'our chaps', who of
course behave with heroic self-discipline and restraint, and 'the
aliens' who are (naturally) terrified and rush the boats in ugly
panic. (The 'great hulking brutes' of Germans, sweeping everyone else aside, bear a family resemblance to the brutal Huns
of popular fiction.) There certainly were Nazis aboard the *Arandora Star*, but there were lifelong and dedicated anti-Nazis too
and a number of German Jewish refugees. And not all the
Italians were Fascists. So the no doubt unintentional slanting of
The Times account anticipates in an interesting way the

subsequent government attempt to rationalize – not to say whitewash – the affair of the *Arandora Star*.

A German Jewish refugee gives a rather different account. He was one of several hundred internees at Warners Camp at Seaton in Devonshire. About two hundred and fifty of these were Nazis: some were seamen, brought to England on the ship *Adolf Woerman*; some were German businessmen caught in England when war broke out; there were even (according to this internee) some Gestapo agents.

There were also some two hundred Jews in the camp. Some of these had been put in Category A and had been interned by the aliens tribunals at the beginning of the war. These included refugees who had come to England without visas and those who had quarrelled with the refugee organizations – in fact the black sheep already mentioned; and others who for various reasons had managed to antagonize the judge at the tribunal.

In addition there were a large number of 'politicals' – dedicated anti-Fascists who had nevertheless been put into Category A. These included ex-International Brigaders from Spain; German trade unionists; Austrian Socialists; German Communist seamen; and many others.

Despite protests, the German Jews and the anti-Fascists were not separated from the Nazis in internment. All requests for segregation were refused; and this witness notes what has been remarked more than once, the formidable discipline and solidarity of the Nazis, the aggressive morale that could have made them a danger in the event of a German invasion.

Early in June the Nazis were sent away; it was said that they were being taken to Canada. On 30 June the remaining detainees at Seaton were brought to Liverpool. They were medically examined and then put on board 'a ship with two guns' (as this refugee describes it). The *Arandora Star*'s normal passenger capacity was doubled: a cabin intended for two accommodated four and so on, *pro rata*. Soon after he went on board, the refugee noticed that the Nazis who had left Seaton early in June were also on board. They were under the command of Captain Burfend of the *Adolf Woerman*. He goes on to say:

We left Liverpool at night. Many had relatives and wives in Liverpool, but could not see them. We were not allowed to walk on the promenade deck where armed guards were on patrol all the time. We had lifebelts in our cabins. But I noticed that there was no boat drill. There were 12 lifeboats with a capacity of 60 each; they were worn out. One of them was a motor-boat. There were very few sailors and officers on board but many soldiers . . . On 2 July at seven in the morning [*The Times* report says the attack occurred at 6 a.m.] a hollow explosion was heard in the engine-room. I tried to switch the light on – in vain.

He dressed and went up on deck. He went towards the lifeboats but was stopped by an armed guard. Then he crossed to the other side of the ship. There, men were throwing pieces of wood into the water. There was no discipline apparent; no officers or sailors to be seen. The refugee noticed that most of the life-rafts could not be used : they were tied down with wire, which could not be loosened without tools, although men were trying to undo them with their bare hands. Panic spread through the ship. He heard shots fired.

Later on I heard that internees were shot at, who wanted to go to the lifeboats, which were reserved for English soldiers only. But as the soldiers were not seamen they cut the ropes with an axe when the boat was only halfway to the water and were drowned.

The Nazis remained under the strict discipline of Captain Burfend. The refugee describes how they marched on to the deck in files of two : 'They had many seamen and brought down about seven lifeboats.' (Possibly this led to the reference to the burly Germans rushing the boats.) The refugee goes on :

I came to the upper deck; no lifeboats were left. Scenes of distress. A man hanged himself; a sixty-two-year-old Jew sat in despair on his suitcase and could not be persuaded to put on his lifebelt. The old and ill people in the decks below had no chance. Among them was the seventy-five-year-old Julius Weiss who had been in England for fifty years . . . I advised two soldiers who were still standing guard with drawn bayonets to throw away their bayonets and to spring into the water. They said they were not allowed to because they had not had an order but I persuaded them . . . As the boat heeled over I climbed down a rope ladder with a plank in my hand into the water. The decision to do so was very difficult for me. I swam away from the ship and saw it sink . . . It took thirty-five minutes from the explosion to the sinking of the ship. The water was full of oil; hundreds of planks and pieces of wood with barbed wire threatened us . . . the water was terribly cold, with fog and slight rain. Cries, prayers, shouts of 'Mother' by old and young in every language (Italian, German, English, Hebrew) depressed us terribly. Old people got heart attacks and died. Bodies swollen by water floated beside me . . . After about three hours a coastal aeroplane sighted us. It cruised about for hours over our heads, as if it wanted to tell us that rescue was coming . . . After six and a half hours I sighted one of our lifeboats. I swam to it. An English sailor, the first mate, was at the helm. I spoke to him in English, told him that I was quite exhausted, and asked him to take me into the boat. He said, 'Full up.' I held on the helm and implored the others in the boat, who drew me, quite exhausted as I was, into the boat.

The decision to deport as well as to intern appears to have been taken some time in June 1940, presumably by the War Office and the Home Office in conjunction. The decision and its implementation were alike obscure until the loss of the *Arandora Star* forced the whole issue into the light of Parliamentary debate. Then M.P.s were granted the unfortunate but hardly uncommon spectacle of ministers of the Crown being forced to disgorge the truth an inch at a time, conceding one painful fact after another – and then, slipping into the lineaments of the morning-coated British Government spokesman stereotype, angrily closing the whole matter as something that had, after all, been intended for the best. That hundreds of innocent lives had been lost was regrettable, but as Lord Cranborne was to say of another ship, the *Struma*, it was inevitable that people should become hardened to horrors. How typical of a crank like Josh Wedgwood to go on pressing the matter!

The government at first maintained (through Mr Cross, Minister of Shipping – not himself connected with deportation) that only aliens in Category A had been deported. Basing his statement on information provided by the Secretary of State for War, Anthony Eden (who was, of course, one of the ministers responsible), Mr Cross told Parliament on 9 July :

I am informed . . . that all the Germans on board were Nazi sympathizers and that none came to this country as refugees. None had Category B or C certificates or were recognized as friendly aliens.

This declaration drew protests from M.P.s who pointed out that many Category A internees were not only not Nazis but in fact had suffered infinite hardship, had risked their lives and forfeited their freedom in fighting Nazism. Mr Joseph Parker mentioned Louis Weber, a leading anti-Nazi in the German Seaman's Union, who had been drowned on the *Arandora Star*. Josh Wedgwood spoke of three dead Italians, lifelong anti-Fascists and enemies of Mussolini, who had been on the ship. Thus, in this first debate, the government's first lies were nailed: all those who had perished on the *Arandora Star* were *not* Nazi sympathizers. Moreover, according to Mr Cross's statement, inspired by Anthony Eden, the names of the dead anti-Fascists were being transmitted to their enemies the Nazis, through the Protecting Power (Switzerland).

Members pressed Mr Peake, the Home Office spokesman, for firmer details as to how the names of those on the *Arandora Star* had been selected; but both he and Sir Edward Grigg for the War Office tried hard to wriggle out of responsibility. Mr Peake prevaricated:

> the question of sending refugees and internees overseas is a decision that is not taken either by the Secretary of State for War or the Home Secretary. It is a decision taken by a Committee of the Cabinet, presided over by the Lord President of the Council [Neville Chamberlain].

Several Members then protested at Chamberlain's absence from the House.

It is tempting to lay most of the blame for deportation on the shoulders of the old appeaser and arch-trimmer, Chamberlain; but it must be apportioned over a wider area. After that first debate M.P.s dug out more facts about who had been on the *Arandora Star* and why and the whole question of deportation came under fire. Karl Olbrisch, a former Reichstag Deputy, who had spent some years in a concentration camp, had been drowned; and there were many others, both Jews and gentiles, who were proved to have been life-long enemies of Fascism. Category B and C internees were proved to have been deported, despite what had been said in Parliament. But the government spokesmen went on wriggling. On 16 July Anthony Eden said:

> It was understood by my department that none of these Germans were refugees, but I am making further enquiries on this point.

A day or so later Sir Edward Grigg promised a complete list of the dead and missing. This was on 17 July, but the list was not forthcoming until August. By then it had been revealed that no proper lists had been kept of those aboard the *Arandora Star*; and that the names of those to be embarked had been selected by means at best haphazard and at worst corrupt. It was said that personation had occurred; that some internees had paid other men to take their places aboard the ship. £15 was a sum commonly mentioned; as much as £100 was said to have been paid. It was also alleged that some internees had been forced on board by violence and the threat of violence. Some refugees had been kicked and beaten before they went on the ship. On 23 July Mr Eden promised to find out who had been responsible for choosing the passengers for the *Arandora Star*, but on 30 July he was still claiming that his department had chosen them from

Germans and Austrians who were in Category A and from Italians who were members of the Fascist party.

He added that all the Germans and Austrians aboard, 473 in number, had been placed in Category A. The next day Mr Peake admitted for the first time that there had been

considerable confusion owing to the amount of impersonation in regard to those sent to the Dominions.

At last on 6 August it was agreed that a special information bureau should be opened. On the same day, in a debate in the House of Lords, Lord Faringdon said:

I consider that whoever was responsible for these men and, after their internment, for their transportation, is accountable for their deaths.

The Duke of Devonshire, speaking in the same debate, was more matter-of-fact. Deportation had been decided on, he said, when the risk of invasion was imminent.

It seemed desirable both to husband our resources of food and to get rid of useless mouths and so forth.

It is not clear whether the duke was aware of the measures Hitler was even then taking to get rid of useless Jewish mouths; but the remark shows the robust freedom from inhibitions that characterized the Tory spokesmen in the Upper House. While their opposite numbers in the Commons paid at least some deference to humanitarian sentiment, these hereditary legislators spoke at times with an almost eighteenth-century realism.

The effect the loss of the *Arandora Star* was to have on public opinion was not immediately apparent, but the various debates that followed it opened up the whole question of deportation and thus of internment itself.

Deportation was first justified by the familiar Fifth Column bogy. On 10 July Mr Peake had told the Commons that Canada had agreed to take between six and seven thousand prisoners of war and internees. They had by then (10 July) 'now arrived there'. He went on to say

We have sent to Canada the most dangerous classes of internees, and where we have had to make up the number we have selected single men under the age of fifty and in preference those who wished to go . . .

The 'most dangerous classes of internees' clearly refers to the Fifth Column scare; 'those who wished to go' to another unpleasant aspect of deportation: the various inducements the authorities put before those whom they wished to 'volunteer' to go overseas. It was suggested to them that Hitler was coming; a Nazi invasion was imminent and naturally the Jews would be the first victims. Why not get out when they had the chance? Others were promised reunion with their relatives. An internee wrote to *The Times* on 6 August 1940:

On 10 July twenty-two married men left this camp [in the Isle of Man] voluntarily for overseas under a guarantee given to them in the name of the Command that their interned wives in Port Erin would accompany them in the same convoy. A week later it was admitted that the guarantees had not been kept. Furthermore letters from Port Erin dated 10 July say that all women there had been told on exactly the same day that their husbands would leave for overseas and it was hoped to reunite them at a later date. Apparently not even an attempt was made to fulfil the given guarantee. The twenty-two men left, trusting the word of the Command, as they had no possibility to communicate with their wives.

In this doubtful area of those who 'volunteered' come the schoolboys, some no more than sixteen, who were deported.

One afternoon early in May Ilsa Geiss was working in the garden of her cottage when she heard the sound of a car coming up the lane. It was a big, official-looking car and she recognized one of the men who got out of it: the police inspector from Colchester who had been so kind when she'd had to go before the tribunal there. The inspector said 'Good afternoon' and introduced his colleague, a detective-sergeant. She noticed an awkwardness in him; later, she thought of the burgomaster on that other sunny afternoon, some years before. 'Mrs Geiss, I have something to tell you . . .' She at once thought: Kurt has had an accident. He's fallen off his bicycle in front of a car and he's badly injured. She never for a moment thought of it being Maria. No, it was Kurt; he was at the Leys School, Cambridge, and he was allowed to use his bicycle within a radius of a few miles. She'd never felt happy about it.

The inspector appeared embarrassed. 'These new regulations. Concerning enemy aliens in the coastal belt. You probably heard it on the wireless. Cambridge comes within the specified area, Mrs Geiss.' But she still did not understand. 'Mrs Geiss, I am afraid your son has been detained as an enemy alien over the age of sixteen years within the provisions of the Order.'

She had wept, she had protested. 'No! He's only a child – a schoolboy!' She had demanded, 'Are we in England or is this Nazi Germany?' The inspector hadn't said anything; at last she had stopped, embarrassed for herself, for him. The inspector continued to look at her. It occurred to her that he had probably had no official orders to come and break this news; he was doing it out of kindness and here she was behaving like this. (She was right; she was soon to hear of other refugee mothers and wives who were to hear definite news of their interned sons or husbands only after weeks of hideous waiting.) Ilsa apologized; she was so anxious to end the inspector's embarrassment that the edge of her own anger was dulled.

A fortnight later she heard that Kurt was in Huyton camp. She got no letter; again the news came from the apologetic Essex police. And then began the worst time of all. Since she had come to live in Essex the postman had become part of the pleasant furniture of her rural life. She didn't get that many letters; her sister Gerda in Highgate usually telephoned the village shop when she was coming down, or Ilsa would call on her on the rare occasions when she went up to London. Now she lived for the post. She remembered a not very successful author of her acquaintance who had told her how the postman had dominated his life for years. Living in a remote part of Essex, struggling to establish himself, every joy and sorrow had come to him through a thin envelope that bore his literary agent's monogram on the flap. Ilsa had thought this absurdly dramatic: now she understood. The author had quoted 'a watched pot never boils', and every morning Ilsa tried to convince herself that she had missed Joe Trower's passing by the end of the lane. Watching from her front window she could see his head and shoulders glide along a short stretch of road between a clump of bushes and a telegraph pole: that meant he wasn't coming. If she didn't see him, it could mean that he had turned up the lane first and there might be a letter for her.

In fact she only got two letters in three months. One was a field service postcard from Huyton; the other a long and (considering the circumstances) not too unhappy letter from Canada. Kurt had been deported without her knowledge and, he maintained, without ever being asked whether he wanted to go or not. The Home Office later insisted that he had volunteered; Kurt said not. He had woken up one morning and been told that the commandant had been ordered to produce a further two hundred men for a draft that was going overseas: Kurt and other younger internees at Huyton were to make up this balance. In fact he did not complain too bitterly: he was young enough to regard the voyage as an adventure and had always cherished vague dreams of being a sailor. But some of the older men had cried and one had talked of suicide. (He achieved it four days later, jumping off the boat-deck in mid-Atlantic.) Another had been cuffed and kicked by the camp guards before he got on the lorry that took them to Liverpool. Kurt did not hear of anyone paying a substitute to go to Canada in his place.

Ilsa's original shock and anger had worn down to a generalized depression and anxiety long before she heard that Kurt was in Canada. And after that her sense of gratitude that he had not died in another *Arandora Star* disaster lightened her mood and gave her hope. As she says, she was of a naturally optimistic disposition; she overcame her bitterness at the paradox of Kurt's being interned as an 'enemy alien' when he was becoming so

British so quickly that she felt a sense of loss, wished he would speak German again, at least occasionally.

The reaction to the loss of the *Arandora Star* led to some attempt to regularize deportation procedures. After it the authorities appear to have tried to get genuine volunteers to go overseas.

Some of those who arrived in Canada complained of the severe climate and of the fact that they were shifted from camp to camp within a very short period. To their delight, however, the greatest hardship all the refugee internees had had to suffer was removed: they were no longer forced to endure their imprisonment with Nazis and Nazi sympathizers. In Canada, for the first time, there were exclusively Jewish and Aryan camps. In August 1940 the War Office sent a liaison officer to Canada. When the machinery of internment began to go into reverse and internees to be released, those in Canada were told that theoretically they were free but that they would have to remain in their camps until there was a ship available to take them back to the United Kingdom.

The German Jewish internees who travelled to Australia on the *Dunera* endured sufferings comparable with those of the unfortunates who had crowded into the Greek and Rumanian coffin-ships that carried them down the Danube to attempt illegal entry into Palestine. The crew of the *Dunera* treated the deportees abominably. They abused them; kept them prisoners in the holds for days on end; demanded money with threats of violence; denied them food and water; subjected the Jewish women to gross sexual insult. The arrival of these internees in Australia, depressed, outraged, and penniless, thousands of miles from the European civilization to which they belonged, is another black episode in the story of the refugees.

But the loss of the *Arandora Star* remained the significant catalytic disaster that changed British opinion. It dramatized the fact that Britain, practically the last free nation left in Europe, had in its attitude to the refugees abandoned the very ideals it was fighting for. The newspaper campaign, followed by the shock of the German sweep across Europe, induced a mood in which 'intern the lot' was accepted as a measure of patriotism and common sense. But that mood had begun to cool by August. After that it was increasingly seen as the most ridiculous nonsense ever devised to take in a people in a moment of great excitement

as Viscount Cecil put it. The harsh measures against aliens caused alarm not only among left-wingers and 'progressives' – the Kingsley Martins and the Josh Wedgwoods – but over a wide area of educated opinion. It was hard to avoid the feeling that the plea of military necessity was being used to excuse totalitarian measures that could be turned with equal ease against any other section of the population. The approach of the government to the refugee problem was seen to have been both muddled and devious from the beginning; and it was hard for decent people not to react with anger to the 'useless mouths' argument. The three months during which measures against 'enemy aliens' reached their peak also represent a highwater mark of influence for the considerable body of xenophobic and anti-semitic feeling in Britain (something to be examined in a later chapter). There was never any question of a plot; this was a mood rather than a movement or a disciplined lobby, but unlike the organized anti-semitism of Mosley's blackshirts it represented a deep-set reservoir of feeling, unorganized but pervasive and influential, and it was to know its greatest power during those months of May, June, and July 1940.

Chapter Six

WAR EFFORT

Although the debate in the House of Commons on 22 August 1940 reflected the high-point of Parliamentary reaction to internment and deportation, in the earlier debate of 10 July Sir John Anderson had already shown signs of modifying his attitude. It was announced on 23 July that the Home Office would consider releasing Category C internees who belonged to the groups that it had originally been decided should not be interned at all. Sir John explained that there was no question of reversing the policy on internment: it was merely being modified to achieve a position that (although this was not said) might have existed had not the government yielded to panic impulses. The Home Office set up an Advisory Committee and an Advisory Council. The committee consisted of Mr Justice Asquith; Sir Herbert Emerson, the High Commissioner for Refugees; and Sir Neill Malcolm, the former High Commissioner for Refugees from Germany. Sir John Anderson explained the functions of the committee: to assist him in 'the control of aliens of enemy nationality'. Its duties were to keep under review the application of the principles laid down in regard to the internment of enemy aliens and to make such suggestions to the Home Secretary as they thought fit; to advise him on any future proposals that might be made for modifying internment policy; to examine and make recommendations upon individual cases or groups of cases 'referred to them from time to time by the Home Secretary'. The Advisory Council was attached to the Refugee Department of the Foreign Office and consisted of Lord Lytton (of the Academic Assistance Council) as chairman; Sir Herbert Emerson (again) as vice-chairman; Sir Neill Malcolm; Eleanor Rathbone, M.P. (with Colonel Wedgwood the most consistent champion the German Jewish refugees had); and a number of others including Mr Graham

White (also a member of the 'refugees lobby' in Parliament) and – no doubt on the principle of checks and balances – Viscount Cranborne and Earl Winterton. The functions of the council were somewhat different from those of the committee. It might suggest measures for maintaining the morale of aliens 'so as to bind them more closely to our common cause'. Other objectives of the council were stated as being to review and to propose measures for the coordination of the various refugee committees and other organizations; to maintain contact with the various government departments concerned with refugees; to advise the Home Office as to the arrangements made for the welfare of enemy aliens in internment camps; and to make recommendations on the problem of finding occupation for enemy aliens in internment camps.

It will be seen that the Advisory Committee and the Advisory Council had different but complementary ends. The crux of all these admirable intentions, however, lay in the brief given to Mr Justice Asquith's committee – to keep under review 'the application of the principles laid down in regard to the internment of enemy aliens'. This still left all executive power with the government, leaving the committee to merely advise on policies decided from above. The scope of the Advisory Council was at first glance rather wider : its terms of reference suggested that the government was now prepared to listen to the people who knew something about internment's victims and effects. But, like the committee, the council had an essentially passive role. The general policy of internment was still in the hands of the government and both the committee and the council had to wait till the government referred specific questions to them.

Ancillary to the formation of the committee and the council was the issue of a White Paper in July. This set out various groups of internees who might be considered for release. Apart from age or infirmity, the criterion was essentially utilitarian – was the refugee in question doing work of 'national importance'? – and later that year Professor Lafitte was to write that the July White Paper was inspired by the same attitude as a farmer has to his horses or his cows – use them or lock them up.

All these measures were of a rather half-hearted and interim nature. As we have seen, the loss of the *Arandora Star* represented a climactic breaking-point for a large body of liberal and humanitarian feeling throughout the country; it found expression in the House of Commons debate of 22 August but it had already evoked protests from the *New Statesman*, the *Evening Standard* ('Why not intern De Gaulle?'), H. G. Wells (an article 'J'accuse'), and many other shapers and leaders of opinion. The first result was a second White Paper issued on 26 August. Although Sir John Anderson still adhered in principle to the policy of general internment, this White Paper widened the range of those eligible for release. These fell into nineteen categories. Three of these were defined by age – under sixteen and over sixty-five (already mentioned in the July White Paper) and those over sixteen but under eighteen if they were living with a British family or at school or living with a parent, step-parent, or guardian 'to whose care the Secretary of State is prepared to allow them to return'. Internees who had been discharged from the British Army 'on grounds not reflecting on their loyalty to this country or on their personal character' and any refugee with a British-born or naturalized son in the Forces was eligible for release. (If the son was himself a refugee in the Pioneer Corps, his parent was *not* eligible for release.) Those refugees who had been fortunate enough to win a place on the American immigration quota would be allowed to visit the United States Embassy to finalize the arrangements and would then be conducted under escort to the port of embarkation, only being 'released' when they actually boarded the ship.

The remaining categories were all determined by utilitarian considerations and specified various groups of refugees engaged on work of national importance. These included those with key jobs in industry; skilled workers in agriculture; employers of twelve or more British workers in work 'certified to be of value to the community'. Professional people like doctors (but only those already authorized to practise – through re-qualification – or approved to study for re-qualification), dentists, and ministers of religion (except of the German Churches); and academics – 'scientists, research workers, and persons of academic distinction for whom work of importance in their special field is available'. Men accepted for service in the Pioneer Corps could be released. And so could those engaged in work for the refugee organizations. The nineteenth and last category of those eligible for release consisted of those considered by a special tribunal to have 'publicly and consistently' opposed the Nazi system. This last class was obviously created to rebut the charge that the British Government had imprisoned some of Hitler's worst enemies.

The composition of this special tribunal was announced in September 1940. The chairman was Sir Cecil Hurst, a former president of the Permanent Court of International Justice at The Hague; Sir Andrew McFadyean, an eminent civil servant and expert on German war reparations; Dr Seton Watson, an expert on Central Europe; and Mr (later Sir) Ivone Kirkpatrick.

This tribunal faced a particularly hard task. More than most of the bodies dealing with aliens, they were chasing definitions. What was 'opposition'? How apply the words 'consistent' and 'public' in such a context? Most Jews were *ipso facto* opponents of a regime that persecuted them, but this opposition was unlikely to have been expressed in the kind of political action that the formula before the tribunal seemed to demand. And what about those who had worked against the Nazis in secret?

In fact this special tribunal seems to have interpreted its brief with humanity and common sense, as did the Advisory Committee and the Advisory Council and also the committees set up by the vice-chancellors of universities, the British Academy, and the Royal Society to judge the eligibility of academics and professional men for release. They performed the especially difficult function of defining 'work of importance in their special field' for those concerned with work in the arts or the 'humanities' far removed from the practicalities of any nation's war effort.

The debate of 22 August marked the defeat of the 'intern the lot' mentality, although this was to become apparent only gradually over the next year. Herbert Morrison succeeded Sir John Anderson as Home Secretary and thus became identified with official attitudes that were to become more liberal towards the refugees. The Socialist and ex-conscientious objector Morrison might be expected to be more liberal on an issue like internment than the ex-colonial administrator Anderson, but to see the change in terms of the personalities of these two very different men would be to falsify its nature. Politicians in a democracy rarely respond quickly to the intangible we label 'public opinion'; it works rather through a kind of subtle infiltrative process. 'Climates of opinion' do not change overnight. The August debate did not effect a general change of attitude to the internment of refugees: it was a signal that such a change was taking place.

It was left to an M.P. speaking in that debate to sum up the whole rationale of internment:

If an archangel appeared before all the members of the War Cabinet at once and said, 'There is one red-headed man in England who, unless care is taken, will do something to injure the State', I think it would be the duty of the War Cabinet to see that all red-headed men were interned. I should say it was their duty to do this at whatever cost in human misery, or whatever risk to what is called British prestige.

Enlistment in the Auxiliary Military Pioneer Corps (usually referred to simply as the Pioneer Corps) had a dual significance for any male German or Austrian Jewish refugee who was fit enough to join. Not only did it afford him an opportunity to serve against the Nazis who had proscribed and persecuted him and forced him into exile but, after August 1940, it offered him a chance of release from internment. Although it has never been suggested that the refugees who exercised this option and were released to join the Pioneers were in any way inferior as soldiers to those who had enlisted earlier, it was argued at the time that the choice presented was unfair. The refugee who chose to escape from internment through enlistment was neither volunteer nor conscript. He could not be expected to feel the simple patriotism of the national of any country, fighting a war against its enemies. If he was accepted for the Pioneer Corps and he happened to be waiting to re-emigrate, he might lose his place on the immigration quota to America when it came up, although he would have the consolation of being able to fight his enemies, the Nazis. (He would fight them, of course, without weapons, since at the beginning the Pioneers were a non-combatant corps. In May 1940 it was decided to arm the *British* members of the corps.) And what, it was further asked, would the refugees conceive to be their aims in fighting – apart from gratifying their loathing for the Nazis? Their war aims would scarcely coincide with those of such comrades-at-arms as the Fascist Prince Stahremberg or the various anti-semitic elements in the Polish Army in Britain.

In fact a majority of the refugees who enlisted in the Pioneers as a condition of release from internment appear to have done so from motives as uncomplicated as those that had moved earlier recruits. They wanted to fight Hitler; they wanted to cancel themselves in the physical life at a time when the exercise of memory and imagination was sometimes too agonizing to be borne. These considerations were more important to them than the question that hung over the Jewish members of the Pioneer Corps – and over them alone, of all the soldiers in the British Army – what would happen if the Germans took them prisoner? They could not expect the same treatment that would be accorded to any other prisoner of war. Of course there were many English Jews in all three services, but although these might be in some danger on capture, the risks they ran were small compared with those incurred by these German and Austrian Jews, assembled together in units which the German authorities knew to be made up of refugees.

During the war of 1939–45 the Pioneers evolved from a group of labour battalions to a highly organized corps, performing duties that would previously have been the function of the Royal Engineers, and there is no doubt that the refugees helped this development. The first recruitment of refugees was made at Kitchener Camp at Richborough in Kent. This camp was a relic of the First World War, a drab congeries of army huts which had not been used for many years. In 1939 a sub-committee of the Council for German Jewry had leased the area from the owners (not the War Department but the steel firm, Dorman Long) as a reception area for refugees, particularly those awaiting re-emigration. It was equipped to receive 3,500 men; skilled refugee craftsmen assisted with the work. The first parties arrived in February 1939 and by the outbreak of war in September the camp was housing its full quota of 3,500 men. Then, in November, the British Government decided to enlist up to 2,000 refugees into the Pioneer Corps and Kitchener Camp was established as a depot for the training of recruits.

One of the first of these recruits arrived in June 1939. He says:

Despite the circumstances in which I arrived there, I have happy memories of Kitchener Camp. I remember the day we arrived. I had been in a concentration camp – the 'little' camp at Buchenwald – after the November pogrom – Crystal Night – and we had been offered the chance of release – if we left Germany. The British Home Office offered to allow us in, if it was guaranteed that we would re-emigrate. Well, I had good hopes of that: I had an uncle and an aunt in New York, and at last they offered me the sponsorship that would get me on to the quota – in time . . . So I had to wait – but it got me the visa for England. It was marked 'for transit only' . . .

I remember the brilliant summer day we arrived. We had come to Dover via Ostend and I remember my first sight of Dover – and of England – the famous white cliffs and the castle like a toy over the town . . . The nearest town to Kitchener Camp was Sandwich and we arrived there by train from Dover. There were buses waiting to take us to the camp and I remember thinking how hot and dry it was, so unlike the idea Continental people usually have of England. I was young then – only twenty-one – everyone in Kitchener Camp was between eighteen and thirty-five – and I didn't know anyone else at the camp, but arrival was a moment of reunion for many people who did know each other – they were excited: laughing and shouting at being together – and free! Yes – because we were, even though we were in this camp and under control and had to get permits to leave for a moment – it didn't matter! – *free*, in a way we could no longer be in Germany . . .

I felt so happy at this that I loved everything about the camp. I didn't mind some of the things the older men disliked and kept complaining about, like the lack of privacy . . . What privacy had there been in Buchenwald? . . . We lived in huts, each divided into two compartments – each compartment held thirty-five to forty men, with a hut leader. Other huts were used as classrooms and there were lessons in English and other languages. We got pocket-money each week: sixpence and a twopenny halfpenny stamp. As I said, one had to get a permit to get out – one could go to London 'on business' – and 'business' was fairly liberally interpreted. We could go on walks into Sandwich and Ramsgate. I was fascinated by the old-fashioned atmosphere of Ramsgate – I'd never seen anything like it before. And Sandwich was a charming little town . . .

That was the time that a number of us made our first acquaintance with the English. They were not so 'different' as we had expected; some of us probably had ridiculous ideas of them as a race who wore little toothbrush moustaches and weighed up all foreigners through carefully focused monocle's – only to find that the damn fellas didn't come up to scratch! In their turn they probably thought of German Jews as noisy and hysterical, shouting and wheedling like Shylock in the *Merchant of Venice*. Everyone was wrong of course; and the strange thing is, quite a number of us who came to Kitchener Camp en route to America never went to America after all . . . We must have liked the English, to stay and become English ourselves . . .

In those few months before war broke out a kind of pattern of life emerged in the camp – with the language classes, the debates, and so on . . . it must have been a bit like the life of the internees on the Isle of Man except that we were free men and they were not – we didn't have the sense of being held prisoners as they did . . . And during the last month or so when it was obvious that war was inevitable and more and more men came from Germany, we did realize how fortunate we were to have got away at all . . . Even the classrooms were crowded with men sleeping anywhere they could find an inch of space . . . We spent our days filling sandbags – millions of them; I used to dream about filling sandbags . . . A separate camp was opened for women and children and a number stayed there for a couple of months till they were transferred to hostels in London . . . Perhaps because we were near the coast the war seemed quite near. I remember the first air-raid alarm that followed on Chamberlain's speech announcing that Britain was at war with Germany . . .

How did I come to join the Pioneer Corps? Two reasons, I think. One that the war had stopped re-emigration – for the time being anyway – and thus one did feel trapped at Richborough. That was what one might call the negative aspect. The more positive one was the chance to do something against the Nazis, even though it was emphasized at the beginning that this was to be a non-combatant corps . . . We knew we were going to be used for labour duties and not for fighting the enemy and yet we felt great pride in being soldiers . . We had an English officer in charge of us and the non-commissioned officers who trained us were old soldiers who had been in the First World War. They were very correct; they didn't bully us – on the contrary, we got the impression that some of them were letting us down lightly because we were 'foreigners' and we would have preferred it if they hadn't. Some of us complained at the amount of squad drill – just marching up and down, 'right wheel', 'left wheel', and so on – we got at the beginning. We would have loved to have rifles and have learned how to use them . . . And yet – unarmed as we were, we did get the feeling we were in the British Army – if only because the whole atmosphere discouraged the few who although they were Jews – perhaps this sounds rather ridiculous in the circumstances – still tried to have a 'German', almost 'Prussian' attitude to being in the Army. Somehow this wasn't possible in the British Army. The atmosphere was all wrong for heroics : it was civil service, almost, with King's Regulations and

Army Council Instructions being quoted all the time . . . The presence of the depot at Kitchener Camp altered the whole set-up there. Those at the camp who did not enlist provided services for the military depot – cleaning the quarters and so on – although like all soldiers we had to do our share of fatigues. However, since we'd been doing these menial jobs ever since we arrived at the camp, this wasn't any great hardship for us . . .

Once we'd got our basic training, of course, we wanted to get away on active service, like any other soldiers anywhere . . . This was in January 1940 and we stayed at Richborough till February when we heard the rumour that we were going overseas. One morning – this was the end of February – about 800 of us were formed up and got into buses which took us into Sandwich. It was all rather like the first day, except that now it was damp and cold instead of sunny, and we went from Newhaven. We were posted to the B.E.F. as Line of Communications troops, although we operated mostly in the Pas de Calais area, which was really the Base. We were doing mainly the preliminary labour for constructional work, sometimes under the direction of the Royal Engineers. A lot of the time we were helping build transit camps and holding camps – putting down concrete paths and digging drains: that sort of thing . . . Then when the Germans attacked and started to move across France, we were moved to Gravelines on the coast near Dunkirk. There were rumours that things were so bad that we were going to be issued with rifles and machine-guns and would help to fight the rearguard action to cover the Dunkirk evacuation, but this didn't happen . . . After a day and a night being bombed on the beaches at Dunkirk we finally got away. When we landed in Britain we were sent to another Pioneer depot in the west of England – because of the removal of aliens from the coastal areas the one at Kitchener had to be closed down . . .

In the debate of 22 August Colonel Arthur Evans, Member for Cardiff South had described how two companies of refugees had in fact taken up arms and fought the Germans. He had been commanding the Havre Defence Force, which had included some 600 refugees. In the final desperate stand against the German onslaught Colonel Evans had decided to arm these non-combatants, giving them a rifle and 50 rounds of ammunition apiece. Within a few hours they had learned how to handle not only the service rifle but also machine-guns and anti-tank rifles, and they manned various strong-points against the arrival of the German armoured columns. 'They conducted themselves,' Colonel Evans

WAR EFFORT 223

said, 'in a manner worthy of the best traditions of the British Army.' He added that once these refugees had returned to England they were again disarmed and put into non-combatant battalions.

The refugee who has already been quoted served for a further two years in the Pioneer Corps. Then, Army regulations having been broadened to allow for transfers and for aliens serving in the Pioneers to be commissioned in other branches, he applied for a commission in 1942.

We were stationed at a big camp at a place called Pollokshields, outside Glasgow. I was a corporal by now and a friend of mine in the company office had informed me that a directive had come round saying that aliens – refugees – could apply for commissions in certain other arms. I think they had men with technical qualifications in mind. I had done a year studying electrical engineering in Frankfurt, so I thought – Why not? I was happy enough in this unit, but it was a negative life: I was at an age when one wants to be tested to one's limit and I was roughly in the position of a foreman in the building trade. The men under me knew just as well as I did what had to be done . . . The real planning was usually done by an officer of C.R.E. [Commander Royal Engineers] 's office in the area. The officer in command of our company never struck me as at all interested in the jobs we, as Pioneers, were doing; in fact, he even seemed to resent them. He had been a regimental sergeant major in an infantry regiment and perhaps thought of the Pioneers as a bit of a come-down. On the other hand he might not have got a commission in his original unit – I'm only guessing now: I have no evidence to support that. Captain — would hand us over to the Engineers, so to speak, for the work we had to do, but all his energies went into what the army calls 'bull'. He was the first Pioneer officer I had encountered who was like this: mostly they were very practical. But Captain — loved parading us in full marching order for inspection. I doubt if even the infantry had as many inspections as we had at Pollokshields. It made life very difficult for us because often we would be very tired and dirty from the actual work we were doing – our denims covered in filth and mud – and you can imagine what our boots would be like . . . And then to get back, with maybe fifteen minutes to eat a meal, and then be required to be out on parade in full band-box bullshit order maybe ten minutes later. (Originally he had us scrub our web equipment white and have our boots highly polished; but this was against regulations in 1942; he had to settle for green blancoed equipment and dubbined boots.) He would inspect our sleeping-quarters and would go mad if the surface of the sand in the fire-buckets was at all disturbed...

Anyway, I went before this officer and made an application for transfer to a Royal Engineer O.C.T.U. [Officer Cadet Training Unit]. He was not sympathetic. He cross-examined me about my engineering studies in Frankfurt and of course he was trying to minimize them, make them sound like nothing! His attitude was: these are your rights; you shall have them – but only according to the letter of the law. He started on to me about the work of the unit – and this confirmed what I had always felt about his attitude to the things the company was actually doing: that the real business of the army was soldiering – by which was meant boot-polishing and button-polishing, not laying drainpipes and making concrete paths. He said, 'If you're going to be an officer, well – you'll have to smarten up! An officer has to know something beside digging trenches. An officer has to be seen to command – he has to make the smartest man in the unit look like a raw squaddie.' I couldn't help feeling that he was outraged at the idea of this foreign Jewboy – from Germany too! – holding the King's Commission that meant so much to him personally... Again, I've no proof I'm right and you may think this the typical persecution complex of the refugee. I can't say that he was unfair to me. He forwarded my application for a commission – but he took care to take me off all Pioneer duties and put me on what I can only call bullshit duties exclusively – guard-commander, dining-hall N.C.O., N.C.O. in charge of indoor fatigues and so on. This ostensibly was to give me necessary experience, to fit me for the regimental duties of an officer, but I wonder...

This refugee eventually got his commission in the Royal Engineers and served in North Africa and Italy. As he says, he never persisted in his original aim of emigrating to America: he was naturalized a British citizen in 1946.

No single testimony is ever wholly representative, but the experiences of other German and Austrian Jews who won commissions in the Forces parallel that of this refugee. Many of them remark on the essentially civilian-turned-soldier nature of the army they served in – a contrast to the Germanic idea of an select officer corps dominating an army that took civilians and ground them into precision parts functioning smoothly at its behest. Few complain that there was any prejudice against them because they were Jews or foreigners, although several describe the rueful attitude of old-sweat officers to their own ambitions. The refugees who were content to remain in the ranks did not, of course, encounter these problems. It is no doubt easier to preserve one's essential selfhood as a private soldier; easier to remain anonymous in the Other Ranks' dining hall than in the Officers' Mess.

Certainly many senior officers took the attitude that the refugees were very temporary guests in Britain. It was decent of them to join us in fighting the Germans, but doing so did not entitle them to call themselves British. C. C. Aronsfeld mentions the War Office dignitary who told an assembled company of Pioneers that he hoped that 'the adventurous spirit which had brought them to this country would take them far afield at the end of the war'.

This was plain speaking. But by 1946 over four thousand refugees had been naturalized and some of them had established their right to be British citizens by the best method of all – by fighting Britain's enemies in the British Army.

One might expect that of all the refugees one group might have escaped internment: the scientists. Not because of any reverence the government might feel for their intellectual attainments or because they differed socially or politically in any way from their fellows, but from purely utilitarian motives. The scientists – particularly the physicists – were in a position to make a unique contribution to the war effort.

The government seemed quite unaware of this. Like every government, it contrived to split itself into diverse and often mutually opposed entities. The Home Office, concerned with the internment of enemy aliens, saw no reason to consult the Ministry of Aircraft Production or the other agencies involved with the successful prosecution of the war on the technical side. The blanket internment of enemy aliens took no account of the scientists working at the Cavendish Laboratory in Cambridge, for instance. Cambridge came within the scheduled coastal area; the scientists in question were enemy aliens; that was enough, they were interned. There were other scientists – some of them of European reputation – living and working outside the proscribed area; as the net was drawn tighter, they too were interned. If Germany had chosen to weaken herself by expelling her best scientists, then British prejudice and hysteria threatened to rob the war effort of the imagination and expertise of some of those same scientists, now exiled in laboratories and universities throughout Britain.

As we have seen, the equivocal Lindemann, making snide jokes about Jews, had yet contrived to rescue German Jewish scientists like Kürti, Mendelssohn, Kuhn, and Simon. There were many others, who reached Britain in many different ways. The famous physicist Otto Frisch had worked at the University of Hamburg; he was forced to leave Germany soon after Hitler came to power and the Academic Assistance Council granted him a fellowship at Birkbeck College. Later he went to Copenhagen to work with the great Nils Bohr. Then, in 1939, he returned to England. Herbert Froehlich left Germany in 1933 and went to the Soviet Union. After less than a year there he came to Britain and worked at Bristol University. Dr Schlesinger came to Loughborough after nearly thirty years as a professor at Charlottenburg to head a department of the Institute of Production Engineers. Professor Rudolf Peierls (son of a former director of the A.E.G. in Germany) also came to Britain after the Nazi takeover. Probably the most dramatic advent of all was that of Hans Halban and Lew Kowarski. They had been working in France with Professor Joliot and in 1940 they escaped to Britain, leaving only hours before the Nazis arrived, sailing on one of the last ships to leave before the fall of France.

All these and many others were in Britain when internment began. Was this unmeasurable total of skill and knowledge to be spilt behind the walls of Brixton, to moulder inside the barbed-wire fences on the Isle of Man?

Fortunately there was one man who was not prepared to allow this to happen. Dr C. P. Snow was working in Whitehall as an administrator concerned with the scientific aspects of winning the war. Already well-known as both scientist and novelist, he was not yet identified with the attempt to bridge the scientific and humanistic elements of our fragmented culture. At once he set about trying to get the interned scientists released.

He faced indifference and an official obscurantism that drew strength from the confusion that attended the fall of France. But he persisted. For days he had to badger the Home Office to find out where individual scientists were interned (it will be remembered that the documentation of internees was often chaotic), and even when he had this information he had to persuade the Home Office that it was in the national interest to reverse a decision only recently arrived at. Officials naturally shrink from making exceptions that will weaken their ordinances and Dr Snow had to convince the Home Office that the experience and talents of this particular group were such that the government simply dare not let these men stay behind bars.

Today Lord Snow says he was fortunate. 'I happened to be in a position where I knew I would be listened to.' Despite this disclaimer, it seems likely that the creator of Lewis Eliot must have brought into play some of the political arts he has analysed in his great novel-sequence. His request was agreed to: certain refugees would be released to do work of scientific importance.

It seemed he had won. Then the Ministry of Aircraft Production announced that the release of the men he had asked for was to be confirmed – but that none of them were to be allowed to work on radar. Radar was, of course, the immediate technical obsession of the British Government and it was rendered immensely urgent by the Luftwaffe attacks on London which had just begun. The security aspects of radar were such, the authorities said, that only those British subjects with native-born British parents were to be allowed to work on it.

Snow had won – and yet it seemed a victory without point. These refugees were to be prevented from working on the very project where their knowledge and talent were so urgently required. They were to be released. But to do what? He was convinced that these German and Austrian Jews were indispensable to the British war effort and yet it had been decided that they could not be used where they were most wanted. How could they be used then?

After some thought he drafted a memorandum to his superiors. He also wrote to a number of British scientists whom he knew. These included Sir John Cockcroft, Professor George Thomson, and Professor P. M. Blackett. Was there any way, he wanted to know, in which the talents of these refugees could be used in the national interest?

In due course the scientists he had approached replied that there were indeed many ways in which the refugee chemists and physicists could be utilized. There was a line of research being pursued on which they could fruitfully be employed. This was a project under the control of the Maud Committee. The Ministry of Aircraft Production decided that as this was of no immediate importance to the war effort they had no objection to refugees being employed on it. They added that the foreign scientists were to be subjected to rigid surveillance as enemy aliens. They must register with the police and report to them frequently; they must not own motor cars, bicycles, or maps; they must stay in the same area and not move from it without official permission; they must obey a nightly curfew and be in their homes by 10 p.m. each night. These were virtually the same restrictions that had applied to Category B aliens, but still more rigorously applied.

This was to be expected. What mattered was that the refugees were, after all, to be used. Among others Dr Frisch and Dr Rotblat were to report to Liverpool University; Dr Brotscher, Dr Halban, Dr Kowarski, and Dr Freundlich to the Cavendish Laboratory at Cambridge. Dr Peierls went to Birmingham University – later he was to be joined by Dr Klaus Fuchs, one of the few gentiles among the refugee scientists, who was later to achieve a dubious fame by passing information to Russia.

The project 'not of national importance' on which these and other scientists were working was to become the Manhattan Project: the development and manufacture of the Atomic Bomb.

From the autumn of 1940 onwards refugees began to be released from internment. At the beginning a trickle, the releases had become a flood by the middle of 1941. The bulk of the internees on the Isle of Man were released under the various categories laid down in the White Paper of August 1940. Others were found jobs through the labour exchange on the Isle of Man. Eight hundred internees came back from Australia; nearly a thousand from Canada. A large number of the younger men, of course, had joined the Pioneer Corps; many more, both men and women, went into wartime industry. Hugo Neher continued to work in a factory in Sheffield, making the sights for anti-aircraft guns. Lothar Kahlmann had been moved from Brixton to the Isle of Man; he was released in the middle of 1941 and sent to a factory at Enfield on the outskirts of London. There he sewed buttons on to army uniforms. Mr Sachs remained in the offices of the chemical firm in Devonshire, achieving an industrious but peaceful war, during which he experienced only one air-raid alarm. Ilsa Geiss was re-united with her son Kurt, who had returned from Canada under the provisions of the White Paper and was being allowed to continue his education. Early in 1941 Helga Zinn was released from the Isle of Man on being accepted for training as a nurse.

These, like all the refugees, had been eager to forget the shock and insult of internment: to cancel the months of corroding idleness in work that would stretch them to the utmost. But both among the internees and the minority that had escaped internment were some who lacked any work in which they could submerge the past – because they were too old or too ill or because they eluded all the occupational pigeon-holes. Mostly they had stayed in London before internment and now they found themselves returning to a different city. When London had welcomed them, however indifferently and coldly, some time between 1933 and 1939, they had been baffled by its general vastness and anonymity and by such details as the fact that Hampstead bedsitters had no central heating or that freezing draughts – a continual subject of discussion but never rectified – appeared to be part of the British way of life. All that seemed trivial now. Large areas of London had been devastated by the first mass raids of summer 1940 and through the winter of that year the attacks grew worse. For those refugees who lacked absorbing employment life narrowed into a routine dominated not by the conventional markers of day and night, meals and sleep, going to a job and returning from it; but by the moment when, dusk having entered fully into darkness, the sirens wailed the Alert. The drone of the bombers would follow within minutes or even seconds and then the anti-aircraft barrage would open up: a sky-filling, brain-deadening bedlam that some found comforting – 'At least you know our boys are hitting back at the bastards!' – and others professed to find more frightening than the bombs themselves.

However loud the barrage, the bombs would begin to fall within the first five minutes. The particular horror of this form of attack lies in the helpless role imposed on those enduring it on the ground: the blind, arbitrary way the bombs come whistling down. In theory, at least, it is possible to flee from an artillery bombardment. Terrifying as it is, those who suffer it know it is directed at them by other men; but an air-raid has a particularly fateful savagery: you can run from the blast of one bomb straight into the path of another. Those who endured the London blitz know that if lightning never strikes twice in the same place bombs certainly can. Yawning, bleary-eyed in the grey blitz morning, people wondered what the next night would bring – what tonight would bring in fact, not eight hours away now . . . Looking at buildings that had escaped destruction night after night, they would reflect that these were places to avoid: they must be hit soon – and imagine being trapped in there . . . When the Alert went, the refugees enjoyed the same alternatives as the native Londoner. They could risk death or entombment in their own home; they could go to a private air-raid shelter in a garden or basement – which might or might not offer some degree of safety; they could go to public shelters, where bunks and other facilities were provided – safer again, perhaps, but public shelters had been hit quite often, with dreadful results; they could laboriously carry food and bedding to the nearest Underground railway station and spend the night there – perhaps the safest choice of all.

Each course had its disadvantages. If the refugee went to a shelter shared with neighbours or to a public shelter he or she might clash with people suffering stresses at least as great as their own. The weight of danger and uncertainty, coupled with enforced propinquity, had a dual effect: it broke down reserve, made strangers talk to each other, created the comradeship Londoners were to recall with a rueful nostalgia many years later; at the same time it aggravated class resentments and jealousies which sometimes exploded in abuse and even threats of physical violence. Many people, including many refugees, avoided the public shelters; they preferred to take a chance in their homes or go to the Underground.

One woman who was released on medical grounds after a short period of internment on the Isle of Man returned to Chelsea in September 1940. After describing the tension and monotony of a life dominated by the air-raid siren she says:

At first I used to go to a shelter at the corner of the street I lived in and the King's Road. There were bunks there and the same people came to the shelter every night and reserved the same bunks. They were families, a lot of them, and most of them knew each other. They were clannish and you could see they resented any 'outsider' who came in. No one was nasty to me because I was a foreigner, but I was conscious of their stare when I entered the shelter – you know the feeling: that people are watching you and not saying anything. The shelter warden too – he was a nice man, an elderly Scotsman who'd been in the First World War – but I could see he would watch me when the Alert was on and we could hear the bombs actually falling. Perhaps he expected me to get hysterical and start screaming – because I was a foreigner! I don't know . . . Some of the English women got pretty hysterical as a matter of fact and I don't blame them, but some put on a big performance as soon as the raids started.

They would sing songs – 'Roll out the Barrel' was one favourite – and a big fat woman would conduct. If you didn't join in loud enough, she'd shout to you to get some air in your lungs and give us the old heave-ho! . . . This fat woman was a Mrs Clegg and although they all laughed at her – *with* her, really – some of the other women seemed a bit afraid of her. The men in the shelter were mostly old and they seemed more subdued. Mrs Clegg was the dominant personality in the shelter. She was always telling dirty jokes too: some of them I couldn't see the point of at all . . . Everyone roared with laughter, but I didn't laugh and, again, I felt that, not laughing, I was disapproved of . . . As I say, no one was ever rude but I didn't feel at home – although 'at home' is a ridiculous phrase to use about an air-raid shelter, I suppose. You understand what I mean, though . . . I decided to find another shelter where the atmosphere was less overpowering – less full of of the cockney good fellowship that a sad, sick woman from Vienna could not appreciate.

Clearly this woman suffered from the chronic feeling of exclusion that beset many German and Austrian Jews during their first months and even years in Britain. Did the occupants of that Chelsea shelter really resent her or did she herself resent their very different manners and attitudes? She goes on:

I felt so unhappy going to that shelter night after night – and, a bit later, by day too – that I decided to go to another one farther from my home. This was in a church in Upper Cheyne Row, the church of the Holy Redeemer. It was in the crypt of the church and as the church was a great massive building I think I and a lot of others felt it would be safe – perhaps being a church helped too, although I'd never been religious in any way . . . Anyway, I started going there, although it was farther from where I lived.

Then one day, in the middle of September I think it was, there was a day-time alert. Again, for some reason, I never feared the day-time air raids so much – until this one! Somehow you seemed more vulnerable at night. It was about a quarter past six, a perfect autumn evening, and we all went down the crypt as usual. It was very crowded – more and more people seemed to be coming to the Holy Redeemer from other shelters. There were bunks in the crypt but of course no one went to them at that time . . . I don't know why, but I felt much safer here than at the other shelter – perhaps for superstitious motives, as I say – and this illusion of safety persisted even after the bombing started. The people were all crowded towards the centre of the crypt: the atmosphere was quite different from the other shelter; there was no singing or jokes; people just talked and everything was much quieter . . .

I happened to be sitting behind a pillar – there were these tremendous pillars going right up from the foundations into the body of the church . . . That pillar must have saved me. Unlike other times – in the other shelter – we didn't hear any individual bombs whistling down, just a great vague roaring from above . . . And then the bomb fell . . . I actually didn't *hear* it at all. I suppose I lost consciousness for a minute or two: it was like getting a tremendous blow on the forehead. I couldn't see anything and I was deaf for some seconds too. My head was ringing; it was like waking up in a strange place and you can't believe you're there. There was a lot of smoke and that made me cough and prevented me seeing much at first. I heard afterwards that the bomb had set fire to a lot of coke that was stored in the crypt for heating the church . . . Then I began to *see* – and sometimes I wish I'd been blinded, at least temporarily, because I can still see what was in that crypt and it was so terrible . . . The bomb had come straight down through the church and into the centre of the shelter . . . The place was piled high with dead bodies – the people had been so close together that the bomb had killed them and pulped their flesh together in one huge sponge-like mass. Heads and arms and bodies were all mangled together. Blood was running along the floor – it was like a burst water-main, except that this was blood from the crushed flesh that had once been living people . . . Blood ran around my legs and soaked me and it was all warm and sticky . . . There was a terrible stench and at the other end of the crypt a child was screaming . . .

Even now, thirty years later, this woman dwells on every detail of her experience with self-tormenting intensity, creating a vision of suffering humanity that recalls the tortured art of Hieronymus Bosch. People were literally blown to pieces on this and many similar occasions. Civil defence workers had the ghastly task of piecing corpses together in preparation for burial. Somehow the portions of shattered flesh and bone had to be assembled into sufficient likeness of a human body for the poor remains to be put into a coffin and decently buried. No one suggested that these pathetic groupings of limbs and heads and torsos were not quite arbitrarily assembled, made up piecemeal from the jumbled remains that filled the mortuaries; but this way, at least, the decencies were observed.

The refugee quoted remained in hospital for a week following the Holy Redeemer raid. On her discharge she went to the country, to stay with a cousin near Bath. This cousin, the widow of a wealthy merchant in Stuttgart, had left Germany early in 1933 and had been able to bring most of her money with her. She insisted that her relative stay with her indefinitely; and so, slowly, this 'sick, sad woman from Vienna' was able to recover. For years after the war she was not able to return to London without experiencing trembling, headache, and other symptoms of anxiety; and when she did choose to live in London again it was in Highgate, a considerable distance from the Chelsea that held such hideous memories for her.

Many other refugees had similar experiences, endured similar horrors during the bombing of London by the Luftwaffe. Those who struggled night after night to the underground stations were usually safe. Some of them say that they were welcomed into the kind of instant community life the air-raids engendered. Indeed, they date their first real contact with English people from those long nights spent huddled together on a railway platform. As one woman recalls:

I'd never really talked with an English person before. Not what you would mean when you'd say *conversed*. Talking to the landlady was hardly conversing. It was just 'Don't do this' or 'You must do that' with her – and 'Yes' or 'No' on your part and that was all. And 'good morning' to the postman and to the odd policeman who knew you because you had to report to his station. No one else. And then in Swiss Cottage station to really talk to English people! The mother of a family maybe: worried just as you were worried; thinking the thoughts you thought. I was happy then –

never mind the feet aching and the children crying and annoying the old woman on the other side of us who wanted to get to sleep.

These shelter friendships no doubt resembled traditional shipboard friendships in that they did not often survive the interlude that created them, but they served to break down the diffidence the refugees often felt towards 'the aloof English'. (Many of them still cherished the stereotype of the reserved, emotionally strangulated Englishman; monosyllabic in talk, arctic in emotion.) True community thrives on shared experience; feelings of brotherhood owe more to sufferings endured together than to any number of rhetorical exhortations.

Comparatively few of the refugees had been able to join the civil defence organizations at the outbreak of war. Some of these few were interned in 1940. When they were released, a number of them went to work in factories or joined the Pioneer Corps. But there were refugees involved in civil defence: in Air Raid Precautions, in the Auxiliary Fire Service, and of course detachments of alien Pioneers were engaged on clearing areas devastated by bombing.

When one remembers that the end of the phoney war and the beginning of the real war coincided with the traumatic assault on the refugees' liberty and emotions represented by internment, it must be said that the contribution of the German and Austrian Jewish refugees to the British war effort was generous and wholehearted. It is tempting but too facile to see in this the beginning of identification, of a complete assimilation with the British way of life. Certainly some of the older refugees were to see in the attitude of the younger generation of refugees a rejection of their German heritage that manifested itself in a disinclination to speak German among themselves and an almost exaggerated assumption of English social *mores* (paradoxically, an identification comparable with the 'gentilism' that is sometimes described as a feature of German Jewry). But this was to come later. And it must be remembered that the majority of refugees were still in Britain on sufferance. In 1940 and 1941 most of them were still officially expected to emigrate to America or Palestine. Although many of them felt grateful to Britain, few as yet felt any strong identification with her. It was not yet a case of 'If I love you, what's that to do with you?'

Chapter Seven

ENTRENCHED ATTITUDES

It is said that Chaim Weizmann met Lord Rothschild in the shelter of the Dorchester Hotel at the height of the blitz. Lord Rothschild was trying to calm his three small sons who were naturally afraid of the din unleashed above and around them. 'Why don't you send the boys to America?' Weizmann asked. 'If I sent those three miserable little things over,' Lord Rothschild said, 'the world would say that seven million Jews are cowards.'

If that answer had come from some penniless German or Austrian Jew, recently released from internment, it could be attributed to the awareness of rejection, the anticipation of hostility, that afflicted many refugees. But Lord Rothschild was British: bearer of a name so internationally famous that it transcended any merely Jewish significance; rich, successful, self-assured. Yet his rueful words indicate some worm of insecurity working behind the surface acceptance.

Any account of the German and Austrian Jewish refugees cannot avoid considering the various anti-semitic elements in British life. One says 'elements' because, unlike the rabid, endemic anti-semitism of Tsarist Russia or the calculated, fanatical anti-semitism of Germany, anti-semitism in Britain has never worked as a single identifiable force in public affairs. Rather has it expressed itself in many different ways at different times. It has appeared among various groups in varying degrees of intensity. Since the time of Edward I and the accusations of ritual murder at Norwich, it has never existed as a mass impulse that caused angry mobs to attack the Jews; among politicians only Oswald Mosley made anti-semitism definite policy. In the century that preceded the coming of the German Jewish refugees, many Jews achieved high places in British life. As we have seen, Disraeli's progress from young oriental exquisite to Earl of Beaconsfield, Prime Minister of England and confidant of the queen drew the eyes of European Jewry towards Britain in a kind of yearning admiration; and his triumph foreshadowed the acceptance of many rich or talented Jews into the English ruling class. In 1871 an Act of Parliament allowed a Jew to hold any office of state and after 1885 Jews could sit in the House of Lords, so that they now had full civil rights. It was during this period that the great banking and financial families like the Montagus, the Barings, the Albus, and the Hambros consolidated their position. There was nothing in Britain to compare with the corpus of pseudo-scientific anti-semitism that was being created in Germany, while the hatred generated by the Dreyfus case in France must have seemed mere Gallic hysteria in English clubs and drawing rooms. Later, Edward VII had his *Hof-Jude* in the person of Sir Edward Cassel.

But there was always some feeling against the Jews: an anti-semitic undertow that expressed itself sometimes subtly, occasionally in crude aggression. Its manifestations are important to the story of the German Jewish refugees because a strand of anti-Jewish feeling – always real, if rarely emphasized or even acknowledged – ran through the thoughts and emotions of the men who formed the Establishment that was to seek to appease Germany; at first to turn its eyes from the German persecution of the Jews and later to impose the stranglehold of a financial guarantee on the refugee organizations; to acquiesce in a newspaper campaign against 'enemy aliens' and then, a few months later, to intern them. At no time could the government be accused of definite anti-semitic bias; but it would be naïve to suppose that certain anti-Jew and anti-foreigner attitudes, working their way downwards through the mass consciousness, did not colour thoughts and affect decisions.

In 1930 Harold Nicolson was a guest at the house of Leonard and Virginia Woolf. The company was discussing the nomination board for the Foreign Office. Someone mentioned how the most suitable candidates would sometimes not come forward for fear of being 'ploughed' for social reasons. Afterwards Nicolson wrote in his diary :

The awkward question of the Jews arises. I admit that this is the snag. Jews are far more interested in international life than are Englishmen, and if we opened the service it might be flooded by clever Jews. It was a little difficult to argue this point frankly with Leonard there. [Leonard Woolf was, of course, Jewish.]

This can be compared with C. C. Aronsfeld's mention of a civil servant in the Patent Office who confirmed Heine's observation that Jews were tolerated in England provided they were kept within certain limits. (In the Patent Office, at that time, there was one Jew in a staff of three hundred.)

Nicolson's diary entry reflects the British ambivalence of attitude towards the Jews – the British Jews, of course, not foreign refugees. Nicolson's attitude is cool, not ill-natured – but it assumes that certain limits have to be set and that the moral propriety of setting them does not arise at all. His use of the word 'clever' is significant ('the service might be flooded by clever Jews'): it strikes one of the basic nerves of anti-Jewish prejudice. Jews are usually cleverer than their gentile neighbours; therefore they are likely to take advantage of them; therefore they must be excluded from the arena. But no one wants to be beastly to them, provided they have the good sense to know their place and stick to it. It is even possible to be friends with them – if they know how to behave.

This is a long way from acceptance, but it is also far removed from the excesses of anti-semitism. It could best be described as a policy of 'containing' the Jews in a firm but gentlemanly manner. Like most deep-seated English attitudes, it is something to be rarely acknowledged and never analysed. It is reflected most clearly in some of the stories and plays that set Jewish characters at odds with an English environment.

Galsworthy's play *Loyalties*, produced in London in 1922, poses the question: what price must the Jew pay to be accepted by English society – in this play, 'society' in its narrowest sense. Galsworthy, with his keener sense of social than of emotional dilemmas, shows that as the price for a qualified acceptance the Jew De Levis must behave with monstrously exaggerated 'good form'. Staying in a country house near Newmarket he is robbed of a thousand pounds. When he reacts with normal and justifiable anger, his hosts are enraged with him rather than with the thief, who turns out to be the most pukka of officers, a brilliant horseman with a gallant war record. Of course all the characters in the play sympathize with the officer, Captain Ronald Dancy. 'Even if he did [steal the thousand pounds] I'll stick to him and see him through it,' one of his friends proclaims. His hostess says, 'When it comes to the point, why shouldn't we [side with Dancy]? It's in the blood.'

While one cannot doubt Galsworthy's detachment and integrity, the force of the play is somewhat diminished by the unlikable character of the Jew De Levis – he is altogether too pushing and vindictive – and the audience's sympathies must swing against him when the thief Dancy commits suicide and the suffering of Dancy's innocent young wife must be attributed to the revengefulness of De Levis. And yet Galsworthy may have intended to strengthen his parable by loading the scales against De Levis who is, after all, the victim, with all the right on his side. What English society seems to be saying to the Jew is: Be like us, in dress, in speech; play our games; think like us – and we will accept you – within limits. But *Loyalties* suggests that the price of such acceptance can be too high to ever be paid; that the acceptance is never genuine when it becomes a question of what one of the characters in the play describes as 'like football – you want your own side to win'.

Loyalties deals with the English Jew coming to terms with the society he was born in. When we come to foreign Jews, the myth invoked is cruder and the authors' attitudes more equivocal. John Buchan, Lord Tweedsmuir, was an admired Establishment figure, another Scot who achieved the highest England had to bestow: soldier, pro-consul (Governor General of Canada), biographer, and novelist. In his Richard Hannay stories there are references that suggest that 'Bolshevik' must be equated with 'Jew' – 'places with names like spells . . . run by seedy little gangs of Communist Jews'. This is of interest not because it proves Buchan was particularly anti-semitic – his viewpoint would no doubt have resembled that implicit in Harold Nicolson's diary-entry – but because it shows that it was almost a matter of habit to link Jews with Bolshevism and Communism – in fact, with every kind of threat to cherished English values.

So much for the merely implicit, the prejudice that sits at the back of the mind: half-recognized, rarely admitted. There were some British writers in the 1920s and 1930s who were openly anti-semitic. Hilaire Belloc and G. K. Chesterton were the most talented and the best known among them. Chesterton and Belloc were very different men, but they stood together in the public mind (Bernard Shaw dubbed them 'The Chesterbelloc'). Both were identified with the same kind of aggressive Roman Catholicism: right-wing but anti-capitalist. Belloc had been educated in France and had served in the French Army. Although he had become more English than the English themselves, he was imbued with the militant anti-semitism that had culminated in the Dreyfus Affair. Both he and Chesterton revived the ancient charges that the Jews were 'cosmopolitan', that they owed allegiance to 'International Jewry' rather than to their fellow countrymen (wherever they might live); and both Chesterton and Belloc played a role in the notorious Marconi scandal in 1912, which involved cabinet ministers and the then Attorney General, Rufus Isaacs, later Lord Reading.

Belloc's writings were more openly anti-semitic than Chesterton's. He wrote two novels (illustrated by Chesterton), *Emanuel Burden* (1904), which describes how a Jew swindles an Englishman; and *The Postmaster General* (1932) which is less openly anti-semitic than its predecessor and is a kind of *roman-à-clef* featuring Herbert Samuel, who had been Postmaster General at the time of the Marconi affair. But *The Jews* (1922) is the most serious statement of his anti-semitic position. Introduced with the usual disclaimers beloved of anti-semites – some of Belloc's best friends are Jews; the book is dedicated to his Jewish secretary – *The Jews* states the theme of 'one race, one country' and, as a corollary, one religion too. The Jews represent an alien element: an intolerable disturbance of the body politic. The Jews are ineluctably 'different': they have a contempt for all non-Jews as 'indelible as the negro's colour'. Belloc sees Bolshevism as a 'Jewish movement' – and here a familiar anti-semitic strand emerges – which had destroyed Russian industrial capitalism to make way for German Jewish industrial capitalism. Belloc says friction between Jew and gentile in Britain is growing; he warns of the likelihood of a pogrom.

The reception accorded to *The Jews* by the critics indicates that anti-semitic attitudes were more acceptable in the England of 1922 than they would be now. Some papers even praised Belloc for 'fairness' and 'moderation' and saw a 'strict desire for justice and truth' in his treatment of Bolshevism (which, it must be remembered, was a potent ju-ju in 1922). *The Tablet*, not surprisingly, was in full accord with Belloc, agreeing with him in attributing the Russian Revolution to the Jews. And Zionism, according to *The Tablet*, was a dangerous error, for it divided the Jew's loyalties between his natural homeland and his National Home in Palestine.

While no one ever called Hilaire Belloc a Fascist, he stands in the same moral relation to the Nazis and their atrocities as do Houston Chamberlain and Gobineau and the other theorists of anti-semitism. As late as 1937, when the Nazis were already well embarked on their persecution of the Jews, Belloc adopted an 'I told you so' attitude. *The Jews* had warned of the dangers of ignoring the Jewish question, he said – rather as if the concentration camps and killing-centres were merely natural catastrophes, which the exercise of prudence could have avoided. Even when the horrors of gassed Jewish babies and 'scientific' experiments on living men and women were revealed, the old anti-Dreyfusard was not too perturbed. He remarked that 'it was the Jews' own silly fault. They ought to have left God alone.'

Most of the bitterness against the Jews no doubt derived from the conditioning of his youth; but since Belloc was all his life obsessed by money – despite his great industry he could never earn enough – one has to speculate as to the part an unacknowledged envy of Jewish 'moneybags' played in his antisemitism.

On a lower level was the work of a Roman Catholic priest, Father Denis Fahey. His *The Kingship of Christ according to the Principles of St Thomas Aquinas* was published in 1931 with an enthusiastic foreword by the authoritarian Dr McQuaid, later to be Archbishop of Dublin ('John Charles' to several generations of Dubliners). In this book Father Fahey advances the familiar right-wing Catholic view that social and religious perfection had almost been achieved in the thirteenth century (when St Thomas was alive and writing). This was the usual Chesterbelloc vision of a medieval paradise; but Father Fahey went on to discuss the French and Russian revolutions. They had been master-minded by Satan; his servants were the Freemasons and behind them all stood the Eternal Jew. All civil and political unrest was brought about to destroy God's rule on earth and of course the Jews were responsible. The book is written in a hysterically racist tone that must have embarrassed more gentlemanly anti-semites like Hilaire Belloc.

Gathering up the strands of anti-semitic feeling and thinking in England in the years before Hitler came to power, one can distinguish the muted anti-semitism of the Tory clubman from the anti-International Jewry propaganda of Chesterbelloc Roman Catholics. But there were several other strands. There was the powerful anti-alien lobby carrying on the tradition of Howard Vincent and William Evans Gordon in the House of Commons and outside it; their resentment of foreigners was strongly tinged by anti-semitism. And there were other groups and individuals; some of them of the Establishment and close to the springs of power; others mere eccentrics, the kind of people the English dismiss as the 'lunatic fringe'.

The Establishment anti-semites were, of course, all archappeasers of Hitler's Germany. Lord Londonderry, who was Air Minister until 1935, was very sympathetic to the Nazis. He often entertained the German Ambassador, von Ribbentrop. He wrote to Ribbentrop on one occasion that he 'had no great admiration for the Jews'. They had caused havoc, he said, in many countries. Lord Londonderry was typical of the extreme right-wing appeaser : hysterically anti-Communist, pro-Nazi, anti-semitic, and of course profoundly anti-democratic. Anti-semitism and a conviction that Parliamentary democracy was finished were two obsessions that united many different people of right-wing views. They met together in organizations like The Link, a pro-Nazi society whose membership included the Germanophil Sir Barry Domville, who went chamois-shooting with Hitler; Lord Lothian, who said that Nazism was 'the result of the denial to Germany of the rights which every other sovereign nation claims' and that Hitler's outbursts were 'the understandable complaints of a man who has been wronged'; Douglas Jerrold (grandson of the Victorian playwright of the same name), a writer and Roman Catholic apologist who had helped to bring General Franco back from exile to start the Spanish Civil War; Sir Arnold Wilson, a Tory Member of Parliament who consistently proclaimed the death of democracy; Francis Yeats-Brown, an author and an amateur of Eastern mysticism; Sir William Morris, former president of the Board of Trade. These influential persons met together to wine and dine and celebrate the Nazis' achievements at a time when the persecution of the Jews in Germany was every day growing more determined and terrible.

Of course not all the appeasers were anti-semitic, but their support for the Nazis forced them to ignore or explain away the persecution of the Jews. The so-called Cliveden set were distinguished more for their slavish attitude towards German policy and their obsessive fear of the Soviet Union than for any anti-semitic prejudice.

Francis Yeats-Brown was an eccentric product of the declining years of the British Raj. An ex-regular officer who cherished literary ambitions, he wrote the now forgotten best-seller *Bengal Lancer* and followed it with several other, progressively less successful, books. One of them was *Dogs of War*, a counterblast to the modish pacifism of the time, although, ironically, Yeats-Brown was very sympathetic to the Fascist countries who would probably be fighting Britain in any future war. Yeats-Brown was not a fanatic; despite his undoubted talents he gives the impression rather of intellectual self-indulgence pushed into stupidity; he represents the kind of naïvety that many thirties figures displayed. He saw what he wanted to see; believed what he wanted to believe. Like so many other retired officers, schoolmasters, even clergymen, he saw in the young Nazis, chanting the 'Horst Wessel Song', stripped to the waist, muscles rippling as they marched through sun-bleached cornfields, the heroic Spartan virtues he was convinced he himself possessed. Such a contrast to the round-shouldered English softies who passed resolutions about on no account fighting for King and Country! He went to Nuremberg as the guest of the Nazis and spoke later of the 'magnetism and mastery' of Hitler. He flirted with Mosley's British Union of Fascists, but had the good sense to drop out well before the war, thus probably saving himself from being detained under Regulation 18b, which was to bring in Mosley and many of the more fanatical Fascist sympathizers. Yeats-Brown was certainly anti-semitic; he mentions that the German liners *Europa* and *Bremen* were crammed with passengers since the Jews stopped travelling on them. As late as 1942 he expressed the hope that 'what was good' in Nazism would survive and that the Jews would not rule the world after the war, as they expected to do.

The most important focus of anti-semitism in Britain was represented by Sir Oswald Mosley and the British Union of Fascists. Mosley's anti-semitism appears to have evolved as part of the development of the political party he founded. Neither he nor the British Union of Fascists as a whole were openly anti-semitic before 1934. There were even some Jews in the B.U.F. in the very early days, notably Kid Lewis, the boxer. Then British Fascism began to need the emotional charge anti-semitism provides. Mosley is alleged to have said that a dynamic creed like Fascism cannot flourish unless it has a definite scapegoat to hit out at, like the Jews. The British Fascists did not bother with elaborate racialist theories; they were content to stress the 'foreignness' of the Jews. There is an echo of Chesterbelloc anti-semitism in their continual talk of Jewish millionaires in the City. Mosley and his men harped on the domination of Jewish capitalism : they translated their words into action in the East End streets, hitting out at Jews who were far from millionaires. When the blackshirts fought the Jews of Stepney and Mile End with nail-studded clubs and jagged bottles, they were of course exploiting and intensifying antagonisms that had existed for many years. When they made the summer night hideous for Judith Kaleman and her children by shouting their hate-charged words from their loudspeaker vans, they were stirring up a situation that had existed since the great influx of *Ostjuden* from the 1880s onwards. In his public speeches Mosley linked anti-semitism with appeasement. Britain had fought Germany once in a British quarrel; Britain would not fight Germany again in a Jewish quarrel. As we have seen, Fascist activities in the East End soon dissolved into racialist violence, culminating in the 'Battle of Cable Street'. The war led to the internment of Mosley and his lieutenants and the British Union of Fascists collapsed.

Considering the eccentric Henry Hamilton Beamish, one may well be treading the lunatic fringe. Of upper-class origins, the son of an admiral, Beamish fought in the First World War and then spent the rest of his life campaigning against the Jews. In 1919 he founded a society called The Britons, whose object was anti-semitic propaganda. He was in Germany during the first days of National Socialism. No one knows how true is his bizarre claim to have 'trained' Hitler, but he was certainly an honoured guest at Nuremberg Rallies. Throughout the 1920s and 1930s Beamish moved around the world, always pursuing his anti-semitic crusade. The book, *The Protocols of the Elders of Zion*, contributed to his fantasies.

Some familiar concepts emerge through the haze of Beamish's utterances . . . The Elders are a secret, self-perpetuating body appointed by King Solomon to rule the Jewish people. The French Revolution was organized by the Jews . . . Jewish families masquerade for generations as Christians, acting as secret agents for the fearful Elders. It is the duty of Jewish men to pollute gentile blood by seducing gentile women and fathering half-Jewish children. Jews are, of course, depicted as super-virile and here one touches the very nerve of racial hatred. Extraordinary sexual prowess is always attributed to the race against whom hatred has to be aroused. According to racialist fantasy, negroes have huge penises . . . This compares with Nazi ravings about the sexual corruption of Aryan women by Jews. With a Jew's alien semen the Aryan women also acquires his alien soul. She can never again, even if she marries an Aryan, bear Aryan children – only racial monsters in whom two souls dwell. This is why Jewish physicians violate Aryan women patients under anaesthetics; why Jewish women allow their husbands to seduce non-Jewish women in the interests of corruption . . .

Beamish was never a political figure in the sense that Mosley and his associates were. He was detained under Regulation 18b and later faded from view to a great extent, although his influence persisted through The Britons. Apparently in conjunction with another organization called The Militant Christian Patriots, The Britons Publishing Society issued on anti-refugee tract, *Refugees Before Britons! A Menace to the Health of the Nation*, which is an extraordinary farrago of rhetorical denunciation. It derides 'the alleged persecution' to which the refugees are said to have been subjected. The real persecution was of the unfortunate Russians who displeased the 'ninety per cent Jewish' government of Moscow during the Revolution. The Jews are described as 'bloody ogres' and why, the writer of the pamphlet demands, does the Jew resent the Jewish saying 'an eye for an eye and a tooth for a tooth' when it is applied to himself? The German Jews are the same Jews as the Bolshevik Jews who perpetrated this mass murder. The Nazis are only giving them back some of their own treatment . . . After several pages in this vein, there

ENTRENCHED ATTITUDES

is a change of gear. The writer resurrects the argument of the biological inferiority of the immigrant. These Jewish immigrants are 'the social wreckage' of other lands who would clog the wheels of British life. They were degenerates who thronged the out-patient departments of hospitals. 'Biologically speaking, they are literally drinking our life blood.' The Home Office were well aware that most of the alien Jewish immigrants were criminals, brothel-keepers, lunatics . . . Who, then, was responsible for thus poisoning the very bloodstream of Britain? The writer gives the answer: Mr Otto Schiff (who, as we have seen, was indeed a leading figure in work for the refugees). Mr Schiff's relative, one Jacob Schiff, was, it was alleged, one of the fiends behind the Russian Revolution . . . Someone had said that the refugees had 'rights'. How could a refugee have 'rights'? – except those of a guest and an unwelcome one into the bargain. Such an idea could only emanate from a muddled brain perverted by 'Talmudic arrogance'. The Home Office were giving away the Britons' birthright for a mess of pottage. In another rapid shift of direction, the pamphlet now attacks the familiar theme of aliens taking British jobs and comments rather enigmatically, 'Truly, the matter is one for the Zoo!' In his peroration the writer lists, among others, 'Freud, Epstein, Steins galore!' as examples of Britain's unwelcome guests, and quotes John O'Gaunt's speech from *Richard II*, winding up with the phrase 'Sic transit gloria Anglia!'

These ravings are not summarized because they are intrinsically interesting, but to correct any impression that the hate-propaganda of a Goebbels or a Rosenberg is necessarily a German thing. The Britons were indeed British and their brand of poison entirely home-grown.

The attacks of the Rothermere newspapers on the refugees have already been mentioned; they set the stage for internment throughout the first half of 1940. Rothermere had certainly supported Mosley for a short time, but it is said he broke with him over the growing anti-semitism of the B.U.F. (It was rumoured that the *Mail*'s Jewish advertisers had threatened to stop buying space if the pro-Fascist line continued.) Soon after the break with Mosley the *Daily Mail* carried two articles praising the contribution the Jews made to British life. A few years later the campaign against the refugees proved that Rothermere's tolerance did not extend to Jews who happened to be also German and refugees.

After the policy of internment went into reverse and large numbers of refugees had been released – many of them to work in industry and in occupations concerned with the war effort – a section of the press began to criticize them again, not with the vigour of the 1940 campaign but spasmodically: an irritable sniping. By 1942 no section of the British press could have been ignorant of what was happening to the Jews in Europe. A newspaper might describe the slaughter of the Jews in Warsaw or Vilna on one page, and on another print some criticism of the refugees. The editor might feel that there was no connection between reporting the holocaust in German-occupied Europe and at the same time running an item about 'arrogant' German Jewish refugees, but the ambivalence was enshrined in a famous cartoon by David Low which appeared in the London *Evening Standard* on 18 June 1943. Entitled 'How the Beastly Business Begins', it shows two housewives, holding shopping baskets. 'It must be the fault of the Jews,' they are saying. In the background are scenes of slaughter and destruction.

The area between anti-alien and anti-semitic prejudice was always an equivocal one. Sometimes it was a deliberate confusion. 'Alien' was understood to read 'Jew' (there is a telling line in one of Chesterton's Father Brown stories where a newspaper editor changes the word 'Jew' to the word 'alien'). At the beginning of Russian-Jewish immigration in the 1880s there had been protests at foreign Jews being allowed to take English names. Now these protests were revived. The *Sunday Despatch* of 15 August 1943 said:

The habit of strange people suddenly acquiring such names as 'Percival Selby Lowndes' or 'Henry York' must be stopped.

This, the paper continued, was essential if 'British unity and fairness of mind' were to be maintained.

It is hard to discern consistent attitudes or motives in such an *olla podrida* of hatred and ignorance – particularly hard to distinguish anti-alien feeling from plain anti-semitism. England never had – never could have had – anything like the Dreyfus Case, the 'Affaire' which served as a catalyst not only for French anti-semitism but for so much that was rotten in France before

ENTRENCHED ATTITUDES

1914. But the case of Leslie Hore-Belisha is an instance of anti-semitic prejudice colouring a political decision in Britain. The men who drove Hore-Belisha from the British Cabinet were the same men who insisted on the financial sponsorship of refugees and who, later, interned them. The Hore-Belisha affair was notable, too, for the intervention of *Truth*, once accused in the House of Commons of being openly anti-semitic, and the consistent enemy of the refugees whom it described in 1939 as 'boorish, insulting, arrogant, and unbelievably ungrateful'.

Leslie Hore-Belisha came from a family of Sephardic Jews, long established in Manchester. A brilliant and sensitive boy, he was much influenced by his mother – indeed, she was to continue to influence him all his life. He served in the First World War and was the first president of the Oxford Union after it. He became a journalist; then went to the Bar; then entered politics. He was made Minister of Transport in 1934, giving his name to the 'Belisha beacons' that adorned London's pedestrian crossings; then, in 1937, Neville Chamberlain gave him the War Office. Chamberlain is said to have thought the Army needed a new broom and that Hore-Belisha was the man to wield it. In fact he was to sweep too vigorously and effectively for his own good. He brought about many improvements in the somewhat sluggish and hidebound Army of the thirties which, it has been said, was busy preparing in 1934 for the war of 1914–18. Indeed the strategist and military historian Liddell-Hart considered that more overdue reforms were carried out in Hore-Belisha's time at the War Office than in the previous twenty years. Chamberlain himself said that Hore-Belisha had done more for the Army than anyone since Lord Haldane.

One of Hore-Belisha's first actions had been to overhaul the obsolete, half-fossilized officer structure. He abolished the half-pay system; gave the troops more physical comfort of every kind (despite protests from backwoodsmen colonels: 'What the hell does the fella think the Army is? A bloody luxury hotel?'); improved pay; fused the Royal Tank Regiment with the various cavalry units into the Royal Armoured Corps, thus blending modern warfare with ancient traditions. He became very popular with the lower ranks; but this popularity caused him to be detested by the Army hierarchy who had in any case been very ready to dislike him. Chamberlain was to say later that Hore-

Belisha had the defects of his qualities and the top brass certainly disliked him for those qualities: he was so impatient, ebullient – so *Jewish*...

Hore-Belisha had wanted younger generals and eventually he got them, but these younger men had the same background and had been trained in the same school as the older men they had supplanted: where the backwoodsmen had opposed Hore-Belisha, the newcomers gave an uneasy acquiescence.

Up to Munich, Hore-Belisha appears to have enjoyed Chamberlain's support. But after Munich he became too impatient. He realized how little time there was and how much there was to be done. He doubted whether, even now, Chamberlain was taking rearmament seriously. On the outbreak of war Hore-Belisha was made a member of the War Cabinet. The long-standing friction between him and the military hierarchy culminated in a row with Lord Gort, who was to command the British Expeditionary Force in France. Gort was jealous of Hore-Belisha's popularity with the troops and Chamberlain warned Hore-Belisha to be careful. Soon afterwards he told him that there was 'prejudice' against him and offered Hore-Belisha the Board of Trade in place of the War Office. Hore-Belisha refused and resigned the next day. Chamberlain wished to offer Hore-Belisha the Ministry of Information but Lord Halifax objected. Such an appointment, he suggested, would have a disastrous effect on neutral opinion, both because Hore-Belisha was a Jew and because his personality and methods would let down British prestige.

There is irony in the fact that Hore-Belisha was driven out – his resignation was generally spoken of as dismissal – in the name of the very causes for which Britain was fighting: decency, justice, and the end of the Nazi persecution of the Jews. The Hore-Belisha affair can be seen both as a rare example of British antisemitism breaking into the open and discharging itself in action, and as a last resentful jab by the appeasers at the new, very different men who were soon to replace them.

In the week of his resignation Hore-Belisha was attacked in a most venomous manner by *Truth*. Its proprietors ensured that a copy of the issue in which the attack appeared was in the hands of every Member of Parliament before Hore-Belisha began his speech of resignation. He was advised by Sir John Simon, however, not to bring the action for libel the article invited. Its anti-semitism was so vicious, Simon believed, that the article would be a gift to Hitler's propaganda machine.

As usual, Joshua Wedgwood reached the nub of the matter. Speaking in the House of Commons on 16 January 1940 he said:

> The Prime Minister denies that the Secretary of State was dismissed because he was a Jew. He cannot deny that the prejudice against him was because he was Jew.

Anti-semitism in Britain, then, was and is something vague but persistent; a common exercise in hypocrisy – 'some of my best friends are Jews'; an obsession half-buried and often denied but still pervasive, taking many protean shapes. As the refugees ceased to be merely bizarre newcomers and became involved in the life and work of England at war, they began to be accepted or rejected by the native gentile population not so much as 'foreigners' but simply as Jews. Of course they themselves did not see the matter in such simple terms. There were many tensions among the refugees; and, despite the magnificent work of the refugee organizations, tensions also between the refugees and the native Jewish community. As Hugo Neher had perceived, the British Jews could stand for a prosperous family, suddenly confronted with an unfortunate cousin who turns up seeking help. The family intends to do its duty by him but the quality of the welcome is somewhat strained.

The government of course still thought of the bulk of the refugees as merely temporary guests. They might be working in British factories or serving in the British forces, but it was still understood that at the end of the war they would move on – to America or Palestine or whatever country was willing to take them. The refugees, collectively, were still a 'problem' rather than a group of people who, slowly and painfully, were being absorbed into British life.

The problem was of course not only one for Britain, but for the world. The events of 1940 – the Fifth Column bogy, the fear of invasion, internment – had trapped any consideration of the refugees into an immediate, local context. But by 1942 the problem could be seen in wider terms, if only because the full horror of Hitler's Final Solution was becoming known. Four million Jews were seen to be standing in immediate threat of annihilation in German-occupied Europe. In November 1942

President Roosevelt had announced that the United States would join Britain and the other allies in forming a War Crimes Commission. The commission would collate and record the acts of war criminals and set about creating machinery for their apprehension and punishment after the war. It was believed that the knowledge that such an organization existed might deter the Nazis from implementing their plans.

Roosevelt appears to have been loth to join in the declaration announcing this, although it was he who had first suggested forming such a commission. But as Arthur D. Morse shows in *While Six Million Died*, Roosevelt consistently evaded doing anything that would really help the Jewish refugees, while at the same time he displayed his genius for publicity by magnifying the importance of such 'initiatives' as the Bermuda Conference which, as we shall see, achieved nothing for the refugees.

In December 1942 Sydney Silverman asked Anthony Eden in the House of Commons whether it had been truthfully reported that the Germans planned to deport all the remaining Jews to Eastern Europe and then put them to death. Eden replied that it was.

I regret to have to inform the House that reliable reports have recently reached His Majesty's Government regarding the barbarous and inhuman treatment to which the Jews are being subjected in German-occupied Europe.

Eden then read the joint allied declaration on war crimes. Then for two minutes the Members of the House of Commons stood in silence, heads bowed, as a gesture to the dead.

In March 1943 Britain and America agreed to hold a conference on the refugees in Bermuda. This was to take place in April and it was announced that there would be a committee with greater powers than had been available to the participants in the Evian Conference. Unfortunately, while the general situation had changed immensely since Evian – the world was now at war and millions of Jews had died or were about to die – in the most important respects nothing had changed. The neutral countries to which the Jews might escape from time to time would still not admit them, while the Allies – notably Britain and America – were still unwilling to relax their immigration regulations to any great extent.

ENTRENCHED ATTITUDES

Given these terms of reference, the problem was really insoluble, and so there was a tendency to look for an answer from outside – something external to the situation that would solve it at one stroke. At the time of Evian it had been a 'change of heart' on the part of the Nazis; now in 1943 it was victory over the Nazis. Both these blessings would have obviously solved the refugee problem, but making its solution conditional on them encouraged evasion : it implied that, lacking them, nothing could be done.

As the *Observer* said :

Today, on April 11, 1943, it must be stated that the British Government has not so far found it within its power to rescue and shelter from the cruel death one single Jewish man, woman or child . . . to arrange for a conference with these terms of reference is only a cruel mockery.

In the weeks before Bermuda Britain suggested to the American State Department that, since the Allies now controlled North Africa (it had been invaded in 1942), 20,000 refugees now in Spain could be sent there, thus enabling Spain to receive comparable numbers of other refugees and thus breaking the deadlock that was costing so many Jewish lives. The State Department refused on the ground that an influx of Jews would obviously anger the Muslim population in North Africa.

Meanwhile, the Americans were assembling their team for the conference. After some difficulty Dr Harold Willis Dodds, President of Princeton University, was appointed, along with Congressman Sol Bloom of New York and Senator Scott Lucas of Illinois. Despite all the evidence that was reaching the White House that it was even now almost too late to save the European Jews, the American delegates were given what Arthur Morse has called 'a mandate for inaction'. Among a number of other restrictions they were ordered not to limit their discussions to Jewish refugees; not to raise questions of race or religious faith when appealing for public support; not to commit the United States regarding shipping-space for refugees; not to bring refugees to America if any space for settlement were available in Europe; not to pledge American funds; and – the most important of all – not to promise any change in the rigid laws that governed immigration into the United States.

The British delegation was headed by Richard Kidston Law (later Lord Coleraine), then Under Secretary to the Home Office. He was accompanied by George Hall, Financial Secretary to the Admiralty. The British delegation, like the American, had their hands tied in advance. The British Government would not approve of a direct approach to the German Government; would not exchange prisoners for refugees or lift the blockade of Europe to permit the entry of relief supplies.

At beginning of the conference on 19 April the leader of the American delegation, Dr Dodds, spoke of the horrors of the Nazi persecution of the Jews. Nothing in history had equalled these horrors. The war had not only deepened the sufferings of the people under German rule, but it had also made it much harder for anyone else to relieve them. After a number of other remarks in the same vein, Dr Dodds reached the real point of his speech: that the problem confronting them was too great to be solved 'by the two governments here represented'. All the conference could do was to point the way and offer such proposals as were practicable under war conditions in the light of what the war effort of the United States could permit.

Richard Law of the British delegation said that only final victory by the Allies could provide a solution to the problem. When that victory was achieved, persecution would be ended and retribution would follow for those accused of war crimes. There were no doubt a number of measures which could, even now, be taken to alleviate the condition of persecuted peoples – but if any of those measures were to postpone by even a month the final victory, then we would be doing an 'ill-service' to the persecuted. These unfortunate people should not be betrayed into a belief that any immediate help was coming – for it was not.

Shorn of their rhetoric, the speeches of Dodds and Law represented a joint Anglo-American declaration that nothing could be done for the refugees. Only a miracle could help them – an immediate victory. Failing that, both the American and British Governments refused to take any relief measures at all.

With the exception of the opening speeches, the proceedings of the conference remained secret. But some details of its deliberations are recorded in the files of the American War Refugees Board and have been quoted by Arthur Morse. The negative impression of the two opening speeches is reinforced. Every suggestion put forward foundered on the restrictive provisos that both delegations had brought to the conference table. No: Allied ships could not carry refugees. No: Portuguese ships could not be permitted to bring refugees to Angola (a State Department man crushed that, on the ground that the Portuguese Government might not like having refugees in their colony of Angola). No: the British would not alter their 'closed-door' policy in Palestine (a Jewish member of the American delegation, Sol Bloom, had suggested they might, only to be silenced by his leader, Dr Dodds). No: no question relating to the Allied blockade of Europe could be discussed at the conference. No: there could be no question of a large influx of refugees into Allied countries as some of these refugees might be sympathizers with the Nazis (this sounds like the old Fifth Column bogy resurrected).

And so it went on. Never could negation have been more unanimous.

The *Observer* was scathing:

Here are the leisurely beach hotels of the Atlantic luxury island, where well-dressed gentlemen assemble to assure each other in the best Geneva fashion that really nothing much can be done ... The opening speeches of the conference have been widely noted in this country, and noted with dismay and anger. We have been told that this problem is beyond the resources of America and Britain combined. If Britain and America cannot help, who can? What is so terrible about these speeches is not only their utter insensitiveness to human suffering. It is the implied readiness of the two greatest powers on earth to humiliate themselves, to declare themselves bankrupt and impotent, in order to evade the slight discomfort of charity.

It is one of the ironies of history that at the very time the English and the Americans were proclaiming their inability to help the Jews, the Germans were launching their final assault on the Warsaw ghetto. The Germans had intended to clear the ghetto in three days; it took them four weeks. The horror of those four weeks has been described elsewhere; meanwhile the English and the Americans were issuing a joint statement on the Bermuda Conference, to the effect that the delegates had been able to agree on a number of recommendations which 'will lead to the relief of a substantial number of refugees of all races and nationalities'. This was so vague that it was given the alibi of security: the recommendations involved 'military considerations' and so had to remain secret.

The head of the British delegation, R. K. Law, now Lord Coleraine, summed up the conference many years later as 'a façade of inaction'. He admitted that it had been totally futile and had achieved nothing for the refugees. He called it a 'conflict of self-justification', and indeed each of the two Allies, Britain and America, excused her own apathy and evasion by seeking to prod the other into some action which neither was prepared to take herself. The result was deadlock adorned by rhetoric – particularly from the White House. While American initiatives towards helping the refugees were always cleverly sidetracked and nullified by Roosevelt and his aides, British efforts were always vitiated by the question of Palestine. The British Government would not budge on this. Thus the State Department could always counter any British proposal with the question 'What about letting them into Palestine?' and Roosevelt was well aware of this.

A fortnight after the end of the Bermuda Conference a refugee committed suicide in London His name was Szmul Zgielbojm, and he was forty-eight years old. He left a note to the Prime Minister of the exiled Polish Government. He could not live, he wrote, while what remained of the Jewish population of Poland were dying in their last heroic battle against the Nazis. Destiny had decreed that he was not to be with them, but he belonged with them in their mass graves. His death was a final protest against the 'way in which the world was looking on and permitting the extermination of the Jewish people'.

Zgielbojm had been one of the most heroic fighters in Poland. His wife and two children had been killed by the Nazis. He had fought in the defence of Warsaw; been captured by the Germans and then escaped, finally reaching England after a dramatic flight across Germany. In England he was a member of the Polish National Council: the 'parliament' of the Polish Government in exile. He had made a notable broadcast over the B.B.C., trying to call the attention of the world to the horrors that were perpetrated. 'The governments of Great Britain and America must be compelled to put an end to this mass murder.'

ENTRENCHED ATTITUDES 255

Now, reading about the well-dressed gentlemen in the leisurely beach hotels agreeing with each other that nothing could be done, Szmul Zgielbojm, the supreme survivor, decided that survival was no longer worthwhile.

Chapter Eight

COMING TO TERMS

'I know what one must do to be Jewish,' says Elie Wiesel, the survivor who has recorded with such tragic simplicity the murder of Jewry. 'He must assume his Jewishness . . . He must assume its past with its sorrows and joys . . . he must bear witness.'

These are eloquent words. No one can doubt their truth. But compare them with Georg Joachim's simple question of many years ago, 'Daddy, am I a Jew?' The contrast is integral to both the past history and the future survival of the German Jews as a separate group with a distinct identity. Their assimilation into German society was as complete as the assimilation of any ethnic group can ever be – so complete indeed that, after the Nazi persecution began, other Jews, particularly in America, became doubtful of the wisdom of such a total integration into any host society. And when the one-sided marriage between German Jew and German gentile was finally sundered by Hitler, the Jews who came to England faced the problem of whether to start assimilating all over again – letting themselves, or at least their children, become more English than the English themselves – or to cling jealously to their identity as German Jews: their German language, their social *mores* and attitudes.

Of course no German Jew was ever able to put the question to himself in these simple terms. Every individual German Jew had obviously established a different degree of assimilation to the Germany he was born in. One speaks of social *mores* that would distinguish the German Jews as a group, but many German Jews were so thoroughly assimilated that they were indistinguishable from other Germans. Those German Jews who had continued to practise their religion with its ritualistic and dietary obligations were naturally more aware of their identity and were sustained by this. However hideous their situation, the gulf that yawned before them was not quite so blank or wide as that confronting those who had forgotten that they were Jews. Of course there were those who, in their extremity, sought traditional props. Ilsa Geiss speaks of the German Jews who started to eat matzoth and bitter herbs and light Passover candles and keep *kashruth* (kosher laws) only when persecution forced them into a realization of their own Jewishness. (She speaks wryly, too, of the rapid conversions to Zionism when Palestine became a possible place of refuge.)

Certainly the German Jews had a distinctive quality: the solidity and earnestness, the intellectual integrity that evoked the nickname *Yaeche*; but *Yaeche* is hard to define, to pin down. Compare it with the colourful, dramatically Jewish tradition of the Jews from Eastern Europe – the tradition that came to such an extraordinary flowering in America: the culture that had its roots in New York's lower East Side in the last years of the nineteenth century. A culture of such ethnic vigour that it was to capture the gentile imagination, not only through a popular musical like *Fiddler on the Roof*, but on another level through the kind of literary renaissance signalled by the work of Malamud and other writers. Expressions like *schmuck* and *schmaltz* and *chutzpah* became popular currency. A kind of Jewish chic had been created, which many gentiles found irresistible in its colour and vitality.

German Jewry could offer nothing so colourful. *Yaeche* could never be so readily identified or dramatized. During their first years in Britain, many German Jews were conscious of this apparent lack of identity. They were German, certainly; Jewish, too – but how define their Jewishness so that the fact had real significance for themselves and for others? They were, after all, being persecuted because they were Jews, and they carried their Jewish ambience before them, as it were, so that it conditioned everyone's response to them. And yet of what did it consist? – which is perhaps only another way of asking the old question, What does it mean to be a Jew?

Those German Jews who were still sustained by religion – whether they were Conservative, Orthodox, or Reform – were of course the most fortunate. They could join with their Anglo-Jewish brethren in the comradeship of a shared faith. But even they, enjoying a bridgehead of common practice and doctrine, felt that Anglo-Jewry was very different in atmosphere from German Jewry. The faith of the German Jew was essentially intellectual: a series of ideas, a religious theory passed from teacher to pupil and accepted by him as the confirmation of his faith. It has been said that the religion of the German Jews was a bookish kind of religion, and that the German Jew found the Judaism of the English Jews *geistlos* – lacking in intellectual depth, although not necessarily lacking in a spiritual way. Traditionally the English Jew had practised Judaism more instinctively and less intellectually, the roots of his faith being none the less strong for that. After 1933 the leaven of the German Jew began to work in Anglo-Jewry, with the German Jews' greater stress on the *Torah* expressed as Judaism – that is to say, as a religion of understanding, of exposition, rather than as a matter of faith and traditional loyalties.

The Jew from Eastern Europe and the German Jew had in common the fact that both were Ashkenazi. But, as we have seen, the group identity of the Eastern European Jews was much stronger. Its greater stress on community life and its more robust, extrovert nature enabled it to survive with its vitality undiminished. By the quality of their background and upbringing many German Jews felt themselves more totally uprooted than the most hapless *Ostjuden* who left Grodno or Vilna after 1881. This must be remembered when one considers the difficulties the refugees faced when they came to grips with exile. Some were acutely aware of this dilemma of identity; others – and this is a measure of the depth of their problem – were hardly aware that it existed.

The first time Sigmund Freud entered the garden of the house his family had rented for him in Elsworthy Road in Hampstead, he raised his arm in the Nazi salute and uttered the words, 'Heil, Hitler!'

The greeting was spoken, his daughter-in-law recalls, with an extraordinary depth of irony and, perhaps, of self-mockery. Freud's sardonic gesture acknowledged the fact that Hitler had at last forced him to live in the land he had thought of settling in many years before. But, as he said, 'One has loved one's prison,' and he had been reluctant to leave Vienna where he had lived and worked for so long.

Freud was no doubt the most distinguished of all the German and Austrian refugees who came to Britain after 1933, but he was hardly representative. Of international fame, comparable with Newton and Marx as an influence on men's minds, he had even in his lifetime achieved the place he was to hold in history. His work made him, like Einstein, a citizen of the world. It did not matter where he lived; he would never have to face any of the problems that bedevilled most refugees. In any case, he was eighty-three and by the time he arrived at Elsworthy Road his life had narrowed into a struggle for survival against the cancer that was to kill him eighteen months later.

Freud's peer, Albert Einstein, had bypassed England completely when the Nazis forced him to leave Germany. He went to America and almost immediately became professor of theoretical physics at the Institute for Advanced Study in Princeton. He stayed there till he died in 1955 : the most famous scientist in the world, although hardly one in a million understood his theory of relativity. With his wild nimbus of white hair, his shabby dress, his pipe, and his violin, he remained the popular stereotype of the vague, lovable scientific genius. Like Freud, Einstein lived and functioned on a plane that made him immune to the ordinary trials of the exile. He was, however, always generous and helpful to other, less fortunate, refugees. He helped in the early development of the atomic bomb; and later wrote an introduction to a memorandum by Leo Szilard, the Hungarian physicist, whose object was to prevent the use of the bomb against Japan and establish some form of control of the new weapon. This memorandum did not achieve its purpose, but Einstein remained a revered father-figure. Paul Tabori tells the story of the British scientist who telephoned Einstein's home from Washington. He could hear the telephone operator say to Einstein's housekeeper : 'Washington for you!' The housekeeper exclaimed in German : 'Washington! Washington? What is wrong *now*?'

Stefan Zweig was also a man of international fame. He enjoyed world recognition as an author; he had all the money he needed – and yet his life as a refugee represents an anguished flight from one retreat to another. As soon as he settled in a place, the worm of fear or despair stirred in him and he had to move on. It is tempting to see in Zweig a man who mirrored in himself the torment and insecurity of the typical refugee, but Zweig had always suffered from an intermittent melancholy. This deepened throughout his years of exile. His devouring, self-indulgent pessimism about German successes has already been mentioned: his prophecies of an apocalyptic triumph for the Nazis have an almost masochistic ring.

His beautiful home on Lyncombe Hill in Bath seems to have become a prison to him. The elegiac calm of Bath and the pastoral quiet of the countryside around appear to have actually heightened Zweig's sense of being trapped. He saw the gracious face Bath presented as only a mask – a mask soon to be stripped off when the sirens sounded and the Stukas came shrieking over; when the bombs came down, smashing these elegant façades; when the panzers ground through these quiet squares and crescents, burning and destroying. After the fall of France, this vision grew stronger and more real to Zweig; eventually it was to become unendurable. But for a time he endured it. He continued on his solitary works, wearing his favourite costume of 'a Stage Englishman': brown jacket and plus-fours with a matching beret. Then he and his wife began to hoard food. There would obviously be famine after the Nazis invaded. Soon the house was crammed with all the tinned and packaged food they could buy under wartime conditions. Although Zweig had always enjoyed meeting and talking with fellow refugees, now he began to avoid them. He was afraid that they might confirm his own vision of a Nazi triumph. All right for them to *think* of it – naturally they thought of it: everyone not an imbecile knew that the Nazis were coming and that they would conquer England. But don't let people *say* it – that made it even more certain, brought the evil day nearer. And so Zweig began to avoid other refugees and, eventually, everyone else. It was time for him to leave Bath; to move on once more.

Even before the fall of France had endorsed his most gloomy imaginings, his depression had been growing. It had been deepened by the death of Freud, which had taken place some nine months previously, in September 1939. Zweig had seen in Freud, as in the murdered Walter Rathenau, the archetype of the Jew of genius: the genius always overshadowed by racial tragedy. Certainly Freud's death brought another degree of darkness, a further narrowing-in for Zweig. He had always admired Freud as a writer and teacher and shaper of men's thought;

and he had visited the old man several times during Freud's last months in Hampstead. At the end he had spoken (some thought at undue length) at Freud's cremation ceremonies.

By 1940 Zweig was seeing new evidence of disintegration all round him. While leaving Europe might in some of his moods strike him as a betrayal, Zweig was by now so much the victim of deep and destructive forces within his own psyche that he could only yield to his most consistent impulse: to fly. He went first to America – one is struck again by the freedom of movement enjoyed by the rich and talented refugee, which contrasts so strongly with the deadlocked impotence of his poorer brethren – and then, as the result of one of those intuitive flashes that Zweig sometimes seemed to live by, to Brazil. Brazil, he had decided, was the ideal retreat. It was free of racial prejudice: new and young and clear-eyed in a way no European country could ever be. He even projected his idealized version of this, his last refuge, in a book called *Brazil – Land of the Future*. It clearly reflected what he dreamed of seeing rather than what, in the limited time available to him, he actually saw. Although the book is pitched on a high lyrical note, its apparent vitality is thin and forced. It does not compare with *Balzac* or Zweig's other biographies. His last work was the nostalgic autobiography *The World of Yesterday*. His depression continued to deepen and, having moved with his wife to the fashionable sub-tropical resort of Petropolis, he died with her in a suicide pact on 23 February 1942.

His biographer Elizabeth Allday sees in Zweig a man conditioned by his Jewish heritage, responding to anti-semitism by cultivating a gentle and compassionate attitude. He suffered anguish from the fact that, while what he sought to teach was ignored, he was acclaimed for saying it so well. Fulfilling his passionate, self-dramatizing nature, he saw himself as the Wandering Jew. He imagined the worst and even willed it to happen, entering into its horrors with a kind of prophetic masochism.

Stefan Zweig, was of course, a man of morbid sensibility. He dramatized the world situation of the Jews in terms of his own fate. But his defeatism reflects a particular kind of Jewish temperament. In the famous author taking poison in far-off Brazil it is not too fanciful to see the medieval Jew dying on his own sword before the crusader can kill him with a shout of *'Hep! Hep!'* The fact that Zweig himself was safe does not make the analogy less valid. Certainly there were suicides among the refugees in Britain that reflected such a reaching after the divine *liebestod* in the very moment of despair. These were men and women who had suffered so much that they found the prospect of internment a final insult that broke the last thread of their will to survive. They had gone on too long. Now there was no hope left.

Professor Lafitte quotes a report from an official of one of the refugee organizations:

The police came to our local refugee committee to ask for £12 for the funeral expenses of . . . , a man of sixty-eight who had committed suicide. His daughter eventually paid. I believe the Jews in Germany were often presented with the corpses to dispose of.

A middle-aged couple poisoned themselves together in Richmond Park because they feared they might be interned and separated. The widow of a professor of psychology killed herself because she had been given notice to quit her house. A teacher drowned herself in the Thames and left a suicide note in which she thanked the British for all their kindness to her and expressed the hope that their country would be victorious. In the debate of 10 July 1940 Eleanor Rathbone mentioned the refugee professor of chemistry who had been tortured in a concentration camp before he escaped to Britain. Once there, he had been working on a scheme for utilizing sisal waste. When he knew he was to be interned, he begged a little time to get ready from the police and then poisoned himself. Questioned about this case in the House of Commons, Sir John Anderson expressed regret but said it was impossible to make the widow any grant out of public funds. A Dr Emile Krasny, an Austrian, was interned in July. His wife, distraught at his having been taken from her, perhaps for ever, committed suicide.

These cases could stand for many more. It might be argued, of course, that suicide always springs from some failure of the will, some destructive impulse in the victim himself, in these cases translated from potential to actual through the pressures to which the refugees were subjected. If this is so, it does not make these deaths less tragic.

A woman who came to Britain as a child says:

My mother and I left Germany in 1936. My parents had separated in 1935. My mother was Jewish; my father was not – I think I've told you everything when I say that. I don't remember well enough to be really sure – you know a child only gets a distorted view of its parents' relationship, unless of course they fight very openly, come to blows almost, and my parents never did that . . . But her being Jewish was the reason they parted. There was never any official divorce, although if my father had tried to divorce her I'm sure everything would have gone the way he wanted. The German courts at that time would have always found against a Jewess whatever the evidence . . . But there was never a divorce. Perhaps my father had some sense of shame about it, I don't know. I get the impression that he was rather a weak man and perhaps the fear of the pressures he would incur having a Jewish wife destroyed a marriage that already had something wrong with it . . .

Anyway, my mother decided to come to England. Eventually she persuaded a cousin in London to sponsor her. I say 'eventually' because I knew she was writing letters to him for a long time. I'm sure he was very reluctant. His father was my mother's brother, who had come to England before the First World War. His name was Werner and he was a doctor in Golders Green. I don't think it was the financial aspect that put him off – at that time my mother had some money from my father anyway – it was more a general dislike of being involved . . . When we did get to England, he didn't invite us to stay at his house as my mother had expected he would, but he did find us rooms in Hampstead. Arkwright Road. That was the first of our landladies. A Mrs Glennie. I think she was Scottish.

My mother couldn't get on with landladies: perhaps it was some feeling of resentment at no longer having her own house . . . Anyway, the pattern with landladies was always the same. They were nice to my mother at first because they thought what a nice quiet woman – as indeed she was. And my mother always said that the landladies were 'very nice' – at first, when she first met them, because she expected ogres. And then – I saw this happen several times – small things, typical landlady things would happen. I suppose, now, they were just the small tensions that come up when people are living in the same house. Things like the stairs light left on; leaving washing on a line in the bedroom – we had no facilities for doing our washing except a bowl in the bedsitter we were in, and you couldn't hang washing in the bathroom which was used by a lot of other people. And then there was the gas-ring we used for cooking. Mrs Glennie had a tremendous neurosis about this being left on. One of the lodgers in a house owned by a friend of hers had blown himself up by lighting a cigarette in a room with a leaky gas-ring, and this landlady had been censured by the coroner. Mrs Glennie was determined that this wasn't going to happen in a house of hers and this made her watch all the time . . . I don't suppose she was a bad person at all, really, but this made for great friction with my mother, who was very sensitive and whose personality had never recovered from being rejected by my father. She got to the point where she was *waiting* for Mrs Glennie to mention the lights or the gas or whatever it was. My mother would get quite hysterical about it and although I was only ten she behaved to me exactly as if I were an adult. She would sit counting – 'One-two-three-four-five-six-seven-eight-nine-ten-eleven' – the idea being that Mrs Glennie would knock and come in with some complaint about the gas or the light or not shutting the front door gently enough (it was supposed to be ready to come off its hinges). I'll never forget my mother sitting there with her head in her hands and her eyes tightly closed, counting, counting . . . I've known her count up to five hundred or a thousand, but the awful thing was, she very rarely had to count above a hundred before there *was* a knock at the door. My mother seemed to have some sort of instinct . . .

She developed such a fear of Mrs Glennie that it was obvious we'd have to leave but when we did her cousin Werner, the doctor, was annoyed. Mrs Glennie was one of his patients and he made a thing of having got us the room through knowing her. That was nonsense, of course; it wasn't at all hard to get rooms in London, then. The impossibility, I now realize, was getting anywhere that mother would have found tolerable . . . She wasn't able to work – didn't even attempt to – for she was over forty and her English wasn't good. Anyway, her personality was disintegrating. She was old-fashioned in one way: she was the sort of woman who's always rather ridiculously dependent on a man. She needed small courtesies like a man helping her on with her coat, holding doors open – and of course in things like writing business letters, dealing with money . . . She needed to feel a man behind her. When we first got to London she would always be telephoning Werner and asking his advice and I see now that she was perhaps seeking a shoulder to lean on – without realizing it of course. Werner would never respond; he would say how busy he was, how a doctor's work was never done, and then he would turn her over to his wife who was English and not Jewish at all . . . Presumably my father had fulfilled this need in her for a man's support and after they parted she wilted away for the lack of it...

Anyway – mother's problems with landladies got worse and our stays in their houses got shorter and shorter each time. We stayed in Hampstead and West Hampstead mostly, although once we went to Willesden Green. Two of the landladies were nicer than Mrs Glennie; one much worse. All the same things happened. The counting became an absolute mania with my mother; she got to the point, once or twice, of stopping her counting and saying the landlady was knocking when there was no one there at all! And she began to take less and less interest in me. Sometimes she didn't seem to know I was there at all. Oh – I don't mean she was unkind, she never was – but she bothered less and less about meals and whether I went to school or not. At first I'd been sent to a school in Heath Road. I didn't get on at all there because I knew very little English . . . Mother took me away from there and she talked of sending me to some school especially for refugee children but nothing came of it. Most of the time I would just sit there with her and at the end I wasn't going to school at all . . . I'd just sit there, in one of those dreadful bedsitters we always had, listening to her talking about the people at Woburn House [the refugee aid committee]. She'd had to go to them because her money had run out and of course we weren't getting any from my father now . . . She didn't like the woman she had to see at Woburn House; she said she treated her, my mother, differently because my mother came from Bavaria and she was a North German . . . When she wasn't talking about the Woburn House people my mother was counting, counting, waiting for the landlady to knock . . .

And then, suddenly, everything improved. We went to stay in a house in Belsize Drive and the landlady there wasn't like a landlady at all: she was a friend. She was called Sylvia Orton and she wasn't a professional like the other landladies: she just wanted to let two rooms in her house and my mother happened to hear of them, I don't know how. Anyway, from that moment everything got better. My mother wasn't afraid of Mrs Orton. She trusted her and Mrs Orton didn't treat mother as if she expected her to bite her at any moment because she was a German . . . Mrs Orton would have been middle-aged then, about fifty, but she treated my mother as if she were twenty and Mrs Orton was *her* mother . . . Mrs Orton wasn't bossy exactly but I think she gave my mother the feeling of everything being taken care of that mattered so much to her . . . Mrs Orton was shocked at the neglect of my education of course and she set about looking for a school for me to go to . . . (I think even then she'd decided to help my mother financially, although I can't be sure.) And then suddenly Mrs Orton had to go away – to the North of England, to relatives. (Later on, when I went to boarding school, I used to think what a lot of 'relatives' English girls had and how unfair it was they should have so many and I shouldn't have any except Werner, who certainly didn't count!) Mrs Orton went off to Northumberland and I've often thought how different everything would have been if she hadn't gone . . . She left us alone in the house. She trusted us – what a contrast to the professional landladies! – and everything was fine for a few days. This, I should have said, was late April, 1940.

Then, in May, came the fall of France. As the news came in, my mother began to change. She got like she'd been when we'd been staying with Mrs Haslip – that was the worst of the landladies – and she got worse and worse. She would crouch by the radio set, hour after hour, shivering and shaking and saying it was only a matter of time before the Germans were in London . . . This was bad enough, and I couldn't comfort her – a child can't comfort an adult and, anyway, for a child, an adult's fantasy is for real: that's why it does a child so much harm to be close to a neurotic adult, no matter how much affection there is . . . I could *see* those German tanks coming down Hampstead High Street when my mother talked about it . . . All this was bad enough – but then they started taking the first refugee men away to internment in the coastal areas and my mother went frantic . . . She knew it would be the women's turn next. Of course I couldn't tell her any different. My mother wouldn't go out; she wouldn't leave the house; wouldn't answer the door even. I had to do all the shopping and of course all thought of school was forgotten, though I suppose the authorities would have caught up with that eventually. Mrs Orton was still away; she kept writing to say that she hoped to get back – next week perhaps – and then she kept putting off coming back because her relatives were still sick. Then, in the last week of May, the women in Category B were taken in. My mother, of course, was in Category C – I understood that even then – and I don't think it was likely that she would have actually been interned – but no one could have possibly made her believe that – even if she'd been seeing anyone else beside me, which she wasn't . . . As it was, during the last day or two she hardly spoke at all – just sat there beside the empty grate with the curtains drawn. All the time she was trembling and talking to herself. I'll never forget how she looked that morning – sitting huddled up, not saying anything when I said 'Goodbye, Mummy' or whatever it was I did say: I don't remember.

By that time I'd even taken charge of the money my mother got from the refugee people. I used to get the tea and sugar and things we needed – my mother had given up cooking proper meals and she'd never tried to teach me to cook . . . Anyway, that day, I remember, I went to Sainsbury's and the United Dairies and several other shops and I was a bit longer than usual. When I got back to Belsize Drive I saw a crowd of people outside the house. Then when I got nearer I saw the broken window and the smoke. I used to think I smelt gas – but I don't see how I could have: I must have imagined that afterwards . . . There were policemen and air-raid wardens in their tin hats. The police stopped me going into the house. They told me there'd been an accident and my mother was in hospital. They asked me if there was anyone else I could go to while my mother was in hospital. I couldn't think of anyone but her cousin Werner and so I went there. They were very kind. Werner's wife broke it to me that my mother had been found dead – she didn't actually say she'd killed herself but of course I knew she had: I think I'd known it from the moment I saw the people in front of the house. No one told me any details about it for a long time afterwards, but what had happened was that my mother had turned on the gas-stove, let the kitchen fill with gas, and then struck a match . . . Exactly the thing Mrs Glennie had been afraid of and of course my mother had got the idea from that . . .

That week Mrs Orton came home – she had to, anyway, for apart from my mother's death, her home was partially wrecked. Mrs Orton told Werner that she wanted to take all responsibility for me. Adopt me in fact. She was extraordinary – how extraordinary I only realize now. She was a real Fairy Godmother. Like something in Dickens. She insisted on sending me off to boarding school straight away. I didn't want to go at the time. I was quite happy at school, though. My English improved quickly and I think I became a real English girl – I didn't think anyone would know I was born in Germany, would they? The other girls all accepted me – up to a point. But when they wanted to be nasty they'd always call me 'Miss Hitler'.

This testimony has been quoted at length because it carries to an extreme so many of the elements implicit in the tragedy of the refugees. The first isolation and bewilderment; the 'poor relation' status; the conflict with landladies and others, to some of whom any foreigner was an unknown and even sinister proposition; the growing paranoia before the threat of internment.

If it seems that internment is given too much importance, it must be said that internment (or the threat of it) was pivotal to the refugee experience. If many refugees appear to be still obsessed by Germany and how they left it, internment also continues to dominate many memories: because it shattered their flimsy sense of security, made them doubt, for a brief but chilling interregnum, the sincerity of their hosts. The young recovered quickly and, as we have seen, there are those among the older refugees who even consider that internment was justified. But there are many who still carry its scars within them.

Many German and Austrian refugees had their first contact with the English through the landlady who rented them a room on their arrival in Britain. There were few refugees who were not depressed by the contrast between their former homes in Germany or Austria and the lodgings they had to occupy in England. The more expensive rooms had small gas-cookers; the cheaper, gas-rings. The bathroom in the average boarding-house was shared with at least a dozen other people; and if those other people left it dirty an attempt to clean it by a fastidious refugee could be much resented. The fireplaces in the rooms were an occasion of frustration and some mystery to many of the refugees. They were used to heating radiators, but central heating was almost unknown in Hampstead bedsitters at that time and few refugees knew how to lay and light a fire, although they soon learned. The English fascination with draughts that required you to discuss them endlessly but never do anything to cure them has already been mentioned. The windows rattled and were often so ill-fitting that there was sometimes a gap of an inch or more between the top of the window and the frame. It took refugees some time to learn to use hot-water bottles as a substitute for more sophisticated methods of heating.

But these discomforts were trivial compared with the question of the landlady. As one refugee said, some landladies were angels; others were devils. Angel or devil, kind or cold, the landlady decided the atmosphere of the house. The stereotype English landlady – eternally watchful, distrustfully padding in carpet slippers, aggression muted by suspicion – has suffered some modification since the early 1930s. Landladies are now rather less likely to be professionals with a whole house to be filled: more likely to be just a woman with a room to let. But to many refugees the landlady remained for a long time the most important figure in their lives. Some, like Mrs Glennie, kept up the traditional lodger-landlady exchanges over gas-rings and lights left on. Others were more subtle in their warfare, and remained to their refugee tenants a constant unseen presence, keeping them tense and apprehensive, awaiting her knock. Children were told, 'Don't make such a noise. *She'll* hear you . . . We don't want her coming up complaining . . .'

But the angels, if less numerous, were more remarkable. Some of them tried to convert their German guests to the English way of life by cooking them Cornish pasties and putting before them dinners of roast beef and Yorkshire pudding. Mrs Orton, although technically a landlady, was as her protégée described her 'a Fairy Godmother', taking on complete responsibility for her from childhood to young adulthood; and such disinterested benevolence was rare but not unique.

Nothing damages the relationship between two human beings more than the suggestion of inequality: the accusation that one partner is giving more – emotionally, sexually, or financially – than the other. Thus a major cause of emotional trauma among the refugees was the fact that wives could often find jobs when their husbands could not; could earn more money, more easily. Normally it was not the wives who resented this, but the husbands: usually middle-aged and usually men who had enjoyed success in a business or profession. Now they had to cut their own life-illusion down to size, undergo the agony of reconciling themselves to the fact that their skill, their success had been geared to a particular place, a particular time. Now no one valued those skills, remembered that success. No one wanted a middle-aged Jew who – in so far as he could speak English at all – spent his time talking about the big things he'd done in Frankfurt or Dresden or Mainz. Whereas their wives (often once pampered, kept from effort and decision to the point of feeling themselves frustrated and useless) now found themselves the breadwinners. One can compare Ann Sachs's success as a housekeeper with her husband's failure as a gardener, although he was lucky enough to find himself an accountant again before his humiliating stewardship of Mr Rayner's lawns and flowerbeds could do him or his marriage lasting harm.

But often the husbands felt their wives' competence as an affront. They grew morose; became unshaven late-risers who projected their aggression and self-pity against the wife who might just be returning from eight or nine hours as a domestic for some exacting Kensington lady. The reproaches exchanged at such times could damage a marriage almost beyond repair.

It was a little better when the wife was doing 'home-work' – invariably the most ill-paid work that is obtainable, because the firms that farm it out know they are skimming a buyer's market, that the people who want to work at home are always those who cannot find any other employment. But even then the wife was nearly always quicker and defter at sticking together the pieces of toys; at making artificial flowers or sewing dolls' clothes. The men got bored, complaining that they were too clumsy for this nonsense; once or twice, exasperated beyond limit, smashing up the fruit of several hours' laborious piece-work.

The situation improved after the internees began to be released, from late 1940 onwards. Internment was, for most of the refugees who suffered it, a test of sanity and the will to survive. Once the test had been endured, the refugee felt himself hardened to accept almost anything; but, paradoxically enough, it was from then on that he really had a chance to come to grips with British society.

The coming of Herbert Morrison as Home Secretary in October 1940 and the formation of the Asquith and Lytton Committees all signalled the end of the mood that had led to wholesale internment. Already, at the end of 1939, the British Government had begun to subsidize the refugee aid organizations; now, at the end of 1940, the government agreed to make a financial contribution during the war, equal to the total sum needed for the maintenance of the refugees at the same rate as was paid to the British unemployed and three-quarters of the total sum expended on welfare, administration, and emigration. In fact, from the beginning of 1941 onwards, the amount actually required for the maintenance of the refugees decreased as more and more were granted work permits and absorbed into different aspects of the British war effort. Release from internment marked for most German and Austrian refugees a new phase in their life as exiles. Whether they were interned or not, the refugees whom we have considered – such as the Sachs family, Lothar Kahlmann, and Helga Zinn – entered a new dimension of their life in Britain in late 1940 or early 1941.

Hugo Neher was an exception. He had gone to the factory in Sheffield before internment had been thought of; he remained there until 1943. It is interesting to compare his experience with that of Lothar Kahlmann, who went to a clothing factory in Enfield after being released from internment in 1941. While Hugo was keenly aware of his position as a German turned Britisher making weapons of war to be used against the Germans (he wasn't naturalized British yet of course, but in his own mind he had committed himself to Britain the moment he stepped ashore at Harwich), Lothar's attitude was more passive, more non-committal. He was a German Jew; he was working in an English factory. So what about it? (It seems mere hair-splitting to distinguish between making uniforms for British soldiers who are being clothed for the ultimate purpose of killing Germans and making sights for guns that will eventually be aimed at Germans.)

Most of Hugo's fellow-workers were men. A great proportion of them had been engaged in the manufacture of optical lenses or in the camera industry before they came to the factory. Hugo came into immediate contact with two men: William Ramsden and Leslie Dudd. Ramsden was at least fifty. He was lean, with sparse sandy hair, and he always wore old-fashioned steel-rimmed glasses and a long apron. He was a Tory in what struck Hugo as an unusual and almost obsolete way: a Tory from the vantage-point of an acquiescent underdog, not from the more usual viewpoint of someone who fancied himself as a topdog, actual or potential. Hugo felt that Ramsden could have crystallized his attitude in the phrase 'that station of life to which God has called us'. 'We don't understand these matters,' he would say, stuffing his pipe full of black plug. 'It's for them who *know* – them in authority!' He would be speaking of the general conduct of the war and particularly of Churchill's sacking of various generals in the Middle East. Ramsden detested Russia and when Hitler turned East in 1941 he was divided between his desire to see the Germans suffer the same fate as Napoleon and his feeling that Hitler's *volte-face* had only paid Stalin out for his treachery in signing the Soviet–German pact. Ramsden never argued: he simply made pronouncements which had the weight of replies by the permanent under-secretary of a ministry. He was very polite to Hugo. Only once did he reveal any anti-semitic prejudice – when he spoke of the Bolsheviks: 'All Russian Jews of course . . .' Then he must have suddenly remembered Hugo's origins, for he let his words trail away and he went on filing the edge of a lens.

Hugo never directly contradicted Ramsden. He merely issued mildly phrased counter-statements. He liked Ramsden; he relished him as an example of a nearly extinct kind of British working man. Ramsden had the outlook of a member of one of the medieval craft guilds: no other comparison could reflect his intense conservatism or his obsessive pride in his work.

There was nothing medieval about Leslie Dudd. He had been employed by the Kodak company and was as skilled as Ramsden in his own way, although he was his antithesis in everything else. Dudd was nearer thirty than fifty; he was a Communist and although, as Hugo knew, there were a number of Jews in the British Communist party, he mixed his Communism with a back-handed kind of anti-semitism. He was as obsessed with 'Jewish capitalism' as Hilaire Belloc was, Hugo thought. (He had read *The Jews* a year or two earlier.) Dudd would hold forth in the Lancashire quack that contrasted with Ramsden's slower, gentler Yorkshire. (Ramsden sounded very like J. B. Priestley, who was at that time giving the broadcasts that compared with Churchill's speeches as a tonic for morale.) By a convoluted dialectic of his own, Dudd managed to excuse the German-Soviet pact on the grounds that 'Stalin knew that Hitler was being backed by the fucking Jewish capitalists' – Dudd pronounced the word 'cap-*it*-alists' – 'I mean, naturally he had to buy some time to prepare, see? Just like Mr Fucking Umbrella Man Chamberlain. And who's to say he wasn't right, now the fucking yiddish bankers have set Hitler on the Russians? They're still playing the same old money game, right?'

Hugo's origins were as obvious to Dudd as to Ramsden. He never called Hugo a 'yid' to his face and for a long time Hugo said nothing, adding his dimension of silence to Ramsden's occasional grunts of disapproval. (Once, as Dudd was going off to his tea-break, Ramsden nodded and said, 'An ignorant man', and this was the only comment he ever made.) At last Hugo decided to attack. He asked Dudd whether he'd ever heard of Buchenwald or Dachau.

'Fucking right, I have!'

'Who do you think are in there?' Hugo demanded. 'Oh – I know you'll tell me some Communists are in there. But – *Jews are in there!* For one Communist there are a thousand Jews. Can you deny that?'

'They're not the Jews I'm talking about! *They're* not in the concentration camps. These are *poor Jews*! Poor little arse-out-of-their-trousers bastards like you and me, mate!'

'They're Jews. That's all. Every kind of Jew. Millionaires *and* paupers. Jews! Jews!' Suddenly Hugo felt very angry. His voice trembled as he added, 'What does their money matter when they stand naked, huddled together, standing on each other's feet, waiting to go into the gas chamber? Does money matter then?'

Dudd said nothing, although his lips parted as if he were about to speak. His tongue came out, lizard-like, and he licked his lips. Ramsden cleared his throat portentously. Hugo felt he had shown his nakedness to the enemy and yet he did not regret having spoken. He said quietly, 'I'm sorry for you, Dudd. You don't seem able to tell the truth from a lie.'

Dudd still did not reply. He turned back to the work on the bench in front of him.

Hugo thought the incident was forgotten. Then, a few days later, Peter Lehman, the only other German refugee working in the same section, approached him. Lehman was a middle-aged Berliner, an optician by profession. With an unusual sense of appropriateness the Ministry of Labour had sent him to this factory.

He spoke to Hugo in German : 'That was a big mistake, wasn't it?'

'I don't think so,' Hugo said. He knew Lehman had heard his outburst.

'Oh, it was,' Lehman said. 'I heard it all and I think you'll find it was a mistake.'

'Is the truth ever a mistake?' Hugo asked.

'Remember who you are and who I am,' Lehman said. 'Guests! On sufferance! Barely tolerated! In fact, speaking like that you were being unfair to me and to every other refugee in this factory or anywhere else.' Lehman appeared to be getting excited. 'Do you think there couldn't be . . . reprisals?'

'That's ridiculous. We're not in Germany now.'

'Exactly!' Lehman repeated in triumph. 'We're in England and we're very glad to be in England – and alive.'

'Well?'

'Well – it's not for us to engage in politics. That's for Englishmen. We – we have no right to speak!'

'England has given me asylum,' Hugo said. 'I tried to join the British Army but I didn't succeeed . . . But I offer England my work; my life if necessary. I intend to be naturalized after the war.'

'You're not naturalized yet. You're still a refugee. You should keep quiet. You're harming us all.'

'I didn't think the British admired cowards,' Hugo said.

Lehman turned and walked away.

Again, Hugo thought the incident closed, but some days afterwards Ramsden approached him and asked him if he would like to come home to tea one evening. (This, Hugo knew by this time, would mean traditional high tea: a substantial meal.) Hugo said he would be delighted. Ramsden nodded. Now he seemed embarrassed.

'I'd love to come,' Hugo reiterated.

Ramsden cleared his throat. 'Happen I'll mention it . . . One thing . . . We won't be having any bacon with the tea.' He paused, looking at Hugo almost appealingly. 'The missis isn't too keen on it.'

By contrast, Lothar Kahlmann neither argued with his fellow-workers nor was invited home by them. They were mostly girls in their late teens and early twenties, and married women in their late thirties and forties. They treated Lothar politely, calling him 'Mr K'; but he remained essentially alone, isolated from everyone by his sex – there were only a dozen other men on the staff and they were all supervisors or executives – his age, his German accent, and his gentle but curiously opaque personality which had kept him a stranger even to the ebullient girls in his cousin Mark's workroom. The women in Enfield all said 'Good morning, Mr K' and 'Good night, Mr K'. The only time when masks were let slip was when Lothar caught two young girls laughing at him. He heard them gurgling and spluttering at the table behind him. He turned round to see what was the matter and they became even more helpless with giggling, refusing to catch his eye but turning as red as lobsters. He went back to his work, more puzzled than angry. Passing their work-table after the girls had gone to their lunch, he saw what had been making them laugh: a crudely-drawn picture of a bespectacled man, obviously intended for Lothar himself, caught in what appeared to be a jungle, but the words below the picture read 'Mr Moses in the Bullrushes'.

Lothar did not mention the incident to anyone – who was there in Britain or indeed in Germany to whom he could have mentioned it? – but it remained in his mind to baffle him. The next morning the girls said 'Good morning, Mr K' as usual and they never laughed at him again; indeed, it seemed to Lothar that they were slightly embarrassed when they met him. The only change was that now they occasionally offered him sweets or bits of chocolate which, after hesitating the first time, he always accepted. Lothar continued to work at his uniforms, doing the non-routine jobs that were beyond the girl machinists. Every night he would take a bus home to his lodgings in a semi-detached house on the outskirts of Enfield. His landlady was a woman in her fifties. Her husband had been a regular staff instructor with the Territorial Army: he was now in the Middle East. They had a son serving in an anti-aircraft unit in Norfolk and a daughter still at home who worked in a solicitor's office in Enfield. Lothar's relations with his landlady and her daughter were most agreeable – and totally remote. Contact between them soon narrowed down to a stylized exchange of 'Good mornings', 'Good evenings', and remarks about the weather. (Like most Continentals, Lothar had read about this weather-talk before he ever came to Britain; it was always depicted as a ritual that symbolized the cold formality of English social life.)

Lothar had always been a great reader of newspapers and magazines; and no longer being able to get German ones, he now tended to go to bed earlier and earlier. He would not have described himself as lonely, for, essentially, he had always been alone. The only time his routine was disturbed was when there were air-raids and he took refuge with Mrs Kershaw and her daughter in the Morrison Shelter in the back room. Lothar crawled into the shelter with them because he knew Mrs Kershaw would be upset if he didn't but he did not believe that the Morrison would save them if a bomb came down. (The Morrison Shelter was named after Herbert Morrison and was a kind of steel table erected indoors. Like the Anderson no protection against a direct hit, it could save lives if the walls of the house collapsed around it.) He was embarrassed by the enforced sociability of these occasions and exhausted by the almost continuous tea-making throughout a long raid. Lothar did not like tea, but – again conditioned by what he had read were taboos sacred to the English – had never dared say so.

Helga Zinn began her training as a nurse in March 1941. All arrangements had been made by the labour exchange on the Isle of Man. Having no friend or relative alive in the world whom she might have wished to see, she went straight from Douglas to the hospital in Lancashire where she had been accepted for training as a probationer.

The hospital, which was dignified with the title of a Royal Infirmary, represented Victorian institutional architecture at its grimmest and it was shrouded with the accumulated soot of fifty years. But to Helga it stood as a vision of freedom, of future achievement and happiness. When she first arrived at the Nurses' Home, she felt dazed at the luxury of having a room to herself again. She wanted to close the door and lock it, and then hug herself at the sheer intoxicating joy of being alone! For the first time she realized that she had never really got used to sharing a room with Maria Seeghers and Marta Geilart and three other women. Such a total negation of privacy slowly destroys a deep-buried part of the self, flays some inner skin that takes a long time to heal. Now Helga absorbed every detail of her small bedroom with delight, even enjoying the view from the window – the grimy brickwork of the Surgical Wing, only a yard or two away. She felt she could not bear it if anyone came and knocked at her door, but that first night no one did.

The next day she met the other probationer nurses. Five were English, two of them from the Home Counties: slim, pale blondes. A few years later Helga would have inferred from their clipped yet breathy accents the tweeded mummies and rose-growing City daddies in the background. The other three were from Cheshire. They had been 'directed' into nursing and they had much less confidence than the southern girls, although they seemed in some undefinable way older. There were also two girls from Dublin: one of them noisy and extrovert, living up to what even Helga could recognize as the stereotype of the harum-scarum Irish colleen; the other so timid that she never spoke at all. It was not until two days later that Leonie Konrad, the other refugee probationer, arrived.

Leonie was about the same age as Helga but looked ten years older. She was short and dark with features that were finely wrought but too massive to accord with any ideal of feminine beauty. Helga thought Leonie's face resembled one of the ancient Semitic masks she had seen in the museum at Munich. In her nurse's uniform Leonie looked disconcertingly exotic. She was an only child and her mother and father had died in the killing-centre at Auschwitz. Sponsored by a refugee organization, she had arrived in England as a schoolgirl some years before. She had not been interned and had worked briefly in a factory before being accepted for nursing. Leonie attached herself to Helga from the beginning, and Helga was at once aware of Leonie's timidity and the hesitancy with which she expressed herself – even in German. After several years her command of English was still very poor and halting.

The sister in charge of the probationers was a Welshwoman called Morgan. She was also small and dark with heavy features – indeed, physically she resembled Leonie more than did any of the other probationers, including Helga herself. No one liked Sister Morgan. Admittedly her relationship with the probationers was that of a sergeant-major to a squad of new recruits, but even allowing for this she was harsh and difficult to please. At this time the training of a probationer consisted not only of elementary nursing duties – learning to make beds, taking temperatures, giving injections – but also of an infinity of cleaning and polishing chores: cutlery, cuspidors, surgical instruments, bedpans . . . Sister Morgan set impossibly high standards for these tasks and decided whether or not these standards had been met in an entirely arbitrary way. She made no secret of her conviction that Leonie Konrad was lazy and probably stupid and was always ready to pounce on her. How far this sprang from the intense irritation she displayed at Leonie's poor English – which, intensified by her awareness of Sister Morgan's hostility, became almost incoherent at times – and how much from anti-semitism Helga could not decide. If it was anti-semitism, it did not extend to Helga herself, for Sister Morgan actually seemed to like and favour her. She treated all the probationers with a merely grudging civility but on the rare occasions when she had praise to give it was usually Helga who got it. Helga wondered if the woman was subconsciously compensating for her hostility to one Jewess by being nice to another. She rejected another explanation: that she was herself the most intelligent and promising of the probationers. She knew she spoke English well now – she'd done all she could to enlarge her vocabulary and improve her pronunciation when she was on the Isle of Man – and she was quick and deft at bandaging or setting a splint. Naturally this pleased her, but she felt uneasy, almost guilty that Leonie was made a scapegoat. Could she deflect Sister Morgan's enmity to herself? She rejected the thought as mere self-dramatization and wondered how she could help Leonie.

Leonie was slow and clumsy in all physical tasks, but Helga believed that this might be because she often did not understand the explanations that were being given and, realizing this and fearing Sister Morgan's anger, fell into a panic. For similar reasons she failed to make any progress with the theoretical part of her training. This was conducted by the sister tutor, a Sister Wilson, who, although more agreeable than Sister Morgan, would still gesture hopelessly when she asked Leonie to identify a particular bone or organ on the wall chart and then encountered the stammering near-incoherence that was Leonie's response to a question she might hardly understand.

The only way to help her seemed to be to improve her English. Helga was convinced that Leonie's reputation for stupidity was now so firmly established in her own mind that it actually prevented her from understanding much of what was said to her. So Helga suggested that Leonie might come to her room for a few evenings a week: then they would speak English. Tactfully, Helga had suggested that the benefits would be mutual but Leonie said, 'Already you speak English fine, Helga . . . It is for you to do the teaching to me and this you know, I think.'

Although they would be exhausted physically after a long day on the wards, they would meet every night in Helga or Leonie's room and work on an English phrase-book and that day's newspapers. The newspapers were particularly useful and Leonie began to make some progress – although Helga sometimes wondered how she could ever escape from the concept of herself as an ugly lumbering girl who could do nothing right. A concept totally unjustified, for Leonie, appropriately dressed and poised, could have been beautiful – had anyone succeeded in persuading her of her own beauty. Helga realized for the first time how relative are 'ugliness' and 'beauty', how often the expression of attitudes already conditioned. She realized, too, that Leonie was, at only a little over twenty years old, imprisoned in her past. Her inward eye was turned backwards, in the manner of a very old man or woman who survives through re-creating the scenes that built their life. Finding the present and the recent past intolerable, she escaped into scenes of her childhood with her dead father and mother. Their laborious English conversations over – and it grew less laborious as the weeks passed and Leonie every day found the *Daily Express* easier to read – Leonie would talk softly and passionately in German, creating a fragile bubble of recollected happiness: the little Leonie playing on the sands at Ruegen Island with her mother and father; sitting under a bright parasol the day her father brought home a little dog to her that her mother (a great reader and perhaps an admirer of Colette?) named Sido . . . But the larger the bubble blew as Leonie delved farther and farther back in time, the more violent (Helga learned) would be the reaction: the anguished dissolution of memory into tears. Her dreaming over, Leonie would sit and cry and cry. All Helga could do was sit beside her, wishing she could cry with her, bereft of anything to say. It was one thing to teach Leonie to read the *Daily Express*; another to create for her a future – or rather, a sense that the future even existed.

Somehow, indeed, Leonie *was* to create such a sense of the future for, years later, Helga heard that she had married and had children. She must have changed a great deal, Helga thought, to have been able to face the responsibility of children – and then she thought again: maybe Leonie's inadequacy had been merely external; facing a test like motherhood she might be more serene than many apparently confident, more capable women. But that was several years away.

During the rest of her training in this hospital she certainly benefited by her greater knowledge of English; she was never to please Sister Morgan but at least she was spared the earlier humiliations. She and Helga remained friends but, to Helga's relief, she grew less dependent on her. After about a year, unrecognizably more confident and competent, she applied for permission to continue her training at a hospital in the south of England, giving proximity to relatives (Helga had not known she had any alive) as a reason.

Helga herself was happier than she would have believed possible. She loved nursing: she was to pass out in both theoretical and practical work with the highest marks of any of the probationers. Now she spoke English so well that she was no longer aware of the different language lying there as a barrier; she began, if the phrase had any meaning, to think in English. She still considered herself German and Jewish but the question of her own racial identity never bothered her until, one day, she agreed to go out with one of the doctors at the hospital. She had been aware of him as an agreeable – but despite his persona of a doctor – rather insipid young man: very Nordic, perhaps even 'German' looking with his fair hair and fair evanescent moustache. He knew Helga as perhaps the most efficient of the junior nurses. Then she happened to go to a symphony concert at the big black Mechanics Institute in the centre of the town: that massive symbol of Victorian cultural endeavour that housed everything from the Lancastrian Players in *The Ghost Train* to displays of Morris dancing. This time it was a performance of Beethoven's *Eroica* by an orchestra recruited over a radius of thirty miles. Helga had heard the *Eroica* many times in Munich and she thought this performance left much to be desired. But as a foreigner and a guest in Britain she would not have dared say this to anyone. Afterwards she saw the young blond doctor going down the steps of the institute in front of her. He turned and looked up at her over his shoulder, then waited for her. She was careful to praise the performance.

'Very good, wasn't it?' he said. 'Surprising to get such a good executant standard among amateurs in an English provincial town.'

Helga agreed. She noticed that his cool doctor's manner had been abandoned: he was almost gushing.

'Of course you must be used to the very best in concert performances, coming from Germany...'

'In Germany at one time,' Helga said. 'Not so much now.'

In fact there was still a lot of good music being performed there; but Helga did not feel she should say that of all the arts music was the one least affected by the Hitler regime; that of all artists musicians were apparently those most ready to collaborate with the Nazis. Was it the ascendancy of Wagner and the perverted ethos he symbolized?

'I don't suppose you've ever heard one of Sir Henry Wood's concerts? At the Queen's Hall?' the young doctor was saying. 'The Queen's Hall is in London of course. You *have* to be in London, really: that's the centre of culture in this country.'

They were well on their way back to the hospital by now. The young doctor went on talking eagerly – even naïvely, Helga thought, and she found this rather endearing. The nicest doctors were always so conscious of being doctors! And then there was the flattering implication that in Helga he had discovered a fellow *cognoscente* among a wilderness of Philistines. She agreed to go out with him the following Thursday, when she had her half-day.

They went out together three or four times. Each time the blond young doctor would be waiting for Helga in his sports car just outside the main gate of the hospital. Then they would drive to some local beauty spot, like the ruined Cistercian Abbey that stood beside the river a few miles from the town. The doctor would bring a picnic-basket packed by his landlady who, Helga presumed, must adore him for he seemed to enjoy an extraordinary standard of comfort and attention at a very low rent.

The doctor's Christian name was George but somehow Helga never got to think him as George; a ridiculous label one of the English nurses gave him, 'Doctor Kildare', kept attaching itself instead. She compromised by rarely calling him anything. Curiously, their relationship never really developed beyond the level of their first exchanges at the concert. They remained two strangers: each made conventional signals to the other; the replies were equally conventional. George didn't talk as much about medicine as she would have expected. He preferred to conduct her on a kind of conversational tour of British life and institutions. The king. The queen. Buckingham Palace. Ascot – with special reference to the Royal Enclosure and those who were allowed into it. Polo at Hurlingham. The Royal Academy Summer Show. Helga gathered that George's family enjoyed the freedom of this world, so he naturally regarded his exile as a houseman in this black northern hospital as grim indeed. He would have gone into the Royal Army Medical Corps but for some slight disability he did not specify. He hardly ever mentioned the other doctors at the hospital and never spoke of Helga's fellow-nurses. Helga wondered how she had managed to slip through the net he interposed between himself and the large majority of other people he considered his social inferiors. Perhaps as a foreigner she did not count? She thought it curious that he never asked her anything about Germany, herself, or her family; never showed the slightest interest in the circumstances that had driven her to England as a refugee. He knew she had been a student in Munich: that was about all he did know about her. He was content to project a conventional image of Germany – an outmoded, nineteenth-century Englishman's Grand Tour image in fact: a Germany of pretty boats sailing down the Rhine; of laughing young men downing great steins of beer (pure *Student Prince*!); of magnificent performances of Beethoven in massive, pillared concert halls (music, indeed, was the only area in which Helga and he had any genuine contact). It was all unreal. Each time she met him she felt more strongly that there was a big blank wall between them, against which their polite words knocked in vain.

The third or fourth time they met George was talking about the relationship between the Kaiser and King Edward VII and he happened to use a phrase he was always using to Helga, 'You Germans...'

'Not any longer!' she said sharply. 'It's not "you Germans" any longer. Not for us Jews! Didn't you know that Hitler deprived us of German citizenship?'

George said nothing.

'I'm a Jewess,' Helga said. 'Oh – the British Goverment still call me a German, but that's just a technicality. I'm not, any more!'

She wondered why he continued silent. At last he said, 'I . . . I admire your honesty, Helga. But you know, you . . .' He was almost stammering. 'You know you don't really look like a Jewess!'

'Don't you think so?' Helga said.

'No – not in the least.' He spoke more confidently now. 'With your blonde hair and fair skin?' He smiled and shook his head. 'And the way you speak!' He gestured enthusiastically. 'You don't have a *Jewish personality*. If I introduced you to anyone—'

'Why don't you mention my nose?' Helga cut in. 'It isn't very big, is it? And it's really quite straight. I suppose you were brought up to think all Jews had big hook noses?'

'I don't think you quite understand—'

'I understand very well. You think you're flattering me, telling me I don't look Jewish!' Helga paused. 'You think I want to "pass" as a gentile like some negroes pretend to be white? Is that the idea? Why, my dear man, I wouldn't pretend to be a' – she groped for the word: she'd read it somewhere, some time – 'a *schickser* for anything! I'm a Jewess. And I'm proud of it.'

George stood motionless, a flush of embarrassment – or anger? – gradually staining his cheeks. At his feet lay the half-unpacked picnic-basket; behind him the river. Helga was to remember the swish of the biscuit-coloured water as it swept through the osiers that lined the banks.

Politeness made them both try to salvage was what left of the afternoon; but of course there was really nothing to salvage anyway. When they had allowed a decent amount of time to pass and had parted outside the hospital with vague mutual promises to meet again that both knew would not be fulfilled, Helga went to her room in the Nurses' Home. She lay down on the bed to think. Since she was not in love with the young doctor there was no emotional problem involved, or rather, there was an emotional problem of a different kind. Suddenly, in a manner so simple that nothing could have prepared her for it, she was confronted by the problem of who she was, what she was. She looked in the mirror and saw her blonde hair and straight nose as a betrayal of something. But how would it help to look like Leonie Konrad? Was Leonie more truly a Jewess than Helga because of her looks? And because she spoke with a German accent? – but then her accent was purely German and had nothing to do with being Jewish.

For months and even years Helga continued to brood over this question. The other nurses had been agog when the doctor took her out; she had to disregard their excited twitterings when he ceased to do so. Of course Helga knew that she had given his remarks an importance they certainly had not possessed for him – but in the fact that he automatically assumed she would not want to look Jewish lay the real enormity of the matter for her. It set so many doubts boiling in her mind. Apart from her looks, which she could not help, was she denying her race, her real self, everything that had gone to her making, by learning English so well, becoming – apparently – so 'English' in every way?

For the first time in her life she wondered about Zionism. Everyone she had known in Germany had always presented it to her as a crank movement: now she wondered. Was Zionism an answer to a Jew's loss of identity, a way of finding oneself?

For the moment she had to go on being English; an English nurse helping in the English war effort against the Nazis. But later – there was the promise of the National Home . . . Perhaps Israel – if and when it came into being – would offer her an answer.

Few of the refugees had the problem of their identity as German or Austrian Jews dramatized for them in such concrete terms as Helga Zinn. But even if they had undergone a comparable experience, many of them might have shrugged it off and not suffered the sense of shock Helga did. This, after all, was the attitude gentiles had towards Jews. They had always had it; always would have it. Who, sitting where they were sitting, would want to be a Jew? Accept it then; the girl should have expected this the first time she went out with the doctor.

Helga, like so many who came alone or as mere children, remained largely isolated from her fellow-refugees. By contrast there were others who lived in a world peopled almost entirely by refugees. These included those who came as families; those particularly dependent on the refugee organizations; and those who involved themselves with the work of the organizations. From the beginning of German and Austrian emigration to Britain, various groups were devoted to keeping some sense of national identity alive.

There were Austrian Centres in various towns, founded under the aegis of the Council of Austrians in Great Britain. The Council of Austrians in Great Britain had been created in 1938: its chairman was Professor Walter Schiff, formerly of the University of Vienna. In January 1939 the council opened two houses in London to facilitate social contact among Austrian refugees and the Austrian Centre in London was opened in March 1939. Although the Council of Austrians concerned itself with mainly cultural functions, it was also involved in what might be described as constructive political action when, in October 1939, it issued a memorandum analysing and criticizing the work of the Aliens Tribunals. A very practical measure by the council was the establishment, at the end of 1939, of a Studio for Arts and Crafts. This offered technical training – for instince, welding and other engineering skills – of a kind desperately needed by middle-class refugees anxious to contribute to the British war effort.

The Austrian Centre offered itself as an ethnic oasis in the grey hinterland of steamy tea-shops and draughty bedsitters. At the centre the Austrian refugees found a library with both English and German books; classes in English and other subjects; concerts and plays. A group of actors and playwrights who had worked at the Vienna Kleinkunstbühne started it again at the Austrian Centre; and, when internment killed this venture, it was succeeded by the Kammerspiele under the direction of a well-known Czech producer.

The centre also offered a restaurant specializing in Viennese food at reasonable prices; a hostel to provide temporary accommodation; and a co-operative workshop for the repair of refugees' clothing and shoes.

There was no German equivalent for the Council of Austrians in Great Britain. The best known of the German refugee organizations was the Free German League of Culture. (By 'refugee organizations' is meant in this instance organizations of the refugees themselves, not the British Jewish groups organized to help them.) The purpose of the league was described as an attempt to bridge the gap between German culture – 'suppressed in our Homeland' – and the native British spirit. The Church of England gave the league a house in Hampstead which was adapted along the lines of the Austrian Centre. The first president was the German author Berthold Viertel. Other well-known artists, writers, and actors were associated with the league, including Oscar Kokoschka, Ludwig Renn, Lily Kann, and Erich Freund. In July 1940 plays and concerts were organized to raise funds for interned members of the league.

Internment and the subsequent dispersal of many refugees in the Forces and over a wide area of industry made it hard to maintain the collective spirit of German Jewry in exile. Later, an organization was founded that has done much to keep this spirit alive. This is the Association of Jewish Refugees in Great Britain; born among a group of refugees in an internment camp. Its secretary is Dr Werner Rosenstock and the 'A.J.R.' as it is known has sought to preserve the essence of German Jewish culture by every means in its power. In fact the A.J.R. stands with the Warburg Institute, the Wiener Library (without whose co-operation neither this nor any of the numerous books about the Nazi persecution of the Jews could have been written), and the Leo Baeck Institute as a refugee institution that has enriched British life.

The refugees outside London were those most likely to be isolated, although they were also those most likely to come into contact with the local gentile population, simply because they were much less likely to be living in a traditionally Jewish district like Hampstead or Golders Green.

There was one section of the war effort that actually brought refugees from various countries together. This was the B.B.C. service of foreign broadcasts to the enemy and enemy-occupied countries of Europe. The centre of this work was Bush House in the Aldwych, London : a vast honeycomb of offices and studios. It was from there that the broadcasts were planned and made; often during the actual bombing under conditions of great inconvenience and actual physical danger. During the blitz, to make the dawn bulletins which went out at 7 a.m., the broadcasters had to sleep in the huge underground dormitories below Bush House. Before each transmission they had to collect the news material and arrange and translate it in readiness before going to the microphone.

Not all the refugees involved in this work broadcast themselves. Some were language supervisors whose job it was to read the translations and original talks and then sit and listen in the studio, making sure that the broadcasters adhered to the original text. Others were employed by the monitoring service at Caversham near Reading. This was instituted by the B.B.C. early in the war and still exists, but its present orientation is naturally different from that of the war years. Then the duty of the monitors was to listen to all broadcasts from enemy and enemy-occupied territory; now the focus is on the Middle East and Eastern and Central Europe.

The predicament of the refugee actor would seem at first to be more crippling than that of the refugee author. The actor's instruments are his voice, his face, his body. He has to interpret the visible surface of life in the country he functions in. Coming to Britain from Germany or Austria, the refugee actor had not only to master a new language but also a new set of reactions to social and emotional stimuli: every society externalizes its feeling in different ways. But on its most basic level the art of the actor presupposes the ability to mimic and mime and, once they had acquired a sufficient grasp of English, a number of refugees began to get work – aided by the fact that many topical plays and films, reflecting the war and the years preceding it, often featured brutal Gestapo men and curt be-monocled *gauleiters*. Thus, ironically, some refugee Jews found themselves earning a living by imitating their persecutors. Of course many of the better known German and Austrian actors and actresses had appeared in England and America; their art was already cosmopolitan by the time they could no longer live in their native countries. Such an actor was Anton Wohlbruck (who became Anton Walbrook and starred on the West End stage and in many British films). Others were Albert Bassermann, Charles Goldner, Walter Rilla (who has also written novels), Lily Kann, and Lucie Mannheim.

One actor's story reflects a splendid instinct for survival. When he arrived in England this actor, a German, knew no English at all. Then, he says:

I had this problem. How to learn English. Of course the way to learn it was to go to school – the Berlitz School maybe or a private teacher. To work at it eight hours a day, six days a week. But this was impossible. I had no money and without money, no time. I was living in one hostel, my wife in another. She was fortunate: she did know some English. Not much, but enough for basics. 'Thank you' and 'Good morning' and 'Can you please tell me where is the Ladies' Toilet.' So, when we meet – and we met every day, wet or fine : I have to walk from the far end of Grays Inn Road to West Hampstead – when we meet she gives me a few words. And, don't forget, knowing a few herself, she can always pick up a few more, but I – at the beginning – I was quite helpless, like a man dropped on Mars listening to the residents talking!

Gradually she gives me a few words – enough to go looking for a job. By this time the permits are not so difficult [the actor and his wife had escaped from Nazi-occupied Austria very late, going through Italy by devious ways to England, arriving late in 1940]. It can't be a job that requires much talking – a smile and a 'Thank you' and another smile – that's about the range. I thought at first of going to the Air Raid Precautions, to see if they want me for digging out the rubble that the Luftwaffe was making of people's houses every night. You don't need much English for that. But no : they don't want me. Security maybe – I haven't been in England long – or perhaps they have enough people already. So I keep looking and then another refugee tells me of a job he has heard of going in Jermyn Street. Liftman. By now I can count up to six in English and there were only five floors in this building. So with 'Good morning' and 'Good night' as well I can get by.

So I went along and I suppose then, at that time of the war, there was difficulty getting anyone, for I landed the job . . . Every day I take people up and down to the different offices and as I press the buttons – 'Going up' 'Going down' – I've learned to say that too by this time – I listen to what they're saying and perhaps, with luck, I understand some of it. Sometimes I'm baffled but, bit by bit, the pieces fall into place. I begin to understand whole sentences. I'm not speaking English yet but I'm a lot better than I was . . .

The next thing my wife makes a suggestion. We're together by now; we have a bedsitter in Kilburn; we can afford it, we're both earning. She's working in a restaurant – washing up and some cooking and she's very good at cooking. So she suggests we could go to a hotel or guest-house where they'd take us on as husband and wife – she cooking and I have enough English now to be porter or so she tells me. So we advertise, or rather she does, and we get several replies : the labour situation is bad in the catering business at the time and we even get a choice of places . . . We decide and we go to north Cornwall. This is quite a big place – much bigger than we thought when we got the reply to the advertisement. It's run by an elderly English couple and they're getting past it now so we find we're doing most of the work. There are seventy meals to cook three times a day : breakfast, lunch, and dinner. This is very heavy on my wife and in addition as a Continental she's not used to the heavy English style of cooking – even with rationing! She's there at the stove from morning to night and I'm rushing in and out with trays serving the guests. Some are charming : friendly, helpful. A few are bastards : barking at the waiter for keeping them waiting! The old couple, the owners, they realize they're on to a good thing and they leave us to do more and more. At the end we're more or less running the whole place; getting up at half past five and going to bed at one. Obviously we can't stand it much longer . . .

Then the old man, the owner, has a stroke and dies : the place goes up for sale. The solicitors ask us if we will carry it on till they find a buyer but of course we refuse. We go back to London and get a much easier job in a smaller house in Baron's Court – only twenty-five breakfasts and no lunches. By now I understand everything that's said to me and I'm beginning to speak English quite well. Believe me – in addition to being waiter, porter, and general factotum I was professional eavesdropper as well! I would get the gist of a conversation while I was delivering one course and then pick up the threads again when I came back with the next. It's the best way to learn a language I know.

After some time in Baron's Court this actor met a refugee film director, whom he had worked for during the director's days with U.F.A. Through him the actor got non-speaking roles in wartime documentary shorts and later played a German general in one of the many heroes-of-the-Resistance movies that were being made at that time.

Though apparently in a more favourable position than the refugee actor, the refugee author was in fact worse off. In theory, of course, it was possible for him to write at night while pursuing another job by day; but any writer has deep inner obstacles to surmount and to many of these Germans and Austrians these obstacles must have appeared unsurmountable. Many who escaped from Germany physically unscathed were inwardly so scarred that they were condemned to a permanent silence. They had stayed too long in the poisoned air of Nazi Germany; and it must be remembered that no German writer of any significance, with the exception of Ernst Juenger, was published during the Hitler years. On 10 May 1933, before the approving, culture-hating eyes of thousands of cheering students, a great multitude of books had been burned in a hecatomb that not only included Germans like Brecht, Remarque, Feuchtwanger, and Thomas and

Heinrich Mann, but such foreigners as H. G. Wells, Jack London, Upton Sinclair, and Proust. Then in September 1933 the Reich Chamber of Culture had been set up. Its seven sub-divisions, the Reich Chambers of Fine Arts, were set down like monolithic tombstones over music, literature, visual arts, the theatre, the press, radio, and the cinema. Even before they left Germany or Austria these writers had suffered wounds that exile was not likely to heal.

An almost impossible choice faced those whose creative powers were still intact. Should they continue to write in German? – lacking, almost certainly, a publisher, and, even if published, any significant audience. Or should they concentrate on perfecting their English with a view to eventually writing in that language?

Writers like Thomas Mann, naturally, continued to write in German. The successive books in his biblical novel sequence about Joseph were published by Fischer Verlag, first in Berlin (the firm's normal home); later, as political pressures worsened, in Vienna; and finally in Sweden. There were other refugee publishers like Querido Verlag and Albert de Lange who functioned mainly in the Netherlands prior to the Nazi invasion; but as the war progressed the outlook for the refugee author writing in German grew steadily darker.

It would be true to say that, with such exceptions as Kafka and Thomas Mann, German literature has never been appreciated by English-speaking readers in the way French literature has. Few German writers who came to Britain as refugees found it possible to break through to an English public while still writing in German. Those who did were those who had been well known through translation before they became exiles, like Robert Neumann, who advised the PEN club on the distribution of the Baldwin Fund for refugees; Julius Berstl, author of *The Sun's Bright Child*, the well-known novel about Edmund Kean; and Richard Friedenthal, the friend of Stefan Zweig, who revised and completed Zweig's *Balzac* after his death, working under very difficult conditions.

For those who thought of writing in English there were some illustrious precedents. The most famous of these was Joseph Conrad, although Conrad is said to have 'thought in French' and to have put foreign phrases into his first drafts right up to the end of his life. But Conrad had served for many years in the Merchant Service before he started writing; and despite the many tensions of his life he never faced the difficulties that were commonplace for the refugees.

Although his masterpiece *Darkness at Noon* was written in German, one refugee was to achieve a reputation for writing in English as notable as Conrad's. But Arthur Koestler was a Hungarian, and Hungarian writers are in a category of their own. The size of the Hungarian public has enforced a cultural emigration on ambitious young men. (No one has chronicled the Hungarian contribution to Hollywood, but it must have been immense.) Before the Second World War, at least, young Hungarian writers usually chose to write in German, as did the young Arthur Koestler, changing later to English. Other Hungarians who have achieved this transition include the versatile Paul Tabori, who settled in Britain before the war and became the associate and biographer of Alexander Korda and the author of many books.

But the Germans – and only to a slightly lesser extent the Austrians – were at a disadvantage compared to the nimble, professionally expatriate Hungarians. Their temperament, their whole approach were against them. Even if they knew English well enough to begin to write in it, what, they asked themselves, did they know of English life?

Here, of course, they confronted a deeper problem than that of language. How much confidence can an American feel, writing of England; or an Englishman, writing of America – despite having a language more or less in common? With how much less confidence, then, could an Austrian or German embrace British life as a subject. The exiled writer is almost compelled to take as his subject exile itself and to dramatize his own stance as an outsider precipitated into an alien society. And a writer in this position has to struggle against accepting the kind of folklore every nation creates about its neighbours. Thus the German or Austrian almost inevitably carried before him various stereotypes of the English. The Englishman was cold and reserved, always two or three drinks below par. In England people masked their emotions – or rather, minimized them to grotesque extent ('the Lion and Albert' attitude – the mother being rather 'vexed' when the lion had gobbled up Albert): the stiff upper lip that, confronted with total disaster, only trembled enough to permit a throwaway 'Not so bad, thanks'. The English never admitted to being keen on anything: the amateur was always preferred to the professional – Gentlemen versus Players. The English class system was the most rigid in the world...

The unfortunate refugee had to penetrate these thickets of legend before he arrived at any understanding of the people among whom he had come to live. And, if he was a writer, he might yield to the temptation to write in a half-facetious, half-patronizing manner about how at last he had come to understand the glacial English heart; how by mastering the art of understatement he had come to be accepted as a 'good chap' even though he was a foreigner...

Not only refugees were bedevilled by this folklore (which it would be interesting to pursue to its early nineteenth-century or even late eighteenth-century roots). H. G. Wells said that one could always confuse Joseph Conrad by saying 'That's humour', humour being a 'damned English trick' Conrad had never learned how to tackle. And indeed the concept of 'a sense of humour' – invariably invoked by those who themselves entirely lack humour – has baffled many foreigners in England besides Joseph Conrad.

A majority of German and Austrian refugees were, however, not writers; nor even doctors or lawyers. A great number of them were businessmen, who in their native countries had run enterprises of varying size with considerable success. Now, in Britain, they were confronted with obstacles as great – although of a different nature – as those that faced the artist or professional man. As Jewish businessmen, of course, they figured in the gentile folk mind as successful and relentless entrepreneurs. Legend credited them with the Midas touch. 'What is the good of your being a Jew if you don't make money for us?' the gentile partner of a Jew is said to have protested.

In fact what applied to all the refugees applied with even more force to the refugee businessman: the earlier he came the better he fared. The earlier he left Germany, the better chance he had of bringing out some working capital. The 'Flight Tax', the discrimination the German Government exercised against Jewish firms from about 1934 onwards, the forced sale of Jewish enterprise with the collaboration of the German banks – everything made it harder for a refugee businessman to start again in another country.

Apart from the big Jewish banking families like the Rothschilds and the Warburgs and industrialists like the Weinmanns whom, as we have seen, the Nazis tried to hold to ransom, there were several categories of business in which Jews had been prominent. Broadly speaking, they had been pre-eminent in what might be called secondary industries, manufacturing goods for both the home market and for export. Statistics which break down by occupations the total of 'enemy aliens' classified by the Tribunals show that one-third of the men examined had been manufacturers on their own account. No less than 1,040 had been in the textile trade; 836 had been engaged in the manufacture of clothing; 225 had been concerned with the manufacture of chemicals for industry; 502 had been making leather goods. The expertise these refugees brought with them from Germany and Austria must have gone some way to offset the capital they could not bring. The refugees infused the textile trade, in particular, with new vigour and new ideas, especially in the dyeing and printing of fabrics; but their contribution extended over a wide range of products – lingerie, corsets, belts, gloves, hats, artificial flowers . . . Some of the refugees who set up firms in Britain had, too, the advantage of business contacts already established all over the world. This applied particularly in the German fur trade, centred, before Hitler's accession, in the city of Leipzig. A number of Leipzig fur merchants who came to England as refugees retained the world trading connections they had enjoyed for many years and thus Leipzig's loss was London's gain. The position of London as one of the world's great fur-trading centres was reinforced and enlarged by the newcomers.

Similarly with the leather-goods industry, which had been centred near Frankfurt in Germany and in Vienna. What had been almost a German and Austrian monopoly became, between 1935 and 1939, a British one.

The Germans had been very successful in making Ersatz goods – 'Ersatz' was a key-word of the era – and this skill, too, the refugees brought to Britain; it was to be of great significance in the development of plastics. It was a refugee who pioneered in Britain the electroylitic recovery of copper from scrap. A whole range of light industry was established by refugees. The Treforest

Trading Estate had been started in a depressed area and given special concessions in an effort to relieve unemployment: it included eleven factories started by refugees. These employed between them over 1,000 workers. Some 220 refugees interned in a single camp on the Isle of Man had, before the war, employed in total over 6,000 British workers.

Not all the refugees who had owned businesses in Germany were able to establish themselves in Britain. Only those with some capital were able to start on their own at once. Many of the others, often unable to obtain labour permits, remained in frustrating idleness for months after their first arrival – only surviving through handouts from the refugee organizations or through their wives working. (Then, from the outbreak of war in 1939 to the start of internment, some were able to get jobs.) As we have seen, internment stands as kind of watershed for the refugees. After it, individuals either began to move towards a successful assimilation with British society or else their sense of alienation ossified into a conviction of exclusion and failure that would prevent them ever coming to terms with their environment. The change of climate that followed the relaxation of internment allowed many refugees to get jobs as clerks, salesmen, or managers, especially in the vacuum that resulted from the calling-up of many Englishmen into the Forces. In these jobs the refugees could display their characteristic German Jewish qualities – as we have said, easy to recognize but hard to define – qualities of industry, integrity, and, perhaps, a kind of plodding realism combined with intelligence. The degree of success they achieved depended on several factors: their ability to master the English language – and not, at the end, to still sound too hopelessly 'German'; their willingness to adapt themselves to British conditions and practices; their success in appearing vital and creative while at the same time muffling any suggestion of the aggressive foreigner who knows it all from way back.

This applied particularly, of course, to those refugees who were employed, but it was almost equally true of those who struck out in business for themselves. Gentile folklore always whispers that 'the Jews help each other. The ones who've got it finance those who haven't,' but although the refugees received much help from the established Jewish community, both initially from the refugee organizations and later from individuals, any successes they made were their own: achieved against all the difficulties that beset any immigrant group seeking a place in the commercial fabric of a foreign country. And, just as 'the Jews always stand by one another' is always exaggerated in any story of Jewish success, so also is the Midas touch that, according to folklore again, can sweep any Jew from rags to riches in a few years.

Ernst Stromberg had been a clerk in an insurance office in Berlin. He lived at home with his elderly mother and his sister. He was arrested by the Gestapo on the day after his twenty-fifth birthday and put in a concentration camp in the aftermath of Crystal Night. He was released to go to Britain, sponsored by a refugee organization on the understanding that he would re-emigrate to Palestine. On arrival he was sent to Kitchener Camp. He had not been there long when he was called to an interview with the Refugee Committee.

He listened patiently while the theory of *Aliyah* was expounded by a member of the committee – in English, which he did not understand – and then translated into German for his benefit by another member of the committee.

'Won't you enjoy being a farmer?' the first committee man asked rhetorically, pausing while the other man put this into German. 'Strong arms and true hearts – that's what we're exporting to Palestine.'

After praising Ernst's physique and saying that he was the kind of young man the Jewish Home needed, the first committee man announced that they proposed to send him to an agricultural centre in Hertfordshire.

Ernst enjoyed the camp at first. He did not mind the early rising; the strong air and wide skies, the dawns and sunsets, gave him, a life-long city-dweller, a novel sense of holiday. The work wasn't hard either. The theoretical side of the training was interesting enough, he imagined, if you could understand it: not all the instructors spoke German and Ernst was making only slow progress in English. But as the weeks passed he began to get bored. Or perhaps not so much bored as uneasy. He worried about his mother and sister and although he didn't miss Berlin exactly – how could an obvious Jew miss a city whose pavements he trod with an uneasy delicacy, looking always behind him, expecting the Gestapo to catch up with him? – as eventually, of course, they had. No. Berlin was a jungle full of animals that wanted to destroy him. He would never go back there.

But after a month or two the farm still bored him. Now his eyes seemed to ache with the emptiness of those wide horizons. Ernst began to realize how *noisy* the country was. Dogs barking, cattle lowing, the wind rattling gates and windows – it irritated him. He began to long for the companionable city noises he had heard through the open windows of his mother's flat on a summer's evening: the grunt and roar of a car moving off; the 'good nights' of homegoing partygoers; the long, reactive clangor of trucks being shunted in a distant marshalling-yard. The city made him feel like *himself* – not like this stranger with sore red hands and dung-encrusted boots.

He didn't find he had much in common with his immediate companions either. He got on well enough with the three other men he shared a room with, but two of them were passionate Zionists and talked all the time of 'Israel'. Ernst had hardly heard of Zionism until a few years ago. He remembered his sister saying that Hitler had made more Zionists than ever Theodor Herzl had. This was the kind of sharp intelligent thing his sister often said, but the subject didn't interest Ernst enough for him to pursue it. There had been two other Jewish young men working in the insurance office and one of them had said that his parents were Conservative, but none of them had talked much of Jewish matters. So now Ernst wondered – Zionism? He was now, he supposed, a Zionist himself. But he felt strange and unfamiliar – just as in another way he didn't feel himself, stuck out here in the country, messing about with pigs and cows, covered in manure half the time. Zionism to his companions was a religion. It filled them, exalted them, gave them something to live for. It meant nothing to him.

He had accepted the idea of going to Palestine automatically. He'd have accepted any conditions then, sitting numb with terror in Buchenwald as he was. Now he felt like someone who has taken another's identity as a disguise and then finds himself forced to keep it for the rest of his life. Ernest knew he didn't want to be a farmer; didn't want to go to Palestine.

He knew English fairly well now and would travel up to London occasionally for a half-day. (There was a good service: the St Albans line up to Euston.) He got to know the geography of central London: he had hardly any money and there wasn't much to do except wander around.

Ernst had been three months at the training-centre when, apparently without giving it much conscious thought, he walked into the principal's office and told him he was leaving. The principal didn't protest as much as Ernst had expected. He simply said, 'I must report this to the committee, you understand that?' 'Yes,' Ernest said and left. He went straight to the railway station and took the train to Euston he always took on his half-days.

After wandering about for three days and spending a night in the crypt of St Martins-in-the-Fields, Ernst got a job in Soho: washing up in a café run by Italians in Berwick Market. He didn't get much but he was paid enough to be able to rent a small room at the other end of the market.

There he stayed for some two months. At first he felt confident that he could go on living like this – lost, anonymous – but then he began to wonder what would happen if the police picked him up. It was a miracle they hadn't, already: the West End always seemed to be full of police. And although Ernst didn't want to go back to the Refugee Committee – they would, quite rightly, be angry with him and would presumably want him to go back to the training centre – equally well he didn't want to go on washing dishes for ever.

He decided there was only one thing to do. He must go to the police himself. They might lock him up; they would hardly send him back to Germany. Nevertheless he was trembling when he walked into Savile Row police station.

He told the inspector there exactly what had happened, concealing nothing. The inspector was elderly and said little: Ernst could not tell what he was thinking. The police kept Ernst at the station for the night, questioning him closely about the manner of his coming to England. His replies seemed to satisfy them; presumably they telephoned the Refugee Committee to check on his statements for they allowed him to go the next day. He had expected the police to stop him working at the café, but they said nothing about this. They did, however, order him to report regularly to the nearest police station; and a few weeks later Ernst was called before an Aliens' Tribunal.

The presiding lawyer was quite hostile. He kept stressing Ernst's 'ingratitude' leaving the training centre. 'We give you our hospitality and this is how you repay us,' he said. Ernst had been warned that he might be put in Category A, which would have meant immediate internment; in the event – possibly because he had been in Buchenwald concentration camp – he was placed in Category B, which meant that he had to stay within a radius of five miles, which was no hardship for him.

Ernst was taken into custody in May 1940. He was interned first at Huyton and later on the Isle of Man. He was released nearly a year later, in April 1941. Perhaps because he had been in Category B he found it hard to get essential work in a factory and he was rejected as medically unfit for the Pioneer Corps on the grounds of bad eyesight (although other refugees appear to have been accepted who were at least equally short-sighted). Eventually he was released to work clearing debris from bombed sites. This was dirty and often dangerous work. Twice Ernst narrowly missed death when walls collapsed and once the great metal ball suspended from the end of a crane that was used to demolish ruined buildings swung too far and nearly crushed him against a wall. There were many discomforts. Like a soldier in the desert who learns to put up with sand in everything, even in his food, Ernst learned what it was to live soaked in a fine dust – dust in his eyes, up his nostrils, on his tongue.

And yet he was not unhappy. He never wished himself back on the training farm in Hertfordshire, even when the process of clearance uncovered the horror of crushed and mutilated human remains that had lain under the debris since the great raids of the previous winter. For the first time the realities of war and death came alive in Ernst's rather sluggish imagination.

In fact the work he was doing seemed to have brought his imagination alive. Easy-going, even lethargic, he had always tended to shy away from the broad view of anything; he preferred to stay in a rut. Now, suddenly, he began to visualize, to compare. He had a vision of this great city of London lying prostrate and shattered after the attacks of its enemies – and yet even now recovering, stirring with life. And what about all the other buildings that had not been destroyed but had merely been damaged? Or those that were intact but empty because their owners or tenants had fled from the blitz?

Ernst took to wandering around London again in what spare time he had. He used to walk through the old middle-class areas:

the inner suburbs that had been declining even before 1939. He noticed that in districts like Harlesden, Kilburn, or Finsbury Park there were many empty houses and many others that had suffered damage in the bombing and needed some repair. There were areas, too, where the destruction of a terrace of houses had created a site where it would be wasteful to erect the same kind of housing again : it cried out for high flats.

There was nothing that Ernst could do about any of this at the moment. He went on dodging falling bricks, treading over splintered glass, filling his lungs with choking dust. But he began to consider, to plan. In 1944 he was able to leave demolition work and with what he had saved buy himself into a semi-moribund firm of estate agents on the top floor of a house in the Harrow Road – not far from the once-notorious and long-vanished Cider House. His partner in the estate agents admitted he had only taken Ernst in because he could think of no other way of getting next month's rent. This didn't worry Ernst. His partner was merely an item of furniture; he had more important things to think of. He began in a small way, specializing in letting rather than selling property at that time. (He was naturally careful to advise the creation of leases long enough to protect the landlord from the Rent Restriction Act.) What Ernst was really anxious to do was investigate the market : to place himself in a position where he could take advantage of the tremendous lust for accommodation that was about to be unleashed. The estate agency was really useful as an observation post, nothing more.

Next he formed a property company with a merely nominal capital but with a Memorandum of Association that permitted a wide range of activities. (His partner in the estate agency was left out of the property company; soon Ernst would ditch him altogether.) Now Ernst started buying cheap fag-end leases of war-damaged property in Paddington and Maida Vale. He heard of a large, only slightly damaged house in Westbourne Terrace; he bought it and turned it into flatlets. He now had some capital behind him – he was not married and lived cheaply in a room in Craven Terrace – and he began to use the classic technique of mortgaging one property in order to buy another and then mortgage that in turn. He used his income from the estate agency and the flatlet house for his own expenses and to cover any deficit in servicing his loans. With his war damage claims on the Paddington properties he was able to create furnished accommodation that commanded high rents and always he funnelled the profit back into the business; by now he had several interlocked but technically independent companies. Later he was able to move both upwards and downwards as it were: upwards into the acquisition of the kind of site he had looked jealously on when he was a demolition worker – a site on which a block of flats could be built; and downwards into buying 'part-possession' houses which could be obtained cheaply from disgruntled landlords who wanted to be rid of a property that was partly occupied by a tenant at a small controlled rent. In the 1950s, as the housing shortage grew worse, these 'part-possessions' were to prove immensely profitable, for often the protected tenant could be persuaded to vacate his tenancy on a payment of some hundreds of pounds: the full-possession house could then be sold for several thousand.

From the mid-1950s onwards Ernst Stromberg was involved in every kind of property transaction, from the most conservative to the most speculative, although he never broke the law or treated his tenants brutally as did so many landlords when they bought properties which already had people in them. The 'property empire' which made him a millionaire by 1960 was created through the oldest and simplest economic rationale: that of the snowball which grows larger as it rolls or of those animals or insects which continually enlarge themselves from what they feed on. Such a process would not, of course, have been possible if Ernst had not foreseen and then exploited a need which led to a continually rising market over twenty years. His story is of interest not only because it shows how the wound of exile may in certain circumstances bring to birth talents which a man has not shown before, but because the 'Midas touch' Ernst displayed apparently owed nothing to any atavistic Jewish shrewdness and certainly nothing to help from any fellow-Jew.

Nothing could be more natural than that the ideal of Irish unity should find its most devoted adherents among Irishmen; what is more surprising is that a minority of other Irishmen view this concept with a scepticism verging on cynicism. Thus – although it would be grotesque to push the parallel too far – Zionism has always evoked almost fanatical support from some Jews and indifference and even hostility from others. Ernst Stromberg's sister may well have been right when she said that Hitler converted more Jews to Zionism than ever Theodor Herzl did. She might have added as a corollary that he had destroyed the liberal attitude among German Jews, murdered the Victorian ideal of progress. Pursuing the question of Hitler's unwitting responsibilities, it might be further added that the state of Israel became a reality at last partly because of the monstrous injury he inflicted on the Jews.

The British White Paper of 1939 was mentioned earlier because it affected the situation of those Jews seeking to escape from Germany and find refuge in Palestine. The events that led up to the foundation of the Jewish state in 1949 lie outside the scope of this book except in so far as they affected the lives of the refugees in Britain – which from about 1945 onwards they did, in a particular unfortunate way.

By 1945 internment was a bad dream to the refugees who had suffered it. In 1945 they were grappling with the grey England that had rejected Churchill and chosen Attlee; a weary civilian England to whom most of the refugees had long ago given their allegiance. It struck them, then, as a particularly sad irony that England should, from this year on, be seen as the enemy of the future Israel. England was the hypocritical tyrant denying Eretz Israel, the consolation for all the black years, 'the slain youths and spoliated maidens'. No wonder the pent-up misery and stagnant passion of years of suffering coalesced and then burst in a great outburst of rage against Britain.

But the refugees remembered that Britain had saved them. However obstructive and legalistic the pre-war Tory Government had been, however harsh and unjust internment – Britain had taken them in. They owed Britain something – something which they proposed to repay through their lives as British citizens. And now, owing to the policies of a British Government (Labour not Tory this time) a divided allegiance had been forced on them. It did not matter whether they were Zionists or not. They were Jews and the British Government – their government now – was fighting the Jews.

The situation had developed after 18 June 1945. On that day the Jewish Agency had once more applied for 100,000 immigration certificates. This application was refused, just as it had been seven years before. From then until the end of the Mandate the British Government sought to maintain this refusal by force. In the end they were using five army brigades with naval and air support to contain Jewish resistance. A long period of guerrilla warfare followed: the era of the Stern Gang and of Jewish terrorism. Lord Moyne was assassinated by the Jewish Irgun – it was said because he had responded to Joel Brand's efforts to save a million Jews from the gas-chambers (by bargaining with Eichmann) with the comment 'A million Jews? Where shall I put them?'

Again, without stressing a tenuous comparison, the emotions of peace-loving British Jews (whether refugees or not) on reading of the exploits of the Irgun must have somewhat resembled those of 'assimilated' Irish people in Britain on reading about the I.R.A.

Eventually, of course, Israel was to come into being; and without lasting bitterness between the British and the Jews. But the fighting in Palestine and the bitter war of propaganda that resulted in the United States – anti-British feeling rose to fever-pitch among American Jews – were a source of tension and emotional sufferings to the refugees at a time when they had a right to expect life to get a little easier.

Chapter Nine

SUMMATION

When Chuter Ede, then Home Secretary, announced that the German and Austrian refugees could, if they wished, become British citizens and remain in Britain, they knew they had come to the end of a long journey. During 1947 10,087 certificates of naturalization were issued to refugees. 1947, in fact, was the peak-year of German Jewish naturalization; and enshrined in this statistic of the ten thousand is the tragedy of the six million who did not survive to go anywhere or become anything.

'Happy is the country that has no history' and all the refugees have less to say about their life in England after the war. Some succeeded, some failed – at least according to their own notions of success and failure – but all in some measure came to terms with life in a new land. For the older refugees the hour had come earlier: they carry Germany with them forever, wherever they go. For them Germany will always be there: a loyalty, a regret, a wound. Their most vivid testimony always concerns Germany: how they arrived at their decision to leave it; how fortunate they were to escape – and yet how full of anguish and uncertainty they were, escaping to safety at the cost, seemed, of their true selves, of everything that gave their lives meaning. And indeed today, nearly forty years after the passing of the Nuremberg Laws, the question of German Jewish identity is more than ever in doubt.

Both in Israel and in Britain that identity is in danger of being lost in the younger generation. In Britain through an assimilation so complete as to amount to rejection, by children who refuse ever to speak German (if they have ever learned it), who seek to erase any trace of Germany from themselves. And in the very different atmosphere of Israel the same result seems likely to be achieved, though for different reasons.

Although there were and are many German Jews in Israel – it is said that every seventh inhabitant of the new state was a survivor from a concentration camp – the German language was banned there at first and everything has worked towards the extinction of their separate identity. Obviously Jews who were born in Germany remain a recognizable group: racial traits and habits do not vanish overnight and the 'organization-minded' nature of the German Jews has remained apparent in Israel; but the specific essence of German Jewry seems likely to be lost within a generation or so. It is doubtful if there is any innate and identifiable element in any group that can survive without maintaining a distinctive group consciousness. And it has been stressed throughout this book that it was precisely such a consciousness that was destroyed by the depth and extent of German-Jewish assimilation. Thus the German Jews found settlement in Israel much harder than did the Jews from Eastern Europe, with their blood-awareness of national and religious tradition, their Yiddish ethos that created for them a distinctive way of life. In fact the German Jews in Israel sometimes seemed to face an *Ostjuden* situation in reverse.

What will become of this patient, brilliant people who were first identified on bottle-tops from the third century; who travelled with the Roman legions; who produced Freud and Einstein, Heine and Marx? Will they be extinguished by total assimilation with the English and other western Europeans; swamped by Eastern Jewry in Israel? The Sephardim have, after all, survived. Can the German Jews perhaps survive as a group in America?

Or does it matter whether they remain as a distinct entity? Is there even evolution of a kind in the merging of Eastern and German Ashkenazim in Israel? And there are even Jews who do not object to total assimilation with the gentile.

Whatever disappears, whatever happens, there will still be Jews – 'Am Yisrael Cha' (the Jewish people lives) – and whether identified or not, German Jews will go on contributing their leaven of intelligence, their 'German' sense of order to the world. However labelled, no human qualities are ever entirely lost. As the Mishna, the collection of Jewish proverbs, says: 'Mankind was created in the form of a single man for the sake of peace, so that no man can say to his neighbour, "My ancestor was greater than yours."'

NOTES

As stated in the Author's Note, a great part of this book is derived from the personal memories of refugees. These notes, therefore, usually refer to printed sources.

CHAPTER ONE

The historical background of the German Jews is derived mainly from Marvin Lowenthal's *The Jews of Germany*, the other material from personal testimony. C. C. Aronsfeld's article 'Refugee No 562 Remembers' vividly suggests the atmosphere of the first years under the Nazis. I am indebted to Mrs Ernst Freud and her sister, Mrs Gerda Mosse, for Leo Baeck's speech dealing with Boycott Day; and to Mrs Freud for her translation of it. The theory of 'alleviation and compliance' was developed by Raul Hilberg in *The Destruction of the European Jews*.

CHAPTER TWO

The history of changing British attitudes towards immigration has been told very fully by Paul Foot in his *Immigration and Race in British Politics* and I have relied largely on this. The evolution of modern aliens' legislation is described in T. W. E. Roche's *The Key in the Lock*; and I must thank C. C. Aronsfeld for information about the German Jewish enclave in nineteenth-century England. Arthur Morse refers to the immigration laws of the United States in *While Six Million Died*. A full account of Montagu Norman's financial bailing-out of the Nazis is given in Margaret George's *The Hollow Men*. Press attitudes to the refugees are documented and analysed in Andrew Sharf's *The British Press and Jews under Nazi Rule*.

CHAPTER THREE

The British Government attitudes towards refugee immigration are the subject of A. J. Sherman's *Island Refuge*. I must thank Mrs Freud and Mrs Mosse for information about Sigmund Freud's last days in Vienna. The stamping of passports with a 'J' is mentioned in the 1967 edition of Gerald Reitlinger's *The Final Solution*. The meeting at the German Air Ministry after Crystal Night is described in Hilberg, as is the Nazis' holding to ransom of the Weinmann and Rothschild interests and the whole question of their expropriation of the Jews. There is a full account of the influence of the Gestapo on Jewish emigration in Prinz's essay on this subject in *Yad va Shem Studies III*, to which I am indebted for many details. There are numerous descriptions of the traffic in illegal immigrants to Palestine and of the disasters that befell the *Struma* and other ships. I have consulted among others Morse's *While Six Million Died* and Tartakower and Grossmann's *The Jewish Refugee*, supporting this with personal testimony.

CHAPTER FOUR

I have relied to a great extent on the *Annual Reports* of the Central British Fund for German Jews for details of appeals made and money raised, and for a general picture of their activities on behalf of the refugees. In his *Rescue and Achievement of Refugee Scholars* Norman Bentwich describes the behaviour of the German academic world, and Paul Tabori gives it a further dimension in his *Gift of the Exiles*. Lord Snow refers to Professor Lindemann and the refugee scientists in *Public Affairs* and was kind enough to enlarge on this in an interview with me. Colin Cross's *The Fascists in Britain* gives an account of the activities of Oswald Mosley and the British Union of Fascists in East London. I am grateful to Mr Wolf Mankowitz for describing to me the conditions of his childhood in the East End.

CHAPTER FIVE

Sherman's *Island Refuge* deals with British Government policies up to the outbreak of war. Morse's *While Six Million Died* is valuable on contemporary American attitudes. Zweig's exile in Bath is described in Elizabeth Allday's biography; and Louis Namier's offer to the British Government in Lady Namier's *Life of her husband*. In dealing with the press campaign against the refugees, I have relied on the newspapers concerned, consulting also Sharf and Professor

Lafitte's *The Internment of Enemy Aliens*. In dealing with internment I have drawn largely on personal interviews, but Professor Lafitte's book remains an invaluable source on internment, its machinery, and its effects.

CHAPTER SIX

I have largely relied on personal statements for that part of this chapter that deals with the military service of refugees, consulting also Norman Bentwich's *I Know the Risks*. For information on the release of refugee scientists I am indebted to Lord Snow.

CHAPTER SEVEN

The anecdote of Chaim Weizmann meeting Lord Rothschild at the Dorchester is taken from Angus Calder's *The People's War*, which also mentions the Hore-Belisha affair. I have relied on contemporary newspaper reports on the Bermuda Conference. Lord Coleraine's summing-up of the conference was made in an interview with Arthur D. Morse, who also gives an account of the suicide of Szmul Zgielbojm. I am grateful to Mrs Freud and Mrs Mosse for information regarding Freud's time in London. Among others, Dr Paul Tabori has described life in wartime foreign service at Bush House. The information about publishers-in-exile was given to me by Mr Michael Hamburger. The apocalyptic denunciation of Britain on behalf of 'the slain youths and spoliated maidens' was uttered by Dr Israel Goldstein and is quoted by Hilberg.

BIBLIOGRAPHY

Allday, Elizabeth : *Stefan Zweig*, London, 1972
Aronsfeld, C. C. : 'German Jews in Victorian England' in *Leo Baeck Yearbook VII*, London, 1962
Aronsfeld, C. C. : 'Refugee No 562 Remembers . . .' in *Jewish Quarterly*, London, Winter 1973
Association of Jewish Refugees in Great Britain : *Dispersion and Resettlement: the story of the Jews from Central Europe*, London, 1955
Association of Jewish Refugees in Great Britain : *Britain's New Citizens 1941–51*, London, 1952
Belloc, Hilaire : *Emanuel Burden*, London, 1904
Belloc, Hilaire : *The Jews*, London, 1922
Belloc, Hilaire : *The Postmaster General*, London, 1932
Bentwich, Norman : *I Understand the Risks*, London, 1950
Bentwich, Norman : *The Refugee from Germany, April 1933 to December 1935*, London, 1936
Bentwich, Norman : *The Rescue and Achievement of Refugee Scholars*, The Hague, 1953
Board of Deputies and Anglo-Jewish Association Joint Foreign Committee : *The Persecution of the Jews in Germany* : two pamphlets, London, 1933
Buxton, Dorothy F. : *The Economics of the Refugee Problem*, London, n.d.
Calder, Angus : *The People's War*, London, 1969
Cecil, Robert, Viscount : *All the Way*, London, 1949
Cohn, N : *Warrant for Genocide*, London, 1967
Colvin, Ian : *The Chamberlain Cabinet*, London, 1971
Council for German Jewry (later the Central British Fund for Jewish Relief and Rehabilitation) : *Reports* for 1937, 1938, 1939, 1940, 1941, 1942, 1945, 1949
Cross, Colin : *The Fascists in Britain*, London, 1961
Donaldson, Frances : *The Marconi Scandal*, London, 1962
Fast, Howard : *The Jews*, London, 1970
Foot, Paul : *Immigration and Race in British Politics*, London, 1965

Fraenkel, Heinrich : *Farewell to Germany*, London, 1959
Galsworthy, John : *Loyalties: a play*, London, 1921
George, Margaret : *The Hollow Men*, London, 1967
Gershon, K. : *We Came as Children*, London, 1966
Gilbert, M. : *The Roots of Appeasement*, London, 1966
Grunberger, Richard : *A Social History of the Third Reich*, London, 1972
Hilberg, Raul : *The Destruction of the European Jews*, Chicago, 1961
Hurewitz, J. C. : *The Struggle for Palestine*, New York, 1950
Jewish Central Information Office : *The Position of Jewish Refugees in England*, London, 1945
Klein, Charlotte L. : 'English anti-semitism in the 1920s' in *Patterns of Prejudice*, London, March 1972
Koestler, Arthur : *The Yogi and the Commissar*, London, 1945
Lafitte, F. : *The Internment of Aliens*, Harmondsworth, Middlesex, 1940
Lowenthal, Marvin : *The Jews of Germany*, Philadelphia, 1936
MacNeil, W. H. : *America, Britain, and Russia 1941–6*, London, 1953
Morse, Arthur D. : *While Six Million Died*, London, 1968
Mowat, C. I. : *Britain between the Wars 1918–40*, London, 1955
Muggeridge, Malcolm : *The Thirties*, new edition, London, 1967
Namier, I. : *Lewis Namier: a biography*, London, 1971
Nicolson, Harold : *Diaries and Letters 1930–9*, edited by Nigel Nicolson, London, 1966
Parkes, James : *An Enemy of the People: Anti-semitism*, London, 1945
Parkes, James : *The Emergence of the Jewish Problem 1878–1939*, London, 1946
Prinz, A. : 'The Role of the Gestapo in Obstructing and Promoting Jewish Emigration' in *Yad va Shem Studies III*, 1959
Reitlinger, Gerald : *The Final Solution*, new edition, London, 1967
Roche, T. W. E. : *The Key in the Lock: Immigration Control in England from 1066 to the present day*, London, 1969
Sharf, Andrew : *The British Press and the Jews under Nazi Rule*, London, 1964
Sherman, A. J. : *Island Refuge*, London, 1974
Simpson, Sir John Hope : *The Refugee Problem: Report of a Survey*, London, 1939
Snow, C. P. : *Public Affairs*, London, 1971
Stocks, Mary D. : *Eleanor Rathbone*, London, 1949
Tabori, Paul : *The Anatomy of Exile*, London, 1972

Tartakower, Arieh, and Grossmann, Kurt R.: *The Jewish Refugee*, New York, 1944
Tenebaum, J.: *Race and Reich*, New York, 1956
Toynbee, A. J. and Toynbee, V.: *Hitler's Europe*, London, 1954
Trevor, D.: *Under the White Paper: Some Aspects of British Administration in Palestine from 1939 to 1947*, Jerusalem, 1947
Wedgwood, C. V.: *The Last of the Radicals*, London, 1951
Wedgwood, Josiah: *Memoirs of a Fighting Life*, London, 1941
Weissberg: *Advocate for the Dead: The Story of Joel Brand*, London, 1958
Weizmann, Chaim: *Trial and Error*, London, 1949
Wheeler-Bennett, John: *John Anderson, Viscount Waverley*, New York, 1962
Wheeler-Bennett, John: *Munich: Prologue to Tragedy*, London, 1948
Wrench, Evelyn: *Francis Yeats-Brown*, London, 1948

GOVERNMENT PUBLICATIONS

Palestine: a Statement of Policy, His Majesty's Stationery Office, 1939
Report of the Anglo-American Committee of Enquiry regarding the Problem of European Jewry and Palestine, His Majesty's Stationery Office, 1947

NEWSPAPERS AND OTHER PERIODICALS

The *Daily Express, Daily Mail, Daily Mirror, Daily Sketch, Daily Worker, The Times, Sunday Express, New Statesman and Nation* among others.

INDEX

A

Academic Assistance Council, 124, 125
Acland-Troyte, Lieut.-Colonel, 151
Adalbert, Bishop, 15
Adams, Sir Walter, 124
Adolf Woerman, the, 204, 205
Advisory Committee ('Asquith Committee'), 214, 215, 217
Aircraft Production, Ministry of, 225
Alexander III of Russia, 46
Alexander, Professor S., 125
Alexandria, 26
Aliens Act of 1826, 45
Aliens Control Labor Law (U.S.A.) 1885, 57
Aliens Restrictions Acts (various), 45, 49, 50, 51
Allday, Elizabeth, 261
Alliance Assurance Company of London, 94, 95
Alivah, 134, 135, 137, 138, 295
Amadeus Quartet, the, 199
Anderson, Sir John (Lord Waverley), 164, 171, 177, 179, 186, 188, 214, 216, 217, 262
Angola, 253
Anschluss, Austrian, 75, 76, 78, 80, 104, 128, 130, 149
Arandora Star, the, 66, 196, 197, 202–4, 212
Argentina, 99
Armenians, 47
Aronsfeld, C. C., 61, 225
Aryanization, 85, 91
Ashkenazi Jews, 52, 56, 120, 304
Asquith, Mr Justice, 214, 215, 270
Association of Jewish Refugees in Great Britain, 286
'Atonement Tax', 85, 99
Attlee, Clement (Earl Attlee), 51, 301
Australia, 196, 228
Austria, 76
Austrian Centre (London), 285
Austrians, Council of in Great Britain, 285
Austro-Hungarian Empire, 75
Auxiliary Military Pioneer Corps, *see* Pioneer Corps
Auxiliary War Service Department, 165

B

Baden, 18, 19
Baeck, Leo, 38, 123
Baldwin of Bewdley, Earl (Stanley Baldwin), 59, 61, 62, 121
Baldwin Fund, 121
Balfour Declaration on Palestine, *Balzac* (Zweig), 261, 290
Bank of England, 60
Bank of International Settlements, 60
Baptism, Christian and German Jews, 19
Barbour, John, 30
Bassermann, Albert, 287
Bavaria, 18
Beaconsfield, Earl of, *see* Disraeli, Benjamin
Beamish, Henry Hamilton, 243, 244
Bearsted, Lord, 74
Belloc, Hilaire, 239, 240, 241, 272
Bengal Lancer (Yeats-Brown), 242
Berlin, 19, 31, 37
Bermuda Conference, 250–5
Berstl, Julius, 290
Bettauer, Hugo, 22
Beveridge, Lord, 125
Billing, Noel, 50
Bingen, 108
Black Death, the, 16
Blackett, Professor P. M., 227
Blackshirt, The, 146
Bland, Sir Neville, 176
Bloom, Congressman Sol, 251, 253
Bloomsbury House, 122
Blunt, Wilfred, 55
Böhmische Escompte Bank, 92
Böhmische Union Bank, 92
Bohr, Nils, 226
Bolshevism, fear of, 24, 61, 62
Bonaparte, Princess Maria, 76
Bouillon, Godfrey de, 14

INDEX

Boycott Committee, 92
Boycott Day, 1933, 32, 37, 64, 160
Brand, Joel, 302
Brazil, 99
Brazil, Land of the Future (Zweig), 261
Brecht, Bertolt, 124, 289
Bremen, the, 242 ...
Bremerhaven, 115
Breslau, 19
British Academy, 217
British Broadcasting Corporation, 286
British Medical Association, 127, 128, 129, 130–3
British Union of Fascists, *see* Mosley, Sir Oswald
Britons, the, 243, 244
Brixton jail, 189, 190
Brotscher, Dr, 228
Buchan, John (Lord Tweedsmuir), 238
Buchenwald Concentration Camp, 84, 273
Burfend, Captain, 205
Bush House, the Aldwych, 286
Byalistock, 47, 53

C

Cable Street, 'Battle' of, 146, 243
Canada, 196, 228
Canterbury, 45
Carlmann, Mr (pseudonym), 140, 185
Casimir the Great, 16
Cassel, Sir Ernest, 55, 56, 236
Categories (A, B, and C) of enemy aliens, 158, 162, 178–80, 186, 188, 192, 193, 204, 206, 207, 214
Catholic Herald, the, 64, 65
Caversham, 286
Cecil of Chelwood, Viscount, 125, 152, 213
Central British Fund for German Jews, *see* German Jewry, Council of
Chamberlain, Houston, 20, 240
Chamberlain, Neville, 59, 82, 154, 207, 247
Charlemagne, 13
Chesterton, G. K., 239, 246
Chichester, Bishop of (Dr G. A. Bell), 152
Children's International Aid Committee, 149, 150
Churchill, Sir Winston, 62, 126, 177, 301
Citadel, The (Cronin), 127
Clarendon Laboratory, Oxford, 126

Cliveden Set, the, 242
Clynes, J. R., 51
Coblenz, 109
Cockcroft, Sir John, 227
Cohen, Colonel Waley, 134
Colchester, 45
Coleraine, Lord, *see* Law, Richard Kidston
Cologne, 15
Colonial Office, British, 72, 75
Coming Up for Air (Orwell), 62
Conrad, Joseph, 290, 292
Conservatism in German Judaism, 19, 257
Court Jew (*Hof-Jude*), 17, 18, 22
Cranborne, Lord, 104, 156, 206, 215
Cross, Mr, 206, 207
Crusades, the, 14, 15, 16, 41
Crystal Night, 83, 84, 91, 98, 105, 219
Cuba, 100

D

Daily Express, the, 64, 154, 171
Daily Mail, the, 154, 174, 245
Daily Sketch, the, 175
Daily Telegraph, the, 64, 154
Daily Worker, the, 64, 65
Daladier, Edouard, 82
Danes in Britain, 44
Danube steamers, 102
Darkness at Noon (Koestler), 291
Das Kaiserreich (Mann), 21
Das Schwarze Korps (S.S. newspaper), 82, 99, 199
Der Jüdenstaat (Herzl), 20
Der Stürmer, 128, 199
Deutero-Isiah, 16
Deutsche Bank, 92
Devonshire, Duke of, 208
Die Stadt ohne Jüden (Bettaver), 22
Disraeli Benjamin (Earl of Beaconsfield), 53, 119, 236
Dodds, Dr H. W., 251, 252, 253
Dogs of War (Yeats-Brown), 242
Domestic Bureau of the Council of German Jewry, 140, 141, 143
Dominican Republic, 102
Domville, Sir Barry, 241
Doran, Edward, 51
Dover, 49, 220
Dresden Bank, 93, 95
Dreyfus case, 23, 236, 246
Dudd, Leslie (pseudonym), 272
Dühring, Eugen, 20
Dunera, the, 212
Dutchmen in Britain, 44

INDEX

E

East Africa, proposed Jewish settlement in, 82
Economic Consequences of the Peace (Keynes) 59
Ecuador, 98
Ede, Chuter, 303
Eden, Anthony, 73, 206-8, 250
Edward VII of England, 54, 55, 236
Eichmann, Karl Adolf, 8, 9, 301
Einstein, Albert, 124, 126, 259, 304
Elibank, Viscount, 177
Emanuel Burden (Belloc), 239
Emerson, Sir Herbert, 214
Essay on the Inequalities of the Human Race (Gobineau), 20
Europa, the, 242
Evans, Colonel Arthur, 222
Evening Standard, the, 216, 246
Everybodys, 128
Evian Conference, the, 81, 82, 250, 251
Extradition Act, 1870, 46

F

Fahey, Father Denis, 240
Fall of France, the, 173, 174, 193
Faringden, Lord, 208
Fiddler on the Roof, 257
'Fifth Column', 172, 173, 209, 249, 253
'Final Solution', the, 12, 17, 41, 82, 115
Fischer Verlag, 290
Fisher, H. A. L. (Lord Fisher), 125
Flight Tax, 90
Foot, Paul, 47, 51
Foreign Dentists Register, 132
Foundations of the Nineteenth Century (Chamberlain), 20
Fraenkel, Heinrich, 199, 202
France, *see* specific towns and cities
Franck, Professor James, 123
Franco, General, 241
Frankfurt, 18, 68
Free German League of Culture, 285
Freja Works, 95
Freud, Anna, 76
Freud, Emanuel, 54
Freud, Richard, 40
Freud, Sigmund, 40, 54, 77, 258, 259, 260, 261, 304
Freund, Erich, 286
Freundlich, Dr, 228
Frick, Wilhelm, 32
Friedenthal, Richard, 290
Frisch, Otto, 226, 228
Froehlich, H., 226

Fuchs, Klaus, 228
Funk, Walter, 84
Fur-Trading, 293

G

Galician Jews, 76
Galsworthy, John, 237-8
Game, Sir Philips, 146
Geillart, Marta (pseudonym), 200
Geiss, Ilsa (pseudonym), 36, 38, 44, 68, 86, 88, 99, 114, 115, 118, 150, 155, 159, 210, 229, 253
Geiss, Professor (pseudonym), 36, 86, 90
Geiss, Max (pseudonym), 36, 37, 38
General Strike, British, of 1926, 61
George, Professor Margaret, 60
German Jewry, Council of, 69, 120, 121, 122, 134, 219
Germany, *see* specific towns and cities
Gershom, Rabbi, 13, 14
Gestapo, the, 96, 97, 98, 100, 102, 295
Gobineau, Count J. A. de, 20, 30, 240
Goebbels, Joseph, 84, 85, 92, 98
Goethe, Johann Wolfgang von, 13, 61, 124
Goldner, Charles, 287
Goldschmidt (financier), 24
Gollancz, Victor, 182, 194
Gordon, William Evans, 48, 49, 53, 55, 60, 241
Göring, Hermann, 33, 84, 85, 92, 93, 104, 105
Gort, Lord, 248
Grant, Madison, 57
Grangemouth, 49
Gravelines, 222
Great Panic, the (Der Grosse Krach), 20
Grigg, Sir Edward, 207, 208
Grimsby, 49, 51
Grotwohl, Herr (pseudonym), 9, 10, 11
Grynszpan, Herschel, 84, 99
Gutman (financier), 24

H

Haavara Agreement, 101, 102, 105, 106
Haifa, 103
Halban, Hans, 226, 228
Haley, Arthur (pseudonym), 108, 109
Halifax, Viscount, 59
Hamburg Amerika Line, 102
Harrisson, Tom, 173
Harwich, 49, 111

INDEX

Havre Defence Force, 222
Heine, Heinrich, 19, 36, 304
Help Us Germans to Beat the Nazis (Fraenkel), 199
Herzl, Theodor, 20, 30, 301
Heydrich, Reinhard, 84, 85, 104, 105, 106
Hermann Göring Works, 93, 94, 96
High Commissioner for Refugees, 73, 74
Hilfsverein der Juden in Deutschland, 97, 98, 99, 100
Hilberg, Raul, 26
Hilgard, Eduard, 85
Hill, Professor A. V., 125
Himmler, Heinrich, 84
Hindenburg, Paul von, 24, 110
Hitler, Adolf, 9, 16, 22, 24, 26, 41, 60, 73, 75, 82, 94, 106, 107, 171, 182, 241, 301
Hoare, Sir Samuel, 59, 152, 153
Holland, Invasion of, 172, 173, 193, 236
Home Office, British, 70, 75, 114, 178, 206, 211, 214, 225, 245
Hore-Belisha, Leslie, 247–9
Hoover, President Herbert, 58
Hof-Jude, see Court Jew
'Horst Wessel Song', 25, 34 192, 242
Huguenots, 45
Hull, 49, 51
Humboldt, Karl Wilhelm, 124
Hurst, Sir Cecil, 196, 210, 211

I

Immigration Act (U.S.A.), 58
Immigration and Race in British Politics (Foot), 47
Inflation, in Germany, 23
Interior, Ministry of, German, 97, 100
Internment of Enemy Aliens (Lafitte), 174
International Labour Conference, Geneva, 72
Irgun, 302
Isaacs, Rufus, *see* Reading, Marquess of
Isle of Man, 187, 196–8, 199, 202, 226, 228, 229, 230, 294
Israel, 134, 301, 303, 304, 305
Italy, 132, 224

J

Jefferson, Thomas, 56, 57
Jerrold, Douglas, 241
Jewish Agency, the, 68, 101, 103, 156, 301
Jewish Board of Guardians, 146

Jewish Colonization Association, 69
Jewish Medical and Dental Association, 128
Jewish Refugee Committees, 109, 121, 122, 136
Jews Temporary Shelter, 120
Jews, The (Belloc), 239, 240, 272
Joachim, Frau (pseudonym), 28, 29
Joachim, Georg (pseudonym), 9, 10, 11, 26, 129, 130, 155, 256
Joachim, Professor (pseudonym), 9, 26, 27, 28, 40, 129, 130
Joint Distribution Committee (in U.S.A.), 121
Joliot, Professor, 226
Jones, Dr Ernest, 77
Juenger, Ernst, 289

K

Kafka, Franz, 290
Kahlmann, Lothar (pseudonym), 31, 32, 33, 40, 118, 119, 144, 145–8, 155, 161, 189, 228, 271
Kaleman, Mark (pseudonym), 118, 119, 145, 146, 147–8
Kann, Lily, 286–7
Kempton Park Racecourse, 188, 199, 202
Kemsley newspaper group, 174, 175
Keynes, J. M. (Lord Keynes), 59
Kingship of Christ according to the Principles of St Thomas Aquinas, (Fahey), 240
Kirkpatrick, Sir Ivone, 217
Kitchener Camp, 219–22, 295
Koestler, Arthur, 65, 291
Kokoschka, Oscar, 286
Konrad, Leonie (pseudonym), 277
Korda, Alexander, 291
Kowarski, Dr Lew, 226, 228
Krupps of Essen, 60
Kuhn, Professor Heinrich, 126, 226
Kulmhof (killing-centre), 90
Kürti, Dr N., 126, 226

L

Labour, Ministry of, 141, 273
Lafitte, Professor F., 174, 215, 262
Landerbank, 92
Lang, Max (pseudonym), 190
Last of the Radicals, The (Wedgwood). 50
Law, Bonar, 62
Law, Richard Kidston (Lord Coleraine), 252, 254
Lawrence, D. H., 49
League of Nations Assembly, 72, 73, 74
Leather goods industry, 293

INDEX

Lehman, Peter (pseudonym), 273, 274
Leith, 49
Leith-Ross, Sir Frederick, 105
Lenard (German physicist), 124
Leo Baeck Institute, 123, 286
Lewis, Kid, 243
Liberia, 102
Liddell-Hart, Captain, 247
Lindemann, Professor (Lord Cherwell), 126, 226
Link, The, 241
London, Port of, 49, 51
London, Jack, 290
Londonderry, Lord, 241
Lothian, Lord, 241
Low, David, 246
Lowenthal, Marvin, 14, 15, 307
Loyalties (Galsworthy), 237
Lucas, Senator Scott, 251
Ludendorff, Erich von, 22
Luther, Martin, 16, 17
Lytton, Lord, 125, 214, 270

M

Madagascar, proposed Jewish settlement in, 107
Madeburg-Anhalt, 84
Mainz, 13, 14, 15
Malamud, Bernard, 257
Malcolm, Sir Neill, 74, 214
Mallon, Dr, 189
Manchester, 5
Manchester Guardian, the, 63, 64, 154
Mann, Heinrich, 21, 290
Mann, Thomas, 289, 290
Mannheim, Lucie, 287
Marconi scandal, 239
Marks, Simon, 74
Martin, Kingsley, 213
Marx, Karl, 46, 304
Mass Observation, 173
May, Erskine, 42, 43, 45, 51
Mayen, 15, 16
Mazzini, Giuseppe, 46
McDonald, James G., 73, 74, 81
MacDonald, Ramsay, 51
McFadyean, Sir Andrew, 217
Mecklenburg, 18
Medical Practitioners and Pharmacists Act, 1947, 132
Medical Practitioners Union, 127
Melchett, Lord, *see* Mond, Ludwig
Mendl, L. (pseudonym), 88, 89, 114, 115
Merchant of Venice, The (Shakespeare), 220
Mischlings, 32
Mishna, the, 305

Mond, Ludwig (Lord Melchett), *Morning Post*, the, 64
Mooragh Times, 198
Morris, Sir William, 241, 242
Morrison, Herbert, 217, 270, 276
Mors, 15
Morse, Arthur D., 250, 251
Mosley, Sir Oswald, 146, 147, 174, 242, 243
Moyne, Lord, 302
Munich settlement, the, 82, 83, 154

N

Namier, Lady I., 156
Namier, Sir Lewis, 156, 182
'Nansen Passport', 72
Nantes, Edict of, 1685, 45
Napoleon I of France, 18, 36
Neher, Hugo (pseudonym), 30, 31, 40, 68, 108, 109, 111, 135–40, 159, 160–1, 181, 185, 228, 249, 271
Neumann, Robert, 198, 290
New Statesman and Nation, the, 162, 216
Newhaven, 49
Norman, Montagu (Lord Norman), 60, 105
Normans, the, 44
North Africa, 224
Northcliffe, Lord, 49, 174
Norwich, 45
Nuremberg Laws, 32, 33, 67, 72, 73, 82, 302

O

Observer, the, 251, 253
Olbrich, Karl, 207
Ouchan Pioneer, 198
Orthodox Judaism, 19, 257
Orwell, George, 62
Ostjuden, 25, 54, 57, 76, 119, 120, 189, 243, 258, 304
Oxford Union debate on Pacifism, 61

P

Palatinates, 45
Palestine, 12, 25, 42, 69, 74, 101, 102, 105, 134, 139, 157, 254, 302
Palestine-Amt, 97
Parker, Joseph, 207
Patria, the, 103
Peace Ballot, the, 61
Peake, Osbert, 176, 207, 209
Peierls, Professor Rudolph, 226, 228
Petropolis, 261
Pioneer Corps formerly Auxiliary Military Pioneer Corps), 180, 216, 218–23, 234

INDEX

Planck, Max, 123
Poland, *see* specific towns and cities
Port Erin, Isle of Man, 199
Port St Mary, Isle of Man, 199
Postmaster General, The (Belloc), 239
Priestley, J. B., 55, 272
Professional Committee of Council of German Jewry, 120, 126, 128
Propaganda Ministry, German, 99, 101
Protocols of the Learned Elders of Zion, 24, 244
Proust, Marcel, 290
Prussia, 18, 19

Q
Querido Verlag, 290
Quota system for immigration to the U.S.A., 1921, 57

R
Ramsay, Captain, 51
Ramsgate, 220
Rath, Ernst von, 84, 99
Rathbone, Eleanor, 164, 181, 214, 262
Rathenau, Walter, 23, 260
Rayner, Mr and Mrs (pseudonym), 141, 142, 143, 169, 170, 187, 199
Reading, Marquess of, 119, 152
Reconstruction of the Civil Service, Law for, 1933, 27, 28, 123
Reform Movement in German Judaism, 19, 257
Refugees before Britons, 244
Regensburg, 16
Regional committees, 164
Reich Chamber of Culture, 290
Reich Chamber of Fine Arts, 290
Reichstag, The, 9, 24
Reichsvertretung der Juden in Deutschland, 69, 97–9, 134
Remarque, Erich Maria, 289
Renn, Ludwig, 286
Reparations, German, 59
Reuter, Jules de, 55
Rhine, Confederation of, 18
Rhineland, re-occupation of, 39
Ribbentrop, Joachim von, 241
Rilla, Walter, 287
Roosevelt, President Franklin Delano, 58, 77, 80–1, 106, 120, 154, 250, 254
Rosenstock, Dr Werner, 286
Rotblat, Dr, 228
Rothermere group of newspapers, 174, 245
Rothermere, Viscount, 174, 245

Rothmund, Dr, 83
Rothschild, Alphons de, 95
Rothschild, Eugene de, 95
Rothschild, Baron Louis de, 94, 95, 96, 152
Rothschild, Lord, 235
Royal Engineers, 219
Royal Society, The, 217
Rublee, George S., 82, 105, 106, 153
Russian–Jewish immigration to Britain, 47, 51, 52, 246
Rutherford, Lord, 125–6

S
Sachs, Leah (pseudonym), 78, 79, 141
Sachs, Marcus (pseudonym), 78, 79, 141, 142, 143, 169, 170, 187–8, 198–9, 228, 271
Sachs, Ann (pseudonym), 78, 79, 141, 169, 170
Sachs, Paul (pseudonym), 78, 79, 141
Salisbury, Marquess of, 47
Salvador, the, 103
Samuel, Sir Herbert, 74
Sandwich, 220
Saxony, 18
Schacht, Hjalmar, 29, 59, 60, 104, 105, 106, 153
Schiff, Otto M., 121, 245
Schiff, Professor Walter, 285
Schlesinger, Dr, 226
Schlie (Travel agent), 98
Schuschnigg, Kurt von, 76
Science and Learning, Society for the Protection of, *see* Academic Assistance Council
Seeghers, Maria (pseudonym), 200
Semon, Sir Felix, 54, 55
Sephardim, the, 120, 136, 304
Shanghai, 39
Shaw, G. B., 239
Sherman, A. J., 43
Shertok, Moshe (later Sharrat), 156
Shirer, William, 76
Sieff, Mrs Rebecca, 134
Silverman, Sydney, 250
Simon, Professor Francis, 126, 226
Simon, Sir John (Lord Simon), 146, 248, 249
Sinclair, Upton, 290
Snow, Lord, 126, 226–8
Southampton, 49, 115
Spain, Moslem, 12
Spectator, the, 63
Speir, Eugen, 199
Spieger, Dr Wilhelm, 29
Spires, 14, 16
Starhemberg, Prince, 218

INDEX

State Department (U.S.A.), 58, 104, 250–5
Stern Gang, 302
Starsbourg, 16
Strauss (financier), 24
Stromberg, Ernst (pseudonym), 295–301
Streicher, Julius, 92, 128
Struma, the, 103
Stuckart, Franz, 82, 84
Stuttgart, the, 98
Suicides, of German and Austrian Jews, 15, 77
Sunday Chronicle, the, 175
Sunday Express, 127, 128, 171
Sun's Bright Child (Bersth), 290
Szilard, Leo, 259

T

Tablet, The, 240
Tabori, Paul, 259, 291
Talmud, the, 13, 52
Taylor, Myron G., 81
Thirty Years' War, the, 17
Thomas, J. H., 51
Thomson, Professor George, 227
Thyssen, Fritz, 29, 60
Tillett, Ben, 53
Times, The, 62, 63, 64, 154, 179, 189, 202, 203, 205, 209
Torah, the, 13, 52, 258
Treforest Trading Estate, 293–4
Tribunals, Refugee, 158, 159, 162
Truth, 174, 247, 248–9
Tweedsmuir, Lord, *see* Buchan, John

U

'Unknown Prophet', *see* Deutero-Isiah
Uruguay, 99

V

Valachi (pseudonym), 190
Vansittart, Lord, 60
Versailles, Treaty of, 61
Vienna, 22, 75, 76, 77, 80, 199, 258
Vienna, Congress of, 18
Viertel, Berthold, 285
Vincent, Sir Howard, 48, 49, 55, 241
Vössiche Zeitung, 25

W

Walbrook, Anton, 287
Waltham Cross, 171
War Crimes Commission, 250
Warburg Institute, 286
Warners Camp, 204
Warsaw ghetto, 26, 253
Watson, Seton, 217
Waverley, Lord, *see* Sir John Anderson
Webb, Sidney (Lord Passfield), 55
Weber, Louis, 207
Wedgwood, Colonel Josiah, 50, 51, 75, 104, 151, 164, 181, 206, 207, 213–4
Wedgwood, Dame Veronica, 50
Weimar Republic, the, 22, 24, 124
Weinemann enterprises, 93
Weinemann, Fritz, 93–4
Weinemann, Hans, 93
Weizmann, Chaim, 53, 182, 194, 235
Weizmann, Vera, 182
Wells, H. G., 216, 290, 292
Weltsch, Dr Robert, 68
Westphalia, 18
Wharf Mills, 196
Wiener Library, 286
Wiesel, Elie, 256
Wilhelm II of Germany, 9, 21, 54
Willis, Mrs (pseudonym), 143,
Wilson, Sir Arnold, 241
Willstätter, Professor Richard, 12
Winterton, Earl, 81, 105, 154, 215–6
Witkowitz Steel Complex, 94–6
Wohlthat, Helmuth, 106, 153
Woolf, Leonard, 237
Wörmann (of German Foreign Office), 85
Worms, 15, 16
Württemberg, 18, 19

Y

Yarmouth, 45
Yeats-Brown, Francis, 241–2
Yellow Press, the, 49, 65

Z

Zbasyn, 83, 84
Zgielbojm, Szmul, 254–5
Zinn, Helga (pseudonym), 143, 144, 165–9, 186, 200, 229, 276
Zionism, 30, 50, 136, 137, 301
Zionist Congress, first, 20
Zweig, Stefan, 155, 182, 259–62